THE STORY OF ARCHITECTURE

THE STORY OF ARCHITECTURE

JONATHAN GLANCEY

DK PUBLISHING

LONDON • NEW YORK • MUNICH
MELBOURNE • DELHI

Project Editors: NEIL LOCKLEY, JO MARCEAU
US Editors: CHUCK WILLS, GARY WERNER
Designer: CARLA DE ABREU
Art Editor: SIMON MURRELL
Senior Art Editor: ROWENA ALSEY
Senior Editor: PETER JONES
Senior Managing Editor: ANNA KRUGER
Senior Managing Art Editor: STEPHEN KNOWLDEN
Managing Picture Researcher: SAM RUSTON
DTP Designers: ROBERT CAMPBELL, LOUISE WALLER
Production Controller: SARAH COLTMAN

*In memory of William Hedgehog-ffox (1981–98),
four-legged friend, mentor, and guide who had a nose
for old churches, country houses and the Jaguars that
connected them, but was sniffily indifferent to the
modern architecture that continues to intrigue me.*

PUBLISHED IN THE UNITED STATES BY
DORLING KINDERSLEY PUBLISHING, INC.
375 HUDSON STREET
NEW YORK, NEW YORK 10014

First American Edition, 2000

4 6 8 10 9 7 5

Library of Congress Cataloguing-in-Publication Data

Glancey, Jonathan.
    The story of architecture / Jonathan Glancey.
        p.cm.
    Includes index.
    ISBN 0-7894-5965-5
    1.Architecture--History. I. Title.

NA200 .G527 2000
720'.9-dc21

REPRODUCED BY GRB, VERONA, ITALY
PRINTED AND BOUND BY TOPPAN PRINTING CO., (S.Z.) LTD., CHINA

See our complete product line at www.dk.com

PAGE 2: WIESKIRCHE, STEINHAUSEN, BAVARIA (1745–54, SEE P.89)

CONTENTS

VILLA CAPRA, NEAR VICENZA, ITALY, 1569

Unité d'Habitation, Marseilles, France, 1946–52

FOREWORD

The Story of Architecture begins in Mesopotamia around 7000 BC and reaches into the global architecture of the twenty-first century. Jonathan Glancey brings two special qualities to bear on his encyclopedic task. First, he has visited most of the buildings about which he writes. The reader might be tempted to take this for granted but, regretfully, there are some who write at length about buildings which they have only seen in photographs and the difference tells. The second factor is his infectious enthusiasm for the subject. Architecture touches all of our senses and as we sit, remote from actuality, turning the pages of a book, Jonathan brings the buildings, and the stories behind them, alive for us.

This book reminds us that our culture is about the making of things, a process which starts with the provision of shelter from the elements. Architecture transcends this basic need and its expression across time and space is as varied as the parallel worlds of plant and animal species. Jonathan is a wonderful communicator and here he explores the underlying principles behind architecture of wide-ranging diversity.

His insights are always lively and stimulating. I particularly like the historical vignettes which trace the culture of the time and place, through musicians, artists, architects, engineers, and clients, all of whom come together to shape the buildings and places. This could well prove to be the guidebook to inspire your next architectural pilgrimage.

Jonathan Glancey aims to bring the story of architecture, and all who play a role in its creation, to the widest possible audience. He succeeds admirably.

LORD FOSTER OF THAMES BANK
LONDON, MAY 2000

PREFACE

THE STORY OF ARCHITECTURE is one of remarkable human endeavor, one of the means through which we try to create order and make sense of our endlessly intriguing, yet messy world. And to provide ourselves with shelter. We all live and work in buildings. From the humblest to the sublime, there is no reason why any of these should be less than inspiring even in small ways. The turn of a stair. The way sunlight falls through windows in mesmerizing patterns on floors. Materials cool to the touch in the heat of summer. The rhythm of an arcade. The pregnant quality of a dome. At its best, Architecture, which is different from mere building, lifts our spirits and sends shivers down our spines; at its worst, it belittles us, although it really shouldn't. Ever. This book is a concentrated summary of buildings,

places, and ideas about architecture that from childhood have drawn me to them like the proverbial moth to a flame. I have visited just about every building in the book, which is more or less how they were chosen. Writing about buildings unvisited seems wrong, but there are some no history of architecture could possibly leave out. There are many others I could have shown, but I have had to be selective otherwise this book would be as big as a small building. Architecture is a huge subject encompassing the history of civilization, so although I've tried my level best, it cannot be truly comprehensive. But I hope *The Story of Architecture* will make you want to see and experience these buildings and others worldwide and to discover more about the many ways we have chosen to frame our lives.

JONATHAN GLANCEY

GRAND CENTRAL STATION, NEW YORK CITY, 1903–13

The famous concourse of Grand Central Station is one of the greatest meeting places in the world. The spectacular main concourse measures 120ft (36.5m) by 125ft (38m) and features a ceiling painted by Paul Helleu depicting the heavens.

INTRODUCTION

EXCEPT ON RARE ESCAPES to desert landscapes, or trekking high in mountains, or sailing the high seas, most human beings are surrounded by buildings. There is, though, a difference – a very important one – between building and architecture. Animals can build. Termites build spectacular high-rise nests in the Australian bush. Birds build nests, too – some, like that of the bowerbird of Australia and New Guinea, of great sophistication and beauty. Bees build spectacular hives; their innate sense of geometry and knowledge of lightweight materials unsurpassed.

Humans, though, developed architecture. This is, to be blunt, the science and art of building, or to be more poetic, the moment that a building is imbued with a knowing magic that transforms it from mere shelter into that of a self-conscious work of art. This art might offend and baffle as well as delight. Yet from the magnificence of the Parthenon and the graciousness of the temples of Mahabalipuram, through the soaring ambition of medieval Gothic cathedrals to the skyscrapers of the twentieth century, Architecture is a continually evolving art. It maps our ambitions in three solid dimensions. It is the greatest visible means by which we celebrate our wealth and health (think of all the great churches and temples raised to thank God or gods and saints that some virulent plague had passed by) and a form of staircase to heaven. From ancient times – about eight or nine thousand years ago – humankind began reaching for the sky with extraordinary structures that resembled either holy mountains (pyramids) or early lightning conductors (towers, steeples) up which their priests could ascend to meet the sky-gods or down which, presumably, the gods could step to Earth.

HYPOSTYLE HALL, TEMPLE OF AMUN, KARNAK, EGYPT, 1530–323 BC
The Temple of Amun has a monumental hypostyle hall at its center. This magnificent space consisted of 122 columns, with a central aisle of 12 columns 72ft (22m) high.

CHARTRES CATHEDRAL, FRANCE, 1194–1220
A key building in the development of High Gothic style, Chartres Cathedral is notable for its stained glass windows which bathe the interior in colored light. The cathedral was a symbol of religious faith and commercial prosperity.

The first real works of architecture we know of are temples. This makes sense. Ever since the Bronze Age when the male (or sky) gods triumphed over the prehistoric earth goddess(es) in most parts of the world, mankind has attempted to connect with the eternal and to build in harmony with the cosmos. The fact that ancient temples are designed to line up with equinoxes and eclipses and other movements and patterns seen in the stars should come as no surprise. Mankind wanted to tune in with the mind that

created the universe. It is significant that in monotheist religions (notably Christianity), God has been referred to as the great and original Architect (no wonder so many architects have had such big egos).

What was equally important was that an understanding or connection to the gods made the land or sea (men fished long before they developed agriculture) fruitful. Stonehenge, for example, an observatory and temple of sorts, was probably the mainspring of a giant theodolite or clock that, connected to a network of megalithic stone circles set around Britain, enabled our ancient forbears to read the stars and thus navigate their ancient trade routes successfully. Today we wear such nationwide technology on our wrists in the form of watches and chronometers.

I mention this, not simply because of my fascination with the rise of civilization, but because it reminds me of just how important architecture has been to our lives and how distinct it is from building. Architecture has always been something of a religion and architects a kind of priesthood. At their best, as you can see and even read about in this book, they have been like shamans or magicians tricking stone, brick, and marble, iron, steel, titanium, and polycarbonates into sensational structures that raise our spirits above everyday concerns. Over the centuries, new technologies have allowed architects to practice their art with ever greater dexterity, but also to make more mistakes than were possible at the time of the building of the pyramids or Stonehenge. And, just as great world religions tend to get watered down and split into sects and warring factions with the passing of generations, so has architecture.

At the beginning of the twenty-first century there are many more people and exponentially more architects than there have been at any time in the history of civilization. This certainly hasn't led to an increase in the quality of architecture. Why? Because we no longer build to connect humankind to God or to make sense of our place in the cosmos, but for any number of mundane, banal, fashionable, and profitable reasons that reduce architecture to a vainglorious and earthly pursuit. It is significant that at the very time in history when technology allows buildings to be more thrilling than they ever have been so many are

São Paolo, Brazil
The largest city in Brazil, São Paolo has a population of over seventeen million. It is the foremost industrial center of Latin America, and one of the most populous cities in the Western hemisphere. During the 1950s, 60s, and 70s, some 20 million people moved from rural to urban areas, and cities such as São Paolo grew at a rapid rate.

so lackluster, so many more demeaning. Indeed, at the beginning of the twenty-first century, the architect's role has declined. To survive, to continue to excite us as great mosques and temples have done over the millennia, architects need to rediscover the high ground of the imagination, to be the shamans and magicians their predecessors were before the Industrial Revolution when mere building became all too easy.

There are, of course, architects working today who are as great as any who have existed in the past. Like any great artist in any field they are few and far between. As for the rest, well, it is up to us to encourage, cajole, prompt, demand, criticize, to ensure that our demanding, greedy, and unbalanced global civilization is housed and set against backdrops that promise to raise us to the realm of the gods. But, of course, we get the architecture we deserve. If we truly want to live banal lives then the artless world of the air-conditioned shopping mall, the cartoon world of theme park and leisure center, the furtive world of the gated suburban housing development with its triple-garaged houses designed in coy "traditional" styles, together with those of the faceless distribution depot, the sad "call center," and the soulless office park beckons. This is a very long way from the gods and from Architecture as most of us would like it to be – a story that was first told some eight or nine thousand years ago.

REICHSTAG, BERLIN, GERMANY, 1999
Norman Foster's mastery of light is evident in the new glass dome created for the Reichstag in Berlin. At the dome's center there is a light-reflecting cone which reflects light downward into the parliamentary chamber.

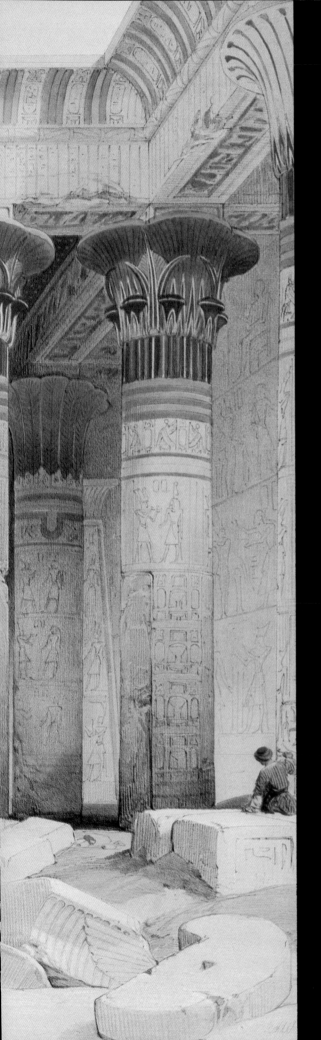

In The
BEGINNING

AT THE BEGINNING OF THE TWENTY-FIRST CENTURY IT IS HARD TO IMAGINE A TIME WHEN THE ONLY ARCHITECT WAS GOD, OR THE GODS, AND THE MANY SPECIES OF HUMANKIND THAT ONCE SHARED THE WORLD HAD NO NEED FOR ARCHITECTURE — OR AT LEAST NOT IN THEIR CONSCIOUS IMAGINATION. IN FACT, THERE WERE SPECIES OF INSECTS AND BIRDS THAT BUILT MORE SOPHISTICATED HOMES THAN OUR HUNTER-GATHERER FOREBEARS. DESPITE WHAT THEORISTS IN EIGHTEENTH-CENTURY EUROPE WANTED TO BELIEVE, THE ORIGINS OF ARCHITECTURE HAD NO MYSTICAL BEGINNING AND THERE WAS NO ONE WAY OF BUILDING SHELTERS AS HOMES OR PLACES OF WORSHIP. ARCHITECTURE EMERGED FROM THE FIRST SELF-CONSCIOUS SHAPING OF HOMES, MONUMENTS, AND CITIES, SOME EIGHT OR NINE THOUSAND YEARS AGO, OR, AS THE GERMAN ARCHITECT LUDWIG MIES VAN DER ROHE PUT IT, "WHEN TWO BRICKS WERE PUT TOGETHER WELL."

GRAND PORTICO OF THE TEMPLE OF ISIS AT PHILAE, NUBIA
David Roberts' 19th-century painting of the Temple of Isis shows the highly decorated, monumental nature of Egyptian temple architecture. No two capitals are the same, yet the actual structure is relatively simple.

THE GROWTH OF CITIES
THE RISE OF CIVILIZATION

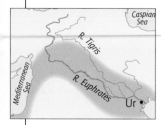

ARCHITECTURE BEGAN when humankind took up farming on a regular basis. Now there was a need for people to live in settled places and to tend the land rather than to hunt and gather nomadically as their ancestors had done and as humans still do in certain parts of the world at the beginning of the 21st century. This new way of life emerged in two places at more or less the same time, along the banks of the Nile River and across the Fertile Crescent, the once lushly green and well-watered land following a curve from the Tigris/Euphrates delta, west along the course of these rivers toward Syria, and then down along the eastern coast of the Mediterranean. It was known to the writers of the Bible as the setting of the Garden of Eden, for that is how it must have appeared. The earliest architecture, and the first cities, were thus in what today we know as Egypt, Israel, Iraq, and Iran.

THE BIRTH OF ARCHITECTURE
Settled down to farm, the peoples of these ancient lands created the first cities, and in those cities they raised permanent homes, shrines, and then temples and palaces. The birth of architecture was thus contemporaneous with the birth of the city and the feeding of the city by the

ZIGGURAT OF URNAMMU, UR, IRAQ, C.2125 BC
Little remains of the upper two stages of this immense structure, but the surviving base gives an indication of the impact it would have made, rising above the featureless plain.

farmlands that served it, as it, in turn, served them. Civilization, as we understand it, had begun its long, sometimes magnificent, and often terrifying ascent.

The very word civilization stems from the Latin word *civis,* meaning a citizen or a city-dweller. The earliest known urban development, and thus the starting point for architecture, was Jericho. Excavations have uncovered houses – built of mud-bricks and doubtless attractive in their day – dating back beyond 8000 BC, and shrines from about 7000 BC. Ancient cities such as Jericho would have appeared quite familiar to our eyes; aside from cars, electricity, ads for Coca-Cola, and satellite television dishes, many small and remote

Middle Eastern and North African towns and villages have barely changed in their appearance over the ensuing 10,000 years.

What drove architecture upward and toward a technological and artistic greatness beyond that of the home was a fruitful marriage of wealth and ambition. The first citizens were soon led by priests and monarchs. Priests appeased and interpreted the will of a pantheon of gods who had the power to make the land bountiful or barren; in turn, citizens looked after the priests who became, in most societies, increasingly wealthy, pampered, and frightening. To protect themselves from the will of other humans living in rival cities and eventually kingdoms, nations, and countries, the citizenry turned to kings who raised armies, fought on their behalf, and protected the land that gave rise to the city. In return, kings were rewarded with or rewarded themselves with great wealth. The priests built temples, kings built palaces, and both built tombs: the architecture we travel thousands of miles to see on vacation – ziggurats and pyramids, temples of brick, temples of marble – reached for the sky and stole our imagination.

THE ZIGGURATS

One of the greatest and most moving of the early temples is the ziggurat (stepped pyramid) of Urnammu at Ur in Sumeria. A temple dedicated to Nanna, the moon god, the ziggurat rose above a densely packed city of some 350,000 people like an artificial mountain, its peak reached by

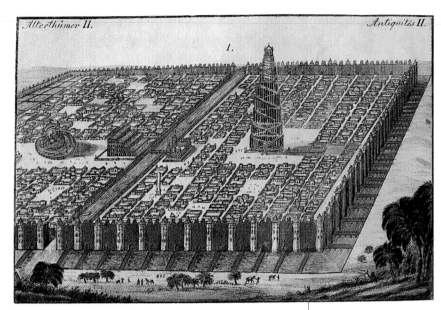

ARTIST'S IMPRESSION OF THE WALLS OF BABEL
The story of the Tower of Babel, related in Genesis 11:1–9, was probably inspired by the ziggurat of Etemenanki. The temple and its walls are recreated here in an 18th-century engraving.

a daunting ceremonial stair. The temple was last remodeled by Urnammu and his successors in c.2125 BC, although this mud-brick behemoth is much older. It seems likely that successive generations built up from earlier bases and thus, accidentally at first, created the distinctive, haunting form of the ziggurat. It has been suggested that each level of the ziggurat would have been planted with trees so that it would have resembled, even more than it does today, a mountain adorned by nature yet bleached by a harsh sun. Perhaps, perhaps not. What we do know is that the great temple would have been visible for miles across the plain, a sign to farmers in outlying irrigated pastures that their priests were intervening with the gods on their behalf.

One of the most famous ziggurats of the ancient world is known to us as the Tower of Babel. This was, in all likelihood, the temple of Etemenanki in Babylon, greatest of all the ancient Mesopotamian cities. The city reached its peak during the reign of Nebuchadnezzar II (605–563 BC). The Tower of Babel would have been a spiral structure, faced in blue-glazed bricks and rising seven stories up from a square base with 295-foot (90-meter) sides. It would have towered over

EARLY WRITING
Writing was essential to the development of early civilizations. It was used to pass knowledge from generation to generation; it led to the first bureaucracies and so to the first cities. Sumerian is the oldest known written language. Developed from simple pictograms, the distinctive cuneiform script (from the Latin *cuneus*, meaning "a wedge") was first used for administrative records from about 3100 BC. This dedication, dating from 2400 BC, is by a queen of the city of Umma for the life of her husband King Gishakidu.

SHIBAM, DESERT CITY, YEMEN
The "Manhattan of the Desert" is nearly 2,000 years old. Most of its mud-brick buildings date to the 16th century AD, but the physical aspect of the city appears remarkably modern.

Nebuchadnezzar's magnificent waterside palace on the banks of the Euphrates, famous for the legendary Hanging Gardens that hung in great, perfumed terraces built on top of a vaulted building. This would have stored water for the plants, as well as ice for the beakers of sherbet drunk by courtiers and the favored princess for whom the gardens, one of the Seven Wonders of the Ancient World, were hung.

BABYLON

Although preceded by other great cities in the Fertile Crescent, notably Ur, Khorsabad, Nimrud, and Nineveh, Babylon was perhaps the first of the world's capital cities to be rigorously planned. The city was walled around, set on the east and west banks of the Euphrates, and crossed by a bridge, part of a great processional avenue that drove through the main temple and palace complex. We know it must have been an impressive as well as a colorful sight since the city's northern entrance, the Ishtar Gate, has

ARTIST'S IMPRESSION OF THE HANGING GARDENS OF BABYLON
Accessed through the royal apartment, the exotic Hanging Gardens, recreated here in a 19th-century woodcut, consisted of a series of artificially irrigated roof terraces.

been conserved. Crenellated with tiny ziggurats along the tops of its walls, the gate is faced in characteristic blue-glazed bricks interrupted by yellow and white bricks depicting lions and fabulous beasts. Perhaps only the gates of the Assyrian city, Khorsabad, of a century earlier were more impressive. Those that led into the Palace of Sargon II (722–705 BC) at Khorsabad were guarded by ineffable man-headed winged bulls; as frightening then as they are today. They are a reminder that these early civilizations could be pretty savage places to be on the wrong day (although this is true of many cities of the 21st century too); walls might be decorated extensively with skins flayed from enemies and rebels caught alive, and avenues lined with those in the torments of crucifixion. These early cities were sophisticated in some ways, yet barbaric in many others.

EARLY STRUCTURES

At this point in the development of architecture, building techniques were universally simple – sun-dried bricks, in general, laid on sun-dried bricks with little use of sparsely available timber and stone, and thus nothing in the way of the structural invention that would appear in Greece and Rome not long after Babylon's glory days. The most distinctive building type of these Mesopotamian civilizations was the ziggurat, and, although impressive in terms of scale, bulk, and mystery, this was a very simple building type indeed compared with, say, a European Gothic cathedral. In fact, it is fair to say that even the greatest building

THE ISHTAR GATE, BABYLON, 605–563 BC
It has been estimated that the processional avenue that passed through the Ishtar Gate extended for more than half a mile (800m). The roadside was decorated with brick lions, the cult-animal of the goddess Ishtar.

of the time, palace or temple, was little more sophisticated structurally than the simplest – the house. In this sense, the ancient Mesopotamian cities would have seemed pretty much alike: the one-of-a-kind, show-off building fighting to celebrate its own identity was still a long way off.

THE PERSIAN EMPIRE

All of these cities and civilizations were eventually swallowed whole by the world's first great empire, that of the Persians founded by Cyrus II (c.600–530 BC). What we see now is the beginning of the idea of fusion in architecture, or stylistic borrowing. Craftsworkers from across the Empire – Assyrians, Babylonians, Egyptians, and Ionian Greeks – joined forces under imperial direction to create a new type of architecture, freer in form, more decorative, and just a little more lighthearted than the somber ziggurats of ancient Mesopotamia.

The greatest monument of this era was the Palace of Persepolis begun in 518 BC by Darius I and completed about 60 years later by Artaxerxes I. Even by this date we do not know the names of individual architects, only the kings and emperors whose glory they celebrated in brick, stone, and terra-cotta. The palace, raised on a mighty platform, was reached by a great rise of shallow stairs – so that horses could ride up it majestically – flanked on either side by rich relief carvings depicting, among other subjects, images of the peoples and the warriors of the new empire. The palace comprised several buildings, including a harem and, most famously, the Hall of the Hundred Columns, a throne room 225 feet (68.6 meters) square, its painted timber ceiling supported by a forest of columns topped with capitals in the guise of bulls and unicorns. Lavishly decorated and brightly colored, the palace complex at Persepolis shows just how far architecture had moved from the elementary ziggurats and defensive walled cities that introduced humankind to the notion and reality of architecture.

Even so, some of the very finest monuments of the wealthy and far-flung Persian Empire were

TERRACE STAIRWAY AT PERSEPOLIS, IRAN, C.518–460 BC
Approaching from the northwest, the palace was reached via the magnificent terrace stairway. The stone pillars at the top of the stairs mark the site of Xerxes' gatehouse. To the right was the apadana *of Darius I (a columned hall serving as a throne room).*

movingly simple, such as the handsome tombs of the Achaemenid kings (fifth century BC) carved into a rock face at Naksh-i-Rustam, a reminder that the greatest architecture, throughout history, has often been the most pared down and thoughtful.

ACHAEMENID TOMBS, NAKSH-I-RUSTAM, IRAN, FIFTH CENTURY BC
The site of Naksh-i-Rustam takes its name from the carvings below the tombs, thought to represent the mythical hero Rustam. An inscription identifies one of the tombs as that of Darius I, the others are probably those of Xerxes I, Artaxerxes I, and Darius II.

ANCIENT EGYPT
PYRAMIDS AND TEMPLES

THE ARCHITECTURE of ancient Egypt is truly a thing apart. Mysterious, consistent, and a law unto itself, it developed slowly over a very long period – some 3,000 years – for most of which time Egypt was free of invaders, wealthy, and well organized. The country's fortune and culture were based on the cycle and flow of the Nile River. Each year the waters of the river rose and brought the valley into bloom. During this time of year, the country went into a kind of agricultural overdrive, producing food that would have to last through the succeeding drought – the dry season – and until the next year. Because there was little or nothing farmers and laborers could do on the land during the dry season, when the river fell, ancient Egypt had a surplus of skilled and unskilled labor for five months of every year. This labor was set to work on the monuments we associate with this enduring and ceaselessly fascinating culture: the pyramids.

The pyramids were designed to house the mummified body of pharaohs and their treasures.

In the Egyptian mind, the soul was immortal and the pharaoh a god. In due course the souls of the royal dead would return to their bodies and make use of the treasures stored for them in their vast stone monuments. The pyramid represented the apex of a religious culture obsessed for 3,000 years with death and the afterlife. The first Egyptian cities were necropolises – cities of the dead – and pyramids stood in the center of walled cities composed of temples and halls linked by long corridors lined with columns, the capitals of which were designed to resemble palm, lotus, and papyrus flowers.

What a strange sight these necropolises would have been. Ordinary people lived along the riverbank in ephemeral and sprawling villages of simple, whitewashed mud-brick houses (models of these were placed in the royal tombs, which is one of the reasons we know so much about everyday life in ancient Egypt). In contrast, the dead set out on the long road to eternal life in some of the biggest and most impressive monuments ever built, set in well-ordered cities.

THE FIRST PYRAMIDS
The pyramids grew out of the earliest royal tombs, known as mastabas. These tended to be stepped structures, but rarely more than 25 feet (7.6 meters) high. One of the earliest pyramids was the Step Pyramid of Zoser at Sakkara (beginning of the Third Dynasty, c.2778 BC) designed by King Zoser's architect, Imhotep, who was deified in the Twenty-Sixth Dynasty. Not only is Imhotep the first architect we know by name, but the pyramid he built was the world's first major monument built in stone. Given that the Egyptians never invented the pulley, this pyramid (like later ones) was an extraordinary feat of construction. Huge granite blocks from Aswan, weighing on average 2.5 tons (2.54 tonnes), were brought up the Nile and then dragged on wooden rollers to the building site. They were heaved up mud ramps formed against the slope of the rising pyramid and levered into position. The accuracy with which Egyptian architects and masons worked has always been something of a mystery; but when you are building not for the next 50 or 100 years, but for eternity, there is no point in doing things by half-measure.

STEP PYRAMID OF ZOSER, SAKKARA, 2778 BC
Rising in six steps, the pyramid forms the focal point of the funerary complex of King Zoser. The pyramid was built by Imhotep, the earliest named architect, who in the Twenty-Sixth Dynasty was deified. This was the first structure to use dressed stone throughout.

The pyramid at Sakkara represents several rebuildings of an earlier mastaba; in its final form, as seen today, it became a six-stepped structure 197 feet (60 meters) high, its base measuring 410 feet x 358 feet (125 x 109 meters). The first of the smooth-sided pyramids was built at Meydum for Huni, last king of the Third Dynasty. This began life as a stepped granite pyramid, but the sides were later encased in slabs of finely dressed Tufa limestone, so that when the work was complete the monument appeared to be constructed of four massive equilateral triangles. The top stones may well have been gilded and the whole device, oriented precisely according to the points of the compass, would have shone in both sunlight and moonlight.

THE GREAT PYRAMIDS OF GIZA

The Fourth Dynasty was the great age of pyramid building. The most famous are the three sited together at Giza to the south of present-day Cairo. These are the pyramids of Cheops, Chephren, and Mykerinos. That of Cheops is one of the wonders of the world, ancient or modern. No less than 480 feet (146.4 metres) high and rising from a base 756 feet (230.6 metres) square, it remains one of the largest buildings of all time. The masons who built the great pyramid were also responsible for the gigantic and strange sculpture we know as the Sphinx, which slouches, half-man (the head of the pharaoh Chephren), half-beast in the precise shadow of its parent. It is interesting to note an inscription that tells us that the Sphinx was first

BOOK OF THE DEAD

This Egyptian collection of mortuary texts was made up of spells and magic formulas and placed in tombs in the belief that it protected the deceased in the afterlife. Probably compiled and re-edited during the 16th century BC, the collection included coffin texts dating from c.2000 BC, pyramid texts dating from c.2400 BC, and other writings. The *Book of the Dead* got its title from Richard Lepsius, the German Egyptologist who published the first collection of the texts in 1842.

PYRAMID OF CHEPHREN, FOURTH DYNASTY

This was the second of the three pyramids at Giza. In the foreground, the Great Sphinx bears the head of Chephren on the body of a lion.

TEMPLE OF AMUN, LUXOR, C.1408–1300 BC
The temple, dedicated to the Theban triad, Amun, Mut, and Khons, was begun by Amenophis III. The great forecourt (above), with pylons, was added by Rameses II. Huge statues of Rameses II flank the entrance. The obelisk was one of a pair.

restored under Thotmes IV in the Eighteenth Dynasty (c.1425 BC): the conservation of old buildings and monuments is nothing new.

And yet for all their enigmatic beauty and geometric brilliance, the pyramids, which reached their peak c.2600 BC (the same time as the great neolithic stone circle was erected at Avebury in southern England), were considered obsolete by about 2000 BC. The New Kingdom of this time ushered in the rock tombs we associate foremost with the Valley of the Kings at Thebes (on the west bank of the Nile and not far from today's Luxor). These magnificent underground structures digging as deep as 315 feet (96 meters) and as far as 689 feet (210 meters) into the rocky Theban

hills were designed, unsuccessfully as it turned out, to baffle tomb robbers for whom the supposedly secret tunnels and chambers inside the pyramids were little more than child's play. Most of the rock tombs (some remain undiscovered at the beginning of the 21st century) were looted; one that escaped was the tomb of Tutankhamun, discovered in all its glory by the British archaeologist, Howard Carter, in 1922.

EGYPTIAN TEMPLES

Beyond the pyramids, the most important Egyptian monuments are the temples built for the popular worship of the gods during the New Kingdom (c.1550–1070 BC). The most famous are the Great Temple of Amun at Karnak (begun in c.1530 BC) and the Temple of Luxor, Thebes (c.1408 BC). These enormous buildings are approached along avenues lined with sphinxes and under frightening entrance gates or pylons that lead into colonnaded halls, courtyards, and sanctuaries. The walls of the pylons are typically "battered," that is, they slope inward from bottom to top. This was a way of building strongly and assuredly with mud-bricks, although it eventually became a style of building that characterized much ancient and revived Egyptian architecture.

The columns were painted and decorated and were much heavier than those of ancient Greece and Rome. The whole effect, especially inside these complex buildings, must have been mysterious in the extreme. The hypostyle hall of the Great Temple of Amun is quite daunting, a forest of no fewer than 134 columns in 16 rows supporting a stone-slabbed roof that rises 79 feet (24 meters) into the sun-flecked gloom. The chamber measures 338 x 170 feet (103 x 52 meters) and is lit by sunlight filtering through a clerestory of pierced stone blocks set between the tops of the walls and the roof. The temples were walled around and their grounds contained houses and stores for priests and servants as well as a sacred lake: the one at Karnak survives. The temple at Karnak was extended over a period of no less than 1,000 years, and yet even experts find it difficult to date its different parts: to say that styles were very slow to change in ancient Egypt can only be a massive understatement.

GREAT TEMPLE OF AMUN, KARNAK, 1530–323 BC
The vast hypostyle hall (c.1312–1301 BC) was built by Seti I and Rameses II. The central avenues are about 78ft (24m) in height and have columns 69ft (21m) high and 11ft 9in (3.6m) in diameter.

Even so, there are a number of distinctive buildings that show very different ways of realizing much the same goal. The Great Temple at Abu-Simbel (c.1301 BC) represents the Egyptians' obsession with overscaled and even outrageous statuary. The temple is cut into a rock-face; its stupendous entrance is designed as a pylon fronted with not one but four 66-foot- (20-meter-) high seated statues of Rameses II, the dynamic warrior-king who had it built. Inside there is a rather eerie 29-foot- (9-meter-) high main chamber, its roof held up by pillars in the guise of the god Osiris.

But where the Great Temple of Abu-Simbel appears to look back to a distant and unreasonable world, the low-lying and crisply colonnaded ranges of Queen Hatshepsut's funerary temple (1520 BC), set against the overhanging cliffs of Der el-Bahari (Thebes), appear to look forward to the noble and highly rational architecture of ancient Greece. The temple was designed by the architect Senmut. It rises in three elongated tiers linked by shallow ramps. Each tier proves to be a shady colonnade. The columns look less like the vegetable-style designs we associate with ancient Egypt and more like prototypes for their Doric Greek successors. The walls are highly decorated with scenes of the life of Hatshepsut, a very dynamic woman, including that of her allegedly divine birth. At the top of the temple is a giant altar to the sun god Ra. The Queen herself was buried in a chamber at the end of a corridor deep inside the cliff-face.

Although the Egyptians thrived for another 1,500 years, their art and architecture tended to ossify and never again reached the peaks of the great pyramids of the third millennium BC, or the temples of the second millennium. But in the structures of ancient Egypt lay the essential building blocks of virtually all architecture since.

HATSHEPSUT

The daughter of King Thutmose I and Queen Ahmose, Hatshepsut reigned from 1503–1482 BC. She attained unprecedented power for a queen, and wore the pharaoh's crown and royal ceremonial beard. Her reign was marked by an expansion of trade: an expedition to the land of Punt brought back gold, ivory, incense, birds, and trees. She also encouraged architecture and other arts.

TEMPLE OF QUEEN HATSHEPSUT, DER EL-BAHARI, 1520 BC

This mortuary temple, dedicated to Amun and other gods, was built by Queen Hatshepsut's architect, Senmut. The fine wall reliefs include representations of the queen's trade expedition to Punt. A processional way of sphinxes linked the temple with the valley.

EARLY AFRICA
TRADITIONAL ARCHITECTURE

DOGON ARCHITECTURE

The Dogon people, who number about 200,000, appear to have lived in the villages of the Bandiagara Plateau in southern Mali for at least 500 years. The main house of a compound is usually rectangular, two-storied, and closed off with a roof terrace. Rough stones are used in building at least the foundation walls. The living quarters of the women and children and the storehouses are grouped around the living quarters of the head of the family. In between, there is a courtyard. The storage towers (above) can only be reached by ladders because their openings are very high up. Interiors are divided into separate chambers by walls going up to half the height of the towers.

SOUTH OF THE SAHARA, African architecture was once, in Western terms, something of a nonstarter. There was a temptation to think that until the arrival of European settlers and colonialists there was nothing here more substantial than a variety of huts; and that even if some of these – those of the Zulu and Ndebele tribes in South Africa, for example – were very beautiful, they could not be classified as "Architecture." What is certain is that without permanent building materials to hand next to nothing of ancient African architecture has survived, although well-planned houses have been excavated from the medieval era at El Ghaba in what was the ancient kingdom of Ghana and in the Swahili town of Gedi in Kenya. If we look at the African continent in terms of modern, environmentally sensitive architecture and consider the materials and practices used to construct its buildings, Africa has much to teach the West.

Despite their scarcity, there *are* monumental ruins to be found in Africa, notably the great Iron Age enclosure at Great Zimbabwe, Zimbabwe (c.1000–1500 BC) – a fortresslike compound – and the Palace of Husuni Kubwa, Tanzania (c.1245). Measuring 481 feet (150 meters) by 241 feet (75 meters), this seaside palace contained at least 100 rooms. These were windowless, built of coral ragstone with dressed stonework around the doors. The royal chambers were barrel-vaulted and ornamented with decorative stonework. The palace had an octagonal bathing pool and was laid out on a geometric grid.

Elsewhere in Africa, there were fairly large cities, palaces, and forts, but as these tended to be built of mud, few have survived. One of the last, Benin City – once the center of a thriving empire – was destroyed by fire shortly after the British colonialists arrived in 1897.

Yet where it has survived or been successfully rebuilt, generation after generation, mud architecture is one of the true wonders of early Africa. Although rebuilt in the last century, the Sankore Mosque, Timbuktu, and that at Djenne – both in Mali – date back to the early fourteenth century. Mud walls, constantly renewable, cover a timber frame, although this is more like scaffolding than anything more elaborate or substantial. They look like giant termites' nests, their minarets hollowed out inside. The mosques of Bobo Diulasso in Burkina and Kong in Ivory Coast are smaller and, due to a moister climate, use larger buttresses and more timber.

A GREENER ARCHITECTURE

This is an ecologically sound, indigenous architecture that is very much back in favor at the beginning of the twenty-first century. The story of architecture is one of stretching new technologies and new ideas to previously unthought-of limits. And yet, there are forms of architecture such as these impressive

CONICAL TOWER, GREAT ZIMBABWE, 11–16TH CENTURY
This 33-ft (10-m) high conical tower stands inside the main enclosure at Great Zimbabwe. Its exact purpose is unknown. The construction of the tower and of the nearby walls illustrate the Zimbabweans' brilliant use of close-fitting granite blocks.

mud mosques that draw us up short and show how much can be achieved working with few resources, little money, and for everyman.

MOSQUE AT DJENNE, 14TH CENTURY
Djenne in Mali was once a major center of trade, learning, and religion. The Djenne mosque, like Djenne houses, has regular buttresses with projecting pinnacles and an impressive stepped entrance.

DOMESTIC AFRICAN STRUCTURES

The most common form of African structure is a circular hut made of clay or stone, crowned with a conical — often thatched — roof. These are found particularly among the agricultural people of the grasslands, such as the Nok in northern Nigeria, who build similarly shaped structures for use as granaries. Other styles of structure include square huts with decorative sculpted poles, such as those in the Cameroon. Elsewhere in West Africa are clay box houses, or impluvia, rectangular buildings with overhanging roofs positioned around a central courtyard into which rain cascades (hence the name).

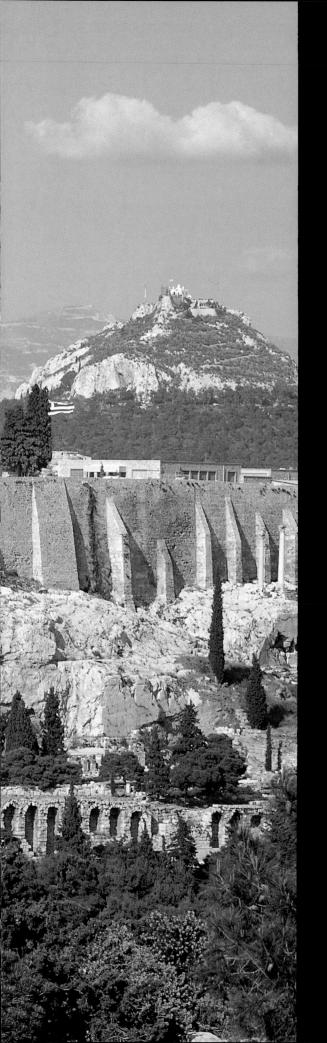

The CLASSICAL WORLD

Before the rise of Classical Greece, architecture seems rather dark and mysterious, a theater of somber and even macabre ritual, an opera of histrionic effects and willful forms. Although this is not strictly true, it is only with the geometric perfection and noble order of Greek temples and amphitheaters that architecture begins to offer a harmonious connection between humankind and the gods, the everyday and the spiritual, the art of building and the magnificent artlessness of nature. Ancient Greece and Rome produced, without doubt, some of the greatest buildings and cities yet. They have continued to fascinate us and to inspire architects and planners worldwide, even in the age of space travel, nano-technology, and the internet.

THE ACROPOLIS, ATHENS
The Acropolis was originally a fortified citadel with its own palace. The first temple to Athena was probably built sometime in the eighth century and the Parthenon that still stands early in the fifth.

ANCIENT GREECE
ORDER AND HARMONY

PERICLES

During his long political career (c.461– 429 BC), the statesman and admiral Pericles brought Athenian democracy to its peak and came close to establishing Athens as the leading state in Greece. From 451 BC, he embarked on a policy of cultural renewal, commissioning a series of public buildings, including the Parthenon, designed to reflect Athenian prominence.

THE PARTHENON is perhaps the greatest and most influential building of all time. It is a thing of immense beauty, as timeless in its appeal as a building can be. A temple devoted to Athena, the Greek goddess of wisdom and guardian of the city-state of Athens that took her name, the Parthenon marked the zenith of ancient Greek architecture. In terms of the ways in which it relates to the city below, the magnificent landscape beyond, to the lesser temples and public buildings gathered around it, and to the human eye, the Parthenon had no rivals in its day and has none at the beginning of the 21st century. It was everything the Greeks wanted

their peerless architecture to be. The building is now a ruin, but being built of marble (with a timber roof), it had survived in pretty good shape from its completion in 436 BC up until the Venetian attack on Athens in 1687, when Greece was under the control of the Turks. The Turks had turned the Parthenon into a mosque in 1458 (complete with onion dome sprouting incongruously through the roof; it had been converted into a Christian church in the late sixth century), and they also used it as a gunpowder store, which blew up. Today, pollution does even more damage: the world's greatest building is vanishing before our eyes.

The Parthenon was commissioned by Pericles sometime after Greek victories over the Persians between 490 and 480 BC. Phidias, the sculptor, was given the task

The influence of the Parthenon on Leo von Klenze's (1784–1864) neoclassical temple is clear. Built for the Crown Prince Ludwig of Bavaria, its hilltop location recalls the Athenian Acropolis (high city).

of coordinating the rebuilding of the temples that overlooked the teeming city and its *agora* (marketplace) below. The temples had been burned by the Persians at an earlier date and subsequently patched up. In turn, Phidias turned to the architects Ictinus and Callicrates, who spent 11 years (447–436 BC) perfecting the great Doric temple in their charge.

Like all architecture, the exterior of the building was much more important than the interior. The climate encouraged the Greeks to spend much time outside meeting one another, so the colonnade – the external corridors of columns that run around all sides of a Greek temple – were all-important. Sunlight played through these and gave the buildings a depth and magic that conventional brick or stone walls lacked. To ensure that their temple looked perfect – perfectly straight and in perfect proportion – to the human eye, Ictinus and Callicrates used the technique known as *entasis* to ever so slightly deform the columns and architraves at the fronts and sides of the building. This distortion (there is not a true straight line to be found in the construction of the Parthenon) causes the eye to see straight lines where otherwise they would appear to curve or sag. It is a brilliant device, and required not only great mathematical judgment on behalf of the architects but immense skill on the part of the masons.

PARTHENON, ATHENS, 447–436 BC
The supreme example of Doric temple design, the Parthenon was built to house the cult statue of Athena Parthenos. The largest temple on the Greek mainland, it marks the zenith of the Periclean period.

Like most, and perhaps all, Greek temples, the Parthenon was brightly colored in reds, blues, and golds. Its statuary would have seemed over-the-top to our eyes. We have become so used to seeing Greek temples as chaste, honey-colored ruins in the landscape that we forget that they were designed to frame and inspire great colorful ceremonies. This was not a society that lived quietly behind closed doors. For the most part, houses were fairly dull or nondescript, leading off narrow twisting alleys in the oldest towns: the open space of the *agora* and the theater of the temples, gathered in picturesque fashion on the acropolis above the city, were busy night and day.

A SYMBOLIC TEMPLE

Symbolically, the Parthenon and its sibling temples represented key aspects of Greek society and culture. The temple was at once a place of gathering and worship as well as a representation of a Greek fighting ship (the basis of Greek power), a domestic loom (the root of every Greek household), and the people (*demos*) themselves – although Athens and the Greek city-states were democracies in a limited sense only. The people were represented by the columns that ran around the buildings as if clustering around the presence of Athena, whose huge statue stood at the heart of the Parthenon. The loom was represented by the temple fronts with their columns set, as with a loom, within a clearly defined frame. As for the fighting ship, that was suggested in the way in which *entasis* caused the columns, and thus the front, of the temple to billow out like a sail. For ancient Greeks, then, a temple like the Parthenon was not just beautiful and impressive but was also a sign and symbol of all the core values that held their civilization together.

The Parthenon's legacy has been vast. Exact representations of the temple have been built in different parts of the world, while its essence – that of a perfect, serene, and detached building – has influenced architects right into the age of the machine, and beyond.

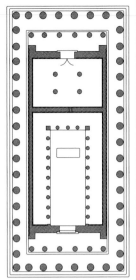

PLAN OF THE PARTHENON

The Parthenon differs from other Greek temples in that the façade, extended under Pericles' leadership, has eight rather than six columns. The number of side columns was increased accordingly to 17. The colonnade encloses the cella, the interior structure, which is divided into two chambers. The larger chamber housed the statue of Athena.

GREEK WARSHIP
Athens maintained control of its empire by means of a fleet of oar-powered warships, or triremes. At the height of its power, in the fifth century BC, the city-state boasted some 300 triremes.

The Parthenon developed fairly rapidly from a style and approach to architecture that had emerged perhaps 150 years earlier; this was the Doric "order" that was probably first used in the design of the Heraion, an acropolis of sacred and civic buildings gathered around the Temple of Hera and dating from c.590 BC. The Doric was what you might call the house-style of the Dorian invaders who came to Greece from the Balkans c.1000 BC. The heyday of ancient Greece and thus Athens itself was between 800 and 323 BC (the latter date being the death of Alexander the Great and the dissipation of the Hellenic empire). The earliest Greek architecture, or architecture in areas later settled by the Greeks, is witnessed in the ruins and reconstruction (in parts) of the Minoan palace of King Minos at Knossos on the island of Crete, dating from sometime between 1625 and 1375 BC. Yet this is labyrinthine architecture, the stuff of nightmares rather than sunlit reason; the Parthenon could hardly be further away in spirit – the Greeks had come a very long way in a thousand years.

PYTHAGORAS

Born in about 570 BC on the island of Samos, Pythagoras was an important philosopher and mathematician whose ideas influenced those of Plato and Aristotle and advanced the development of mathematics. He believed that numerical ratios are the basis of order in the physical world. This concept, which Pythagoras applied to the musical scale, is manifest in the harmonic proportions of Greek architecture.

CLASSICAL ORDERS

At the heart of Greek architecture were the Classical "orders" – the types and styles of columns and the forms of structure and decoration that followed on from them. We know them as Doric (as in the design of the Parthenon), Ionic, and Corinthian, which developed one after the other. Each stemmed, initially, from different parts of Greece: Ionic came principally from the

ARTIST'S IMPRESSION OF THE ACROPOLIS, ATHENS
This 19th-century lithograph is a reconstruction of the Athenian Acropolis at the end of the fifth century BC. Visible are the Parthenon; the Propylaea, the gateway to the sacred precinct; and, on the right, the Erechtheion, an Ionic temple dedicated to the cults of Athena, Poseidon, and the legendary King Erechtheus.

Ionian islands; Corinthian was a late development. The three types of columns were developments of the Egyptian columns, which symbolized bunches of reeds tied together. The capitals of Greek columns were, again, representations of natural forms, as in the rams' horns of the Ionic or the stylized acanthus leaves of the Corinthian. They gave the temples and principal civic buildings of Greece (and, later, Rome) quite different characters: without a doubt, Doric columns are serious and rather masculine, while Corinthian columns suggest delicacy and femininity.

THE GREEK SPIRIT

Greek architecture is, unlike the Egyptian and Mesopotamian styles that preceded it, both serious and lighthearted. For the first time we can look at buildings and see a sense of gaiety and humor. Earlier architecture never smiles. But then Greek society, notably at its height in the fifth century BC, had begun to produce architects, mathematicians, philosophers, artists, and playwrights of the very highest order: it also produced wits and satirists. Now, perhaps, civilization can be said to have truly begun: people were able to laugh at themselves.

The Greek temples were literally the high point of Greek cities, although the buildings themselves were never tall. The Greeks chose and perfected

THE CLASSICAL ORDERS

Of the three Greek orders, Doric is the earliest and the most massive; the column has no base, a fluted shaft, and a plain capital. The Ionic column is a lighter development of the Doric; the fluted shaft has a base and a volute capital. The Corinthian, with its plinth and fluted shaft, is a variant of the Ionic, and distinctive in its ornate capital.

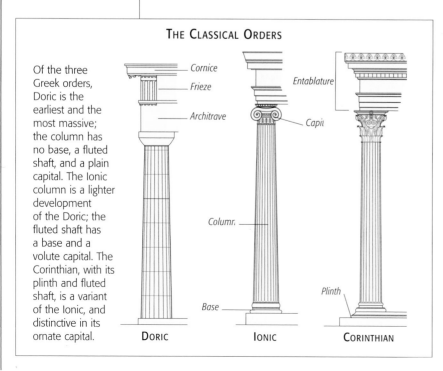

Cornice
Frieze
Architrave
Entablature
Capi
Column
Base
Plinth

DORIC   IONIC   CORINTHIAN

seats, exactly as in the arrangement of sports stadiums more than 2,000 years later. The gymnasium was another important building type. It was often associated with a school; that at Priene is still dotted with the names of ancient Greek schoolboys who carved them into the walls of their open classrooms. Such buildings were equipped with running water.

OTHER GREEK TEMPLES

Some of the best-preserved Greek temples are not to be found in Greece but elsewhere along the Mediterranean coast. What is popularly known as the Temple of Neptune (its actual dedication was to the goddess Hera), at Paestum on the Italian Coast south of Naples, is one of the best preserved of all. The double-tier of columns inside this heavy Doric temple remains intact. Because relatively few tourists come this way, the Temple of Neptune can be experienced as those who first rediscovered these buildings in the 18th century would have done. They are, as yet, free from the theme-park, *son-et-lumière* treatment given to all too many ancient monuments. At Paestum, it is still possible to catch a glimpse of life in ancient Greece. The temples there, and houses and temples farther west along the Mediterranean, show not only how trade and empires spread at an early date, but also how architectural styles and precedent spread with them. Although there was a long pause between the height of Greek civilization and the Greek Revival of the late 18th and 19th centuries, the architecture of the Parthenon was eventually to reach every part of the world.

ATHLETICS

Agones (public festivals in honor of a god or hero) played an important role in Greek society. The chief attractions at these events were chariot racing and athletics. Of the four major athletic festivals – Olympic, Pythian, Nemean, and Isthmian – the most important was the Olympic Games, held every four years in honor of Zeus and begun in 776 BC. The importance of the games is reflected in the buildings erected to house the events. Impressive stadiums survive at Delphi, Olympia, Epidaurus, and Athens. The amphora above shows four athletes taking part in the pentathlon.

a system of design and construction (post-and-lintel) that suited them even though, despite rumors to the contrary, they were quite able to make arches and other sophisticated forms. Beneath them spread not only the *agora* with their colonnades (*stoas*) – behind which were shops, offices, workshops, and places to eat – but also the assembly halls, stadiums, gymnasiums, and theaters that no Greek city worthy of the name lacked. The model Greek citizen was meant to be healthy in mind and body, a classical all-arounder. These ancillary buildings remain some of the most beautiful and usable structures in the world. The theater at Epidaurus, for example, designed by Polycleitos and built c.350–330 BC, seats 13,000 people on 55 rows of stone seats that wrap around the "orchestra" (or dancing floor for performers) and face the *skene* (stage building), itself long since vanished. The theater, though, remains in use, and its acoustics are perfect.

Nearby is the Epidaurus stadium, another important Greek building type. In later designs (c.325 BC), the audience sat around the track on tiers of stone seats with the entrance to the stadium gained by tunnels passing under the

THEATER, EPIDAURUS, C.350–330 BC

By the fourth century BC, theaters had achieved a uniform design – that at Epidaurus is an excellent example. Now, instead of temporary wooden seating, concentric rows of stone seats were built in a large semicircle surrounding the "orchestra" and stage area. The "orchestra" at Epidaurus is 67ft (20.4m) in diameter.

ANCIENT ROME
THE MASTER BUILDERS

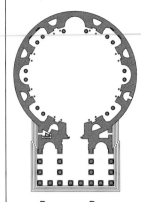

PANTHEON PLAN
The diameter of the Pantheon's floor plan is equal to the height of its dome. In theory the building could hold a perfect sphere, the original Pantheon building being dedicated to the gods of the then-known planets. The portico incorporates elements from an earlier temple building.

CONCRETE
It was the Romans who first used concrete, mixing volcanic soil with lime, and interspersing it with another material, often broken tiles. Concrete enabled them to make large structures – such as domes – spanning vast areas without direct support. Roman concrete was not reinforced like our modern-day equivalent and therefore could not bear direct loads. Its invention, however, revolutionized the shape and possibilities of architecture.

THE PANTHEON is to ancient Roman architecture what the Parthenon is to ancient Greek. It represents the high point of Roman design and structural engineering. It epitomizes the difference between Greek and Roman ways of building. The Pantheon (AD c. 118–28), a giant domed temple deep in the beating heart of Rome, was designed possibly by the emperor Hadrian himself. It is a deeply impressive structure, a phenomenal work of construction, making brilliant use of concrete, but it could never be described as beautiful. Impressive, yes; fascinating, of course; but while the Parthenon is exquisitely beautiful, the Pantheon is a brute in comparison. Why? Because for the Romans architecture was a much more practical affair than it was for the Greeks. The Romans conquered Greece and although they admired and borrowed much in terms of dress, politics, architectural style, learning, and general culture, their engineering feats stretch far beyond those of the earlier Greek civilization with its elegance and grace.

The Romans were the toughies of the ancient world; practical, hard-working, soldiering people. They conquered the whole of the known Western world, connected its extensive parts by a network of superbly engineered roads, and gave their large cities running water – brought from hills and mountains 50 miles (80 kilometers) away and more by extensive aqueducts. They provided public baths, public lavatories, sewers, and public transportation. They built blocks of flats (*insulae*, or islands) originally made of timber and mud bricks, later of concrete, rising up to eight floors high. They made great use of underfloor heating and, in general, their buildings and engineering infrastructure were superior to any previously known, and were to go unchallenged for many centuries after the fall of the Roman Empire in AD 476.

PLASTIC CONSTRUCTION

Roman architecture reflected this common-sensical and no-nonsense attitude towards life, city making, and empire building. The Pantheon is thus a vast building, daringly engineered: its 139-foot (43.2-meter) diameter dome was the world's most ambitious until Brunelleschi raised his over the body of Florence Cathedral between 1420 and 1436. The dome is built of concrete. The Romans made widespread use of this material; it enabled them not just to build domes – which were popular in the design of aristocratic houses as well as in such important civic buildings as the Pantheon – but to construct complete vaults and huge arched constructions such as the Colosseum (AD 70–82). They thus became the masters of what we can call "plastic" construction: in other words, concrete – a malleable, plastic material – enabled them to build freely and on a massive scale. Unlike the earlier Mesopotamian and Greek cultures, they were unrestricted by the need or desire to use post-and-lintel construction methods. They were free to build as they pleased. And how they built.

EARLIER INFLUENCES

Essentially, the Romans adopted Greek and to an extent Etruscan architecture. The Etruscans were the masters of central Italy until subdued by the Romans. Their architecture, influenced by the Greeks, was more flamboyant and primitive; their beautiful funerary monuments, however, have yet to be surpassed. The Romans made great use of the Doric, Ionic, and Corinthian orders, adding two of their own: Tuscan, a modified Doric (from the Etruscans) and Composite, a combination of Ionic and Corinthian. Because concrete allowed them to build

PONT DU GARD, NÎMES, FRANCE, LATE FIRST CENTURY BC
Perhaps the finest surviving example of Roman engineering, this 900-ft- (274-m-) long aqueduct carried water to the city of Nîmes on a channel raised 180ft (55m) above the Gard River.

INTERIOR OF THE PANTHEON, ROME, 1734

This painting by Giovanni Paola Panini (1691/2–1765) shows the Pantheon after its conversion to a church. Originally it was a temple dedicated to the gods of the seven planets. The "eye" in the centre of the roof served to carry off smoke from a central altar and symbolized the sun in the heavens. The cladding and statuary of the lower section are later additions from the Christian era.

VITRUVIUS

Born towards the end of the first century BC, Roman architect and engineer Marcus Vitruvius Pollio was author of the treatise *De architectura*, which he wrote in the first half of the first century AD. The work drew not only on Vitruvius' own experience, but also from the style of earlier Greek architecture. It is divided into ten books on themes such as city planning, building materials, temple construction, and hydraulics.

AMPHITHEATER, EL DJEM, TUNISIA, EARLY THIRD CENTURY AD

Similar to the Colosseum in Rome, this amphitheater is the largest Roman monument in Africa. Smaller than the Colosseum, less emphasis is placed on the decorative external orders, so that the arcades are the predominant features.

without the need for columns, they often used the column as a decorative element in temples, baths, and arenas. Eventually they made flat or half columns that were a part of the wall; these we call pilasters, and they have been a feature of Classical architecture ever since.

Although the Romans built many temples, they were best at making cities. The empire saw these spread throughout the Classical world and, if you had been alive and traveling through the Roman Empire at its peak in, say, AD 200, you would have found its cities, from Londinium (England) to Leptis Magna (Libya) almost homogenous. Building materials and thus forms of design and construction did vary throughout the empire – bricks in Britain, stone in North Africa – yet the essential elements were much of a muchness. Indeed the finest surviving Roman temple (aside from the Pantheon) is the Maison Carrée at Nîmes (see p.124), in the south of France, while many of the most impressive Roman ruins are to be found in modern-day Turkey, Libya, Tunisia, and Syria.

THE CITY OF ROME

Roman cities were big and crowded. At its zenith in c. AD 200, the population of Rome itself exceeded one million. Most citizens lived in *insulae*, a good example of which can still be seen in Ostia, the port of ancient Rome. Until the great fire of Rome of AD 64 (when Nero was said to have played his fiddle while watching the imperial capital go up in flames), these were largely jerry-built of timber and mudbricks by unscrupulous developers: death by fire or structural collapse was a common occurrence.

HOUSES AT HERCULANEUM, ITALY

The ancient city of Herculaneum southeast of Naples, was, like Pompeii, destroyed by the eruption of Vesuvius in AD 79. As at Pompeii, houses here were built in insulae, *large blocks of apartments arranged around courtyards. The city was laid out on a grid system, a fact that suggests Greek influence.*

A law of AD 64 insisted that, in future, *insulae* had to be built with fireproof concrete floors and walls. Ever since, the Roman *insulae* has formed the basis of city apartment blocks the world over.

Merchant, professional, and military families tended to live in city houses grouped around two courtyards. These presented an anonymous face to the street (indeed, entrances were often set between shops), but would have been relatively peaceful within, although we know from his letters that Julius Caesar found Rome impossibly noisy at night and was often unable to sleep. The way these houses were planned has been handed down to us in the design of courtyard housing in European city centers ever since.

IMPERIAL PALACES

The houses of great landowners and emperors were something else altogether, and the greatest and most influential was Hadrian's Villa (c. AD 118–34) near Tivoli, a day's ride south of Rome. This picturesque arrangement of pavilions, libraries, baths, and pleasurable follies spread through more than two miles of gardens. At every turn there would have been a visual surprise: the art of landscape architecture had never been so

GETTY CENTER, LOS ANGELES, 1984–97
Richard Meier's dramatic hilltop campus of galleries and research facilities with its five pavilions, walkways, courtyards, and gardens takes its inspiration from Hadrian's Villa. As with the earlier complex, the Center explores not only the relationship between exterior and interior space, but also that between architecture and landscape.

sophisticated. The Villa has fascinated architects since the Renaissance and has formed the basis of such equally ambitious projects as the Getty Center, Los Angeles, designed in the spirit of Hadrian by Richard Meier. Hadrian and Trajan his predecessor were two of the greatest emperor-

HADRIAN'S VILLA, NEAR ROME, C. AD 118–134
Covering 300 acres (120 hectares), this complex of buildings near Tivoli, outside Rome, was built as a country retreat for the emperor Hadrian and was where he spent his final years. The site included many full-scale reconstructions of architecture from Greece and Egypt.

architects. Hadrian left us the Pantheon, his villa at Tivoli, his massive cylindrical tomb (AD 135–39) in Rome (now the Castel San Angelo), and the Pons Aelius (AD 134) that still crosses the Tiber to give access to his tomb.

EMPEROR TRAJAN

Trajan, a successful and much traveled soldier, commissioned such wonders as the bridge at Alcantara, Spain (architect: C. Julius Lacer); it still carries a roadway on six massive brick arches 154 feet (48 meters) above the Tagus River. One of his most enduring monuments is the column that bears his name in Rome. Erected in AD 112, the 112-foot (35-meter) column celebrated Trajan's victories in the Dacian wars. A spiral stair wound up inside the column to a viewing platform (now topped by a statue of St. Peter). Outside, a continuous frieze depicting episodes in the Dacian campaign followed the spiral of the stairs.

These are superbly realized, but of far greater significance is the superb architectural lettering used for inscriptions on the base of Trajan's column. Trajan's lettering is the basis of modern typography; the text you are reading now is set in a typeface derived from Trajan's.

The Romans were great builders of victory monuments and these have formed the basis of most major victory monuments since the Renaissance. The Arch of Septimius Severus in Rome, for example, is clearly the basis of Marble Arch in London and the Arc de Triomphe in Paris. Obsessed by notions of

TRAJAN'S COLUMN, AD 112
This military column was erected to commemorate the Emperor's victories in Dacia. The surface has carved relief showing scenes from the campaigns. It was originally surmounted by a statue of Trajan (replaced in 1587 by one of St. Peter).

ARCH OF SEPTIMIUS SEVERUS, AD 203
This triumphal arch built to commemorate the tenth anniversary of the accession of Septimius stands in the Forum in Rome. The inscription originally mentioned Septimius' son Geta, this was later removed when Geta was killed by his father's successor Caracalla.

personal hygiene, the Romans brought water into the heart of their cities and built sewers to remove waste. Their aqueducts and public baths are great wonders; their scale remains daunting. Great stadiums such as the Colosseum and racetracks like the Circus Maximus are superb examples of structural engineering and powerful reminders of how emperors kept the population happy, and thus controlled, with their famous policy of "bread and circuses." Yet the Baths of

ARC DE TRIOMPHE, PARIS, 1806

Napoleon's monumental victory arch stands at the heart of Paris and deliberately evokes the triumphal arches of the Roman emperors with their elaborate relief carving, but here the whole project is on a massively enlarged scale.

Caracalla (AD 212–16, see p.143) and Diocletian (AD 298-306) are architectural wonders of the very highest order.

The baths were opulent structures built on a Herculean scale, lavishly finished in rich marbles and set about with statues, fountains, and gardens. The main building of the Baths of Caracalla measures 722 feet (225 meters) by 369 feet (115 meters). This leviathan stood behind the walls of a massive leisure complex complete with stadium, gymnasium, library, and lecture halls. It is hard to imagine how delightful such buildings would have been: nothing like them has been built since, although Pennsylvania Station (see p.143), demolished, in New York City was designed at the turn of the twentieth century by the architects McKim, Meade, & White as an homage to the Baths of Caracalla. The Roman Baths of Diocletian were even bigger than those of Caracalla.

THE BASILICA

If the baths, circuses, and stadiums were three of the most popular meeting places in ancient Rome (and the forum, of course, the Roman equivalent of the Greek *agora*) the basilica was the other. The basilica was the main covered public meeting place and was used for many functions – law court, trading room, and meeting hall among them. Their design was based on that of the imperial baths and the grandest was the Basilica of Constantine (AD 307–12). This comprised two aisles and a nave covered in vaulted concrete ceilings. The nave was 257 feet (80 meters) long, 80 feet (25 meters) wide and 112 feet (35 meters) high; in other words it was as large as a medieval cathedral, and, to our eyes, would have resembled either a Renaissance cathedral or a cathedral-like railway terminal. This is the

right reaction, because the Roman basilica was the basis of the first major Christian churches. In fact, the Basilica of Constantine at Trier in Germany (early fourth century AD) is the link between the architecture of ancient Rome and of Byzantium and the Romanesque architecture of the future. Constantine was, of course, the emperor who converted the Roman Empire to Christianity in AD 313.

BASILICA OF CONSTANTINE AT TRIER, GERMANY, LATE FOURTH CENTURY
Begun in AD 326 as a full-scale cathedral, this large rectangular hall built of red sandstone, interspersed with layers of brick shows the Roman ability to construct vast open interiors without aisles or supporting internal pillars.

From DARKNESS To LIGHT

BETWEEN THE FALL OF THE ROMAN EMPIRE AT THE END OF THE FIFTH CENTURY AD AND THE RISE OF THE GREAT MONASTERIES AND GOTHIC CATHEDRALS, THE DARK AGES ENFOLDED EUROPE. BUT THESE SKETCHILY DOCUMENTED CENTURIES WERE NEVER QUITE THE SHADOWLANDS THAT THEY HAVE BEEN MADE OUT TO BE. IN BYZANTIUM THE EASTERN EMPIRE FLOURISHED, IN MAGNIFICENT MONASTERIES FROM IRELAND TO RUSSIA, CLASSICAL LEARNING WAS COSSETED AND NURTURED, AND THE ARAB ACHIEVEMENT IN SOUTHERN SPAIN BROUGHT NEW LEARNING TO EUROPE. THESE ARE JUST THREE EXAMPLES OF THE CULTURE, ARCHITECTURE, AND CIVILIZATION THAT, FAR FROM DYING, FLOURISHED IN TIMES OF GREAT UNCERTAINTY AND WAR. LIGHT CONTINUED TO SHINE AMID THE ENCIRCLING GLOOM AND SOLDIERY.

HAGIA SOPHIA, ISTANBUL
Completed in the six years after 532, Hagia Sophia stands in a major earthquake zone. Only 21 years after it was built, the dome collapsed, quakes destroyed the dome again in the ninth and fourteenth centuries.

BYZANTINE ARCHITECTURE
THE EASTERN EMPIRE

JUSTINIAN I

After the Roman Empire converted to Christianity, Constantinople became the capital in AD 330. Justinian I (c.482–565) was Byzantine emperor from AD 527 to 565. His lasting contribution to public buildings was largely a result of social concern, repairing existing fortifications, bridges, and aqueducts, and rebuilding cities such as Antioch, which had been devastated by earthquake. His greatest commission is Hagia Sophia in modern Istanbul. His image is remembered in the mosaics at Ravenna (above).

BEFORE THE SACK OF ROME in AD 410 the Roman empire had split into western and eastern halves. The latter had its capital in Constantinople (Istanbul today). The city became a beacon of civilization and a center of Christianity in what had become a barbaric world, an era we have long called the Dark Ages. The early Christian churches in Rome and the western empire were based on basilicas. Although subsequently altered, the best of these to have survived are St. Sabina (AD 422–32) and St. Maria Maggiore (AD 432–40) in Rome and St. Apollinare in Classe (AD 534–49) in Ravenna. But, in the sixth century, as darkness descended on western Europe, Justinian I, the emperor of the eastern empire, revolutionized not just church building but architecture as a whole with one of the most magnificent and adventurous buildings of all time, the church of Hagia Sophia (AD 532–37) or Divine Wisdom.

This was the largest by far of the 30 or so churches he raised in Constantinople during his reign. Its domed structure was to become the basis of such great Renaissance cathedrals as St. Peter's, Rome, and St. Paul's, London. The architects were Anthemius of Tralles and Isidorous of Miletus. They were skilled engineers and mathematicians, although even then the dome partially collapsed about 30 years after its completion; this, however, was put down to the speed of construction dictated by an ambitious emperor rather than any fault in the calculations of the architects themselves.

What Anthemius and Isidorous did was to create a vast place of congregation, a space under great vaulted ceilings and the astonishing central dome, free from interruption by columns and intervening walls. The result is as breathtaking today as it was in the sixth century, even though the church has lost much of its decorative luster and the windows high up in the walls have been made smaller. The concrete dome was said (by the court historian Procopius) to be "suspended by a golden chain from heaven." Only slightly less prosaically, it was supported by four pendentive vaults, which sprang from the four lofty arches that defined the enormous central space below the dome.

Lavishly decorated, the Hagia Sophia showed a number of breaks from the Classicism of Rome; the columns, for example, were topped with capitals decorated with serpentine foliage. Clearly the pragmatic, if ordered, architecture of the West was being seduced by

ST. MARK'S, VENICE, C.1063–73 AND LATER

With its five domes – each carried on a group of four piers – and Greek cross plan St. Mark's clearly shows the influence of Byzantine architecture. This new style had been brought to the city through Venice's extensive trade links with the East. The model for St. Mark's was probably Justinian's Church of the Holy Apostles in Constantinople.

the sensuality and more organic architecture of the East. The Turks, who captured Constantinople in 1153, destroyed many Christian churches, but were deeply impressed by the Hagia Sophia; they turned it into a mosque, which it was to remain for another 500 years. Today it is a museum.

THE SPREAD OF THE DOME

Over the next 500 years, domed architecture spread throughout what became the Byzantine empire, and variations on the theme of Justinian's Hagia Sophia appeared throughout Greece, Macedonia, Serbia, Armenia, Georgia, and later Venice and Sicily. Then it was to spread to Russia, too, and, although in highly bastardized form, the influence of Hagia Sophia could still be felt as late as the beginning of the eighteenth century. Rarely has one building – the Parthenon and the Pantheon aside – had such a pervasive influence. The Hagia Sophia went on to influence the design of some of the greatest mosques as well as cathedrals, but perhaps the most famous "copy" is the delightful St. Mark's, Venice, entirely rebuilt in c.1063–73; in fact the domed and turreted Venetian wonder is more closely based on Justinian's rebuild of Constantine's Church of the Holy Apostles (c.536–65), which was demolished to make way for a mosque in the 15th century.

HAGIA SOPHIA, ISTANBUL, AD 532–37
Part of the genius of Hagia Sophia lies in the fact that the weight of the central dome is dissipated through the smaller domes that surround it. The result is a huge central space uncluttered by columns, while the dome itself appears to float in space.

PROCOPIUS
The Byzantine historian Procopius (fl. first half of the sixth century AD) produced works that are an indispensable source for the period. He was adviser to the military general Belisarius on his campaigns and may have been prefect of Constantinople in 562. His chief works include Wars, *dealing with the wars against the Goths, Vandals, and Persians and* Buildings, *describing the structures erected by Justinian throughout the Byzantine empire.*

Nevertheless, the influence is there as it was in hundreds of provincial churches throughout the fossilizing Byzantine empire.

It was long believed that the ruins of Hagia Sophia-like churches must exist somewhere in Armenia, a land that became Christian before Rome did. Instead we find remote and beautiful fortified churches based on a highly centralized plan and capped with roofs that are more towers than domes; yet the spirit of Justinian's architecture is there somewhere in the stones of such delightful buildings as the Church of the Holy Cross, Aght'amar, Georgia (AD 915–21), which stood as a place of sanctuary and a beacon of Christianity in a fierce and mountainous world, as frightening now as it must have been 1,000 years ago. The plan of this Armenian church was clearly expressed in its form, representing the cross on which Christ was crucified. In the

ST. FOSCA, TORCELLO, ITALY, C.1100
Standing at Torcello, just outside Venice, this church is unusual in that it is a domed construction sitting over a cross plan, but the arms of the cross, seen here on either side of the dome itself, are very short. The church stands next to a basilican cathedral and campanile.

Eastern Church, the Greek cross plan was gradually adopted for most churches – four equal arms – while the Western Church adopted a cruciform plan that was a more literal depiction of a crucifix; this can be seen in any number of Western churches and cathedrals up until the mid-twentieth century. A more sophisticated variation on the domed, Greek cross plan than that of Aght'amar can be seen in the exquisite church of St.Fosca (c.1100) on the island of Torcello in the Venetian Lagoon. This peaceful brick church, very much of a piece, is surrounded by an octagonal portico.

SECULAR ARCHITECTURE

Of domestic architecture from the early Byzantine period precious little survives. However, we can assume that palaces, baths, theaters, and sports buildings continued along the lines of their Roman predecessors for very many years; if anything, they would have been more lavishly decorated.

One of the most magical survivors is not a palace or basilica, but the Great Water Cistern (Yerebatan Saray) that stood under the Basilica in the center of Constantinople. This magnificent cathedral of water was fed by aqueducts: 400 domed vaults are supported by 12 rows of 28 columns some topped with Corinthian-like marble columns. The effect is stupendous – an underground temple that appears to reach for ever, its supporting columns reflected in the water. This is truly the realm of Neptune.

The Cistern is a good example of the esteem in which the ancient world held such engineering marvels, and, as water was the source of life itself, surely it was only right to celebrate it with an architecture to match. Such celebration of

CHURCH OF THE HOLY CROSS, AGHT'AMAR, GEORGIA, AD 915–21
This late Byzantine structure places greater emphasis on height than earlier structures. There is also substantial exterior decoration shown in relief ornamentation on friezes and around the walls.

public utilities was not to return until the nineteenth century. In the Europe of the Dark Ages (with the notable exception of the Islamic caliphate of Andaluz based in Granada, Cordoba, and Seville), running water and sewers were forgotten and there was, even in the medieval world, a sense that bathing was somehow wrong because sensual and thus sinful.

RUSSIAN ARCHITECTURE

Christianity came to Russia late, in the tenth century. It brought with it the forms of Byzantine architecture, but these were always cruder, tougher, and certainly more barbaric in feel than anything seen on the roads and rivers that lead back to the heart of the Orthodox Church in Constantinople.

The Russian Orthodox Church was later to separate from its parent. The obvious stylistic contribution of Russian churches was the onion dome; this was originally shaped to cope with the heavy snows of the Russian winter. It is also significant that Russian churches presented a massive and hunched-up appearance, as in the example of the Cathedral of St. Demetrius, Vladimir (1194–97). Here, though, the high walls are movingly and lovingly decorated with relief carvings, because, soon enough, they were

needed as sanctuaries and fortresses by local people trying to escape the Mongol invasions (these started in 1237). The fight against the invaders lasted for at least the next 300 years, only then did the "Russias" unite under one language and with a new capital at Moscow.

The degree to which Russia found her own voice over the ensuing 300 years is most enjoyably witnessed in the gloriously exotic cathedral of St. Basil (1555–61) commissioned by Ivan the Terrible from the architects Barma and Posnik. Based not on a Greek cross plan but an eight-pointed star, the cathedral seems to belong to some extraterrestrial cult. It was plainer in its infancy, but was added to over the next century. What it shows, however, is how far one architectural idea – Justinian's Hagia Sophia – could be stretched, distorted, and turned into something quite different, if distantly related, over the course of 1,000 years.

CATHEDRAL OF ST. DEMETRIUS, VLADIMIR, 1194–97
The cathedral was built by the order of Prince Vsevolod (1170–1212), who was baptized as Demetrius. Vladimir is one of the cities of the Golden Ring northeast of Moscow. These independent principalities led to the foundation of separate bishoprics and schools of architects. The church is the only surviving part of Vsevolod's palace complex.

RUSSIAN ICONS
In the classical Byzantine and Orthodox tradition, iconography is not realistic but a symbolical art; expressing in line and color the theological teaching of the church. Russian iconic art dates back to 988, the year when Vladimir, Grand Duke of Kievan Russia, married a Byzantine princess and converted to Christianity. It took its inspiration from Greek sources and became the art of the clergy. Identifiable schools appeared in places such as Vladimir, Rostov, and Kiev. The Icon of the Archangel Gabriel (above), often called that of the *Golden-Haired Angel*, is from the late 12th century.

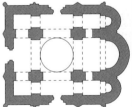

CATHEDRAL OF ST. DEMETRIUS
The groundplan is elongated in the longitudinal axis. The cathedral is a single-domed cross-in-square with a western tribune, high corner bays, three apses, and four cruciform piers. Three Romanesque recessed portals lead into the interior.

MONASTERIES
THE LIFE OF SECLUSION

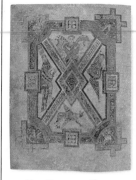

THE BOOK OF KELLS
One of the finest achievements of the great age of Irish monasticism is the *Book of Kells*. Created by Irish monks in the 8th and early 9th centuries, and later taken to the monastery of Kells in Ireland, it is perhaps the finest illuminated manuscript of this remarkably productive time. Written on vellum, it contains a Latin text of the Gospels in Insular Majuscule script accompanied by magnificent and intricate whole pages of decoration with smaller painted decorations appearing throughout the text.

SOME OF THE GREATEST of all medieval buildings were the monasteries of the great Catholic religious orders represented by the Benedictines, Carthusians, Cluniacs, Cistercians, Augustinians, Knights Templar, and Knights Hospitaller. They built cathedral-like churches surrounded by citylike clusters of cloisters, refectories, dormitories, libraries, hospitals, and guest rooms. They were famous for their hospitality and, in later years, for their great wealth. These were monasteries were seats of learning as well as of devotion. They were rarely as corrupt as post-Reformation tracts and novels liked to suggest, and certainly neither the hotbeds of sex and debauchery depicted by scurrilous authors like de Sade in the eighteenth century, nor anything like the frightening places conjured by early Gothic horror writers like William Beckford (*Vathek*, 1786) and Matthew Lewis (*The Monk*, 1796).

GALLARUS ORATORY, DINGLE, IRELAND, 8TH CENTURY AD
This perfectly preserved boat-shaped monastery is windowless and narrow with a small single doorway. The shape probably derives from the dry-stone methods of construction.

The word monastery comes from the Greek word *monasterion* meaning "living alone." The earliest monks were the recluses and hermits of third- and fourth-century Egypt. Over a period of 200–300 years they began to form communities. Some of the earliest surviving monastic buildings are to be found on the Dingle peninsula in southwest Ireland. Monks came to Ireland from Wales with St. Patrick, and from here their ideas and architecture filtered back to England from AD 635, when Aidan was sent to evangelize the north of England. These early buildings were rarely more than simple, rugged stone shelters designed to keep off the strong winds and insistent rains of the west coast of Ireland. They were also refuges in times of trouble and violence.

One of the best surviving of the early Irish monastic buildings is the Oratory of Gallarus at Dingle, County Kerry. Dating probably from some time in the eighth century AD, it resembles an upturned boat or a stone roof of a large house that has long ago sunk into the peaty soil. It features a square-topped door on its west side and a single, round-topped window on its east side. As much a work of landscape art as a prayer hall, it has its own elemental beauty.

THE CISTERCIAN ORDER
The great medieval monasteries emerged with the birth of the Cistercian order in France. The Cistercians were a puritanical order who broke away from the Benedictines in 1098. They wore

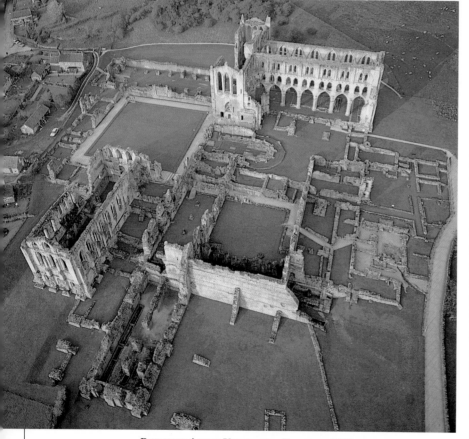

RIEVAULX ABBEY, YORKSHIRE, FOUNDED 1132

The Cistercian style was characteristically massive and austere. The abbey at Rievaulx has fragments of transepts and nave that are the earliest remains of Cistercian architecture in England.

undyed white robes and their buildings were beautiful but severe – no stained glass, decoration, or sculpture. One of the finest Cistercian abbeys is the ruin at Rievaulx, Yorkshire, England, built in 1132. The original buildings were simple, yet the inspired visual relationship with their magnificent surroundings elevates them to a high level of artistic achievement. In stylistic terms, it is interesting to note how the Cistercians brought French ideas to English architecture deep in the countryside some while before these arrived in the cities – as at Canterbury Cathedral. As the story of architecture moved toward the industrial age, it became increasingly rare to find the country leading the city in terms of stylistic development.

The choir at Rievaulx was rebuilt in a more sumptuous style in c.1225–49. Over the next 300 years, the English Cistercians became increasingly wealthy landowners, waxing fat on the income derived from their successful long-term investment in sheep farming. England's wool industry was one of its most important sources of income before the Industrial Revolution.

Christian monasteries evolved in a variety of styles across Europe. The Gothic style became dominant from its inception in 1135 at the Abbey of St. Denis, near Paris, when the Abbot Suger (see p.57) began rebuilding his Carolingian basilica, but elsewhere other equally memorable forms were adopted. The Greek and Russian monasteries of the Orthodox churches followed the model set by the Byzantine architecture created in the reign of Justinian I (see p.38). The Katholikon, Mount Athos, built at the end of the tenth and the beginning of the 11th centuries, is a classic Byzantine design, a small mountain range of domes set beneath an enchanting backdrop of hills and mountains. The plan of the domed church is that of a cross set within a square with apses at either end.

MOUNT ATHOS, GREECE

The center of Eastern Orthodox monasticism is located spectacularly on an isolated peninsula. The precinct contains 20 monasteries surrounded by a wall, like that of a fortified village. It is entered through a long, vaulted passage protected by iron gates.

ROMANESQUE
THE TRANSITION TO GOTHIC

CHARLEMAGNE

The architecture of the cultural revival initiated by Charlemagne (AD 742–814) is sometimes referred to as "Carolingian Romanesque." This early style laid the foundations for that which would flourish in the 11th and 12th centuries. For example, the massive entrance structure, or westwork, on Charlemagne's Palace Chapel, Aachen (Aix-la-Chapelle), would evolve into the towered façade of German Romanesque churches.

THE DEVELOPMENT of the Romanesque style in western Europe came out of the depths of the Dark Ages. For several hundred years, tribes of Goths and other northerners swept across Europe destroying cities, aqueducts, and any sign of Classical learning; but in AD 800, the pope crowned Charlemagne head of the Holy Roman Empire. This one-time illiterate Frankish king and warrior had himself been educated by English monks from York. He learned of the ancient world, and his greatest wish became to recreate the Roman empire.

If Charlemagne failed to do that, what he did do was encourage a new wave of ambitious church building throughout much of western Europe.

HALLMARKS OF ROMANESQUE CONSTRUCTION

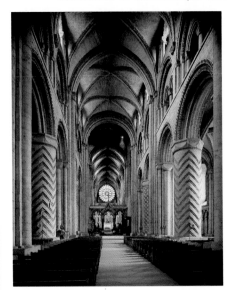

The spirit of the Romanesque is exemplified in the nave of Durham Cathedral, shown left. Although features such as the ribbed vaulting and concealed buttressing anticipate Gothic, the solidity and simplicity of the structure are hallmarks of Norman architecture. The huge piers and round arches that support the three-story nave are decorated with typically Norman moldings.

The Romanesque style that emerged, based on massive structural elements and Roman vaults and arches, was particularly suited to the northern warlords who had invaded Europe in the tenth century. The Normans (the Romanesque style is called Norman in Europe and the United States) adopted and developed the new Romanesque style with military vigor. The Normans were Vikings who settled in northern France in AD 911, Britain in 1066, and later in southern Italy and Sicily. They had, of course, sailed to North America, too, but had not settled there.

A MONUMENTAL STYLE

One of the greatest of Romanesque buildings is Durham Cathedral (1093–1133), which stands high on a craggy hilltop and commands the surrounding landscape like a castle, a role that many Romanesque cathedrals were to play. Its interior is cavernous and spectacularly so: the pointed, almost Gothic, ribs that hold up the vaults are in turn supported by rows of massive columns, alternately round and compound (composed of several smaller columns). The surfaces of the round columns are deeply incised by ax carvings – zig-zags and diamond patterns predominate – while the round arches above them are decorated with dog-tooth and

DURHAM CATHEDRAL, ENGLAND, 1093–1133
This view of Durham Cathedral shows the monumental west façade in its elevated position high above the Wear River. The western towers, adjoining the Galilee Chapel, rise to 145ft (44m). To the right is the central crossing tower, which was rebuilt in the 15th century.

other patterns that look as if they have been made with a giant pastry cutter. Much Romanesque decoration is of this kind, carved into the structural fabric of the building rather than being added to it.

The severity and military masculinity of this form of architecture can be seen, too, in buildings that one might expect to display a gentler nature; the Baptistry, Cremona (1167) is a good example. A design of great, elemental beauty, the Baptistry is an octagonal building, decorated solely by pilaster strips that run down to the base from an arcade that runs around it under a pitched roof. The Romanesque style spread throughout Italy, although the austere severity of St. Ambrogio in Milan (c.1080–1228) in the north of Italy, for example, contrasted strongly with the evident warmth of St. Nicola, Bari (c.1085–1132) in the south.

PISA CATHEDRAL, ITALY, 1063–1118 AND 1261–72
The world-famous complex of buildings at Pisa is one of the finest examples of Tuscan Romanesque, reflecting the wealth and prestige of the city. The cathedral's west façade, with its delicate arcading and polychromatic marble decoration, is very distinctive.

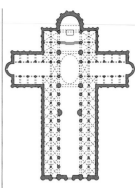

PLAN OF PISA CATHEDRAL
The simple basilican plan of early Christian churches – timber-roofed nave and side aisles – was elaborated at Pisa with the addition of transept arms. At the junction of the transepts with the nave was the crossing, which could be surmounted with a dome or tower.

REGIONAL SCHOOLS OF ARCHITECTURE

In Germany, Romanesque churches had the habit of looking like knights in armor, which seems appropriate. The imperial cathedral of Speyer (1030–61 and later) looks as if it is ready to charge into battle, its four towers rising over its pitched roofs like lances – one expects flags to flutter from them. The upper walls of Speyer are characterized by an exterior gallery set behind arcading, a feature of contemporary Italian cathedrals including, most dramatically, Pisa (1063–1118 and 1261–72). In Britain and Normandy, however, similar arcades were built into the internal walls looking over the nave. Norman architecture was massive, but not inflexible.

With the triumph of Gothic design, the style faded, but by this time it had begun to incorporate all sorts of decorative devices and structural tricks; these were brought to western Europe by the first Crusaders, by pilgrims, and by those, in Spain, in contact with the Islamic influence of Andaluz.

In Spain the situation is complicated by the fact that Christian refugees from the normally tolerant Islamic caliphate built churches such as St. Miguel de la Escalada, León (AD 913). This style is based on the mosque at Córdoba but with Visigoth influences picked up in their new homeland.

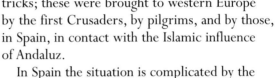

SPEYER CATHEDRAL, GERMANY, 1030–61 AND LATER
A powerful monument to the authority of the German empire, everything about Speyer Cathedral – founded by Emperor Conrad II – is on a vast scale. The two crossing towers are characteristic of German churches of the period.

ISLAM
MOSQUES AND PALACES

ISLAMIC ASTROLABE
By the time of Mohammed's death in AD 632, Islam had spread through much of Arabia. Islam made great advances in the study of philosophy, astronomy, mathematics, geometry, and engineering, especially since this research aided trade and navigation. Research led to the refinement of the astrolabe, a navigational tool originally invented by the Greeks. This example dates to the 14th century AD.

"Enter thou among my servants and enter thou My Paradise"
THE QUR'AN, SURA 89

IF ONE WERE TO CHOOSE to live anywhere in the Europe of the Dark Ages, it would surely have to be Andaluz, the Islamic domain of southern Spain. Here was a land not only of religious and intellectual tolerance, but of wonderful gardens, running water, hammams (Turkish baths), and an architecture of lightness and delight that the rest of Europe was not to experience for hundreds of years.

The Arab invaders, galvanized by the prophet Mohammed (born AD 570) pursued their *jihads* (holy wars) across North Africa, and it was only at the battle of Moussais-le-Bataille, near Poitiers, in AD 732 that the French, led by Charles Martel, were able to stop their seemingly inexorable march on Paris. What they brought to Spain, aside from a high level of civilization (remarkable for a people who only shortly before had been

THE ALHAMBRA, GRANADA, SPAIN, 1338–90
Inside, the Alhambra is a luxurious palace with sumptuously decorated state rooms, courtyards, and formal gardens. The Patio de la Acequia (above) is a long rectilinear garden enclosed by walls along the sides and an arcade at either end. The garden, with raised paths in the form of a cross and a fountain at its center, forms part of a summer palace called the Generalife.

DOME OF THE ROCK, JERUSALEM, AD 688–92

Standing in the center of Temple Mount, the Dome of the Rock is Islam's earliest monument. It was built not as a mosque for public worship, but as a "mashhad" (a shrine for pilgrims).

Multipatterned ceramic facings cover the exterior. Pierced marble and ceramic lunettes fill the window openings. The sumptuous interior is decorated in glass mosaic and quartered marble.

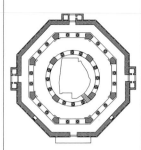

DOME OF THE ROCK: PLAN

The building has a geometrical plan; a dome approximately 60ft (18m) in diameter and mounted on an elevated drum rises above a circle of 16 piers and columns. Surrounding this circle is an octagonal arcade of 24 piers and columns. Four portals lead into the ambulatory.

living a nomadic existence in the desert), was a truly gorgeous architecture. Every major Islamic building was a kind of representation of a desert oasis, each guarded by fortress walls, yet inside abundant in flowing water, lush gardens, and shady alcoves.

THE GREAT MOSQUES

The first Islamic architects adopted local forms: the Dome of the Rock in Jerusalem (AD 688–92), for example, shows the influence of Byzantine design. Built as a shrine around the rock from which the Prophet is said to have made his leap into heaven, the Dome is an octagonal structure topped with a glittering dome (anodized aluminum since 1967, gilded lead before that) that rises above two internal colonnades. Originally sheathed in shimmering mosaic and marble, the walls were reclad in geometric marble tiles under Ottoman rule in the 16th century. Nevertheless, the Dome has a lightness of touch and being that was shared by very few European buildings of the Dark Ages.

The greatest mosques, however, were of course built elsewhere. The largest ever built was the Great Mosque at Sammara, Iraq (begun AD 848). Today, only ruins survive, but these are deeply impressive: an outer wall, 510 x 780 feet (155 x 238 meters), surrounded the prayer hall, which was overshadowed by a gigantic spiral minaret up which a horseman could ride. It is hard now to imagine this great, quasi-military space echoing to the sound of the muezzin's call, the prayers of the submissive, and the play of water. To Arabs, people of the desert, water has always

GREAT MOSQUE, SAMARRA, IRAQ, BEGUN AD 848
The largest mosque ever built is generally regarded as the work of the Caliph Al-Mutawakkil. The cone-shaped minaret is encircled by an outer ramp in the form of a spiral.

been celebrated, and forms an integral part in the design of many Arab buildings, and the gardens and courtyards that flow in and out of them.

The principles of the design of Samarra were taken by Ahmed Ibn Tulun to Cairo where he built the new city in the late ninth century, modeling it on his Iraqi homeland. The most impressive building he left was the Mosque of Ibn Tulun (AD 876–79), a spacious courtyard or parade ground building made of brick faced with stucco, probably built by craftsworkers who had traveled from Iraq to Egypt.

MOSQUE OF CORDOBA

The finest Islamic monuments in Spain are as different in character as chorizo is from cheese. The Mosque of Cordoba (begun AD 785) is the first major building by the Umayyad dynasty after they had fled to Spain from Syria via Tunisia.

The style of the prayer hall was so distinctive – quite mesmeric – that it was extended all but seamlessly during the course of three major additions in the ninth and tenth centuries. The completed prayer hall covers exactly the same space as the orange-scented courtyard that fronts it. Inside, row after row of arcades, formed by columns supporting elongated horseshoe arches, create ever-changing vistas that delight and baffle the eye. Each step the visitor takes alters the way columns and arches appear to intersect; it is a remarkable experience spoiled not so much by the Spaniards inserting a vulgar chapel into the heart of the prayer hall, but by the inane, overloud chatter of tour guides and the flashing of thousands of cameras. The dazzling visual effect of the apparently interlocking architecture of the prayer hall is enhanced by the treatment given to the horseshoe arches:

FORM AND FEATURES

ORIENTATION

The mosque is conceived around an axis directed toward Mecca. The mihrab, a small central niche that marks the nearest wall to Mecca, is where the leader of the congregation (the imam) makes his prayers. This act must be observed from other parts of the prayer chamber. The congregation assembles in lines traversing the main axis and takes its cues from the imam. The mosque has a fountain for ritual washing before prayers. From the minaret, the muezzin calls the faithful to the five daily prayers.

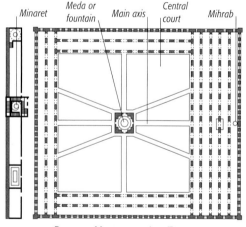

Minaret | Meda or fountain | Main axis | Central court | Mihrab

PLAN OF MOSQUE OF IBN TULUN

DECORATION

Characteristics of Islamic buildings include ogee arches, onion domes, and walls decorated with carved stone, paintings, inlays, or mosaics. As figurative art is not allowed in Islam, buildings are ornamented with geometric, calligraphic, and plant motifs. Even elements with naturalistic origins, such as leaves, are so stylized as to be unrecognizable.

TILEWORK, FRIDAY MOSQUE, YAZD, IRAN

STONEWORK, TOMB OF NUR ITIMID AL DAUL, AGRA, INDIA

Minaret

Pointed arches

Main axis

Central court

MOSQUE OF IBN TULUN, CAIRO, AD 876–79

STALACTITE CEILING, MASJED-E EMAN, ESFAHAN, IRAN

alternating brick and stone bands. The relentless arcades finally give way to three highly decorative sanctuaries of elaborate design – they come as a complete surprise.

THE ALHAMBRA

The most ambitious and most beautiful of all Islamic buildings in Spain is, without doubt, the Alhambra (1338–90), a richly decorated and elaborate palace and fortress set high on a hill jutting into a valley, with the snow-covered peaks of the Sierra Nevada as a backdrop. The Alhambra was built by the Nasrids, the last surviving Muslim dynasty in Spain; they surrendered to the forces of Ferdinand and Isabella in 1492, the year Cristóbal Colón (Christopher Columbus) "discovered" America and claimed it for Spain.

Two main courtyards – the Court of the Lions and the Court of the Myrtles – sparkle with running water and give way to garden terraces, pavilions, elevated walkways, towers, and turrets that offer delight compounded by delight. This was the finest representation of an oasis created by Arab architects and is perhaps the most perfectly thought-through marriage of man-made landscape and architecture, light and shadow. At the beginning of the 21st century, the courts and gardens of the Alhambra

MOSQUE OF CORDOBA, BEGUN AD 785
The covered prayer-space of the Mosque of Cordoba is a forest of arcades 19 bays wide. The arcades are doubled, a second arcade standing clear above the first. The lower arches are of horseshoe form and have voussoirs of white stone and red brick.

still give pleasure to millions of visitors, and remain a suggestion of where global architecture might wish to go in the next century.

THE ALHAMBRA, GRANADA, SPAIN, 1338–90
From the outside, the Alhambra at Granada is a heavily fortified citadel, with severe, castellated, rammed-clay ramparts. The walls, with their 23 towers and four gates, once enclosed mosques, gardens, prisons, seven palaces, and even the Royal Mint.

NORTH AFRICA
PURE WHITE FORMS

AGHLABID DYNASTY
The Aghlabids ruled Tunisia and eastern Algeria from AD 800 to 909. Their capital city was Qairouan in Tunisia. Aghlabid buildings had largely unadorned masonry or brickwork – limited decoration came in the form of carved stone, stucco, and wood. Mosques featured internal arcades, low roofs, and courtyards with square minarets. The Aghlabids invaded southern Italy before they were defeated and replaced by the Fatimids.

THE ARAB INVASION of North Africa occurred in several waves and over many generations. The principal effect on architecture was the construction of vast and often magnificent mosques along the south coast of the Mediterranean, and in the towns and cities built between it and the uninhabitable dunes of the Sahara desert. Among the earliest are the Great Mosque at Qairouan, Tunisia (begun AD 836), the Mosque of Three Doors, Qairouan (AD 866), the Great Mosque at Sfax (AD 849), and the Zaytuna Mosque, Tunis (from about AD 860). These featured the spacious paradeground-like courtyards common to early mosques and, in keeping with a religion that had developed as a military force and fought *jihads*, or holy wars, had the look of elegant army barracks. They were and remain impressive spaces and elegant, elemental structures.

Later invasions of what are now Morocco and Algiers saw the development of more elaborate mosques making great use of horseshoe arches and rich, shell-like decoration. Impressive examples of this later style can be found at Tlemcen (from c.1080), the Quttubiyya Mosque, Marrakesh (1147), and the Almohad and as-Jedid mosques, Fez (1276–1307).

SIMPLE STRUCTURES
And yet some of the most moving and ultimately influential North African buildings of the period between the Arab invasions and European colonization are some of the simplest. These include the endless small white courtyard houses that can be found the length of the southern Mediterranean seaboard and which date in essence from biblical times. The Mediterranean was from ancient times a major shipping and

GREAT MOSQUE, QAIROUAN, TUNISIA, BEGUN AD 836
The original building was reconstructed in the ninth century, when bays were added to the courtyard face of the prayer hall, and a central dome constructed over it.

MOSQUE OF THREE DOORS, QAIROUAN, TUNISIA, AD 866
This small town mosque has a triple-arched portico with horseshoe arches. Above the arches there are Kufic inscriptions topped by a bracketed cornice.

trade route and ideas about how to build and how to live traveled quickly and readily from Mesopotamia to Morocco and ultimately to Spain. The famous white villages of Andalucia leading up from Algeciras and grouped around Jimena de la Frontera are dominated by a long decayed Moorish fortress that could easily be in North Africa. From the tops of the fortress towers, the Atlas Mountains can be seen on a clear day. The white rendered North African houses were to have a profound influence on the mind and works of Le Corbusier (see p.182–83), as were the simple barrel-vaulted Tunisian farmhouses on those of Louis Kahn.

PURE FORMS

The sequence of barrel-vaulted mosques built on the beaches or overlooking them on the Isle of Jerba, Tunisia, is among the most special to be found anywhere in the world. For here is the essence and foundation of architecture, pure Platonic forms that are nevertheless warm and joyous. Composed of cylinders, cubes, pyramids, they are deeply satisfying in terms of their geometry and proportions. More than this, however, they are clearly made by hand. The abstraction of their pure white geometry – no other colors are used, nor decoration of any sort – is offset by their handcrafted character. No decoration is needed, not so much because this would be a distraction from prayer or some sort of offense to God, but because the play of sunlight and shadow on these perfect forms is embellishment enough. This, and the mosques' setting by an ocean that appears gold in the middle of the day, azure in the evening, and the white sands and scent of orange blossom that fringe them.

Here is architecture at its most elemental and in many ways its absolute best, in harmony with its natural surroundings, heedless of the tides of passing fashion, a perfect equation balancing form, function, and beauty. Jerba, located in the Gulf of Gabes, is perhaps the ideal location for such dreamy architecture: it was, after all, the mythical land of Homer's lotus-eaters, who lived a life of indolent forgetfulness. The rest of architecture can be indolently forgotten here, if only for a day or two.

KIMBELL ART MUSEUM, FORT WORTH, TEXAS, 1969–72

The Kimbell Art Museum, designed by the American architect Louis Kahn (1901–74), has six barrel-vaulted galleries. These were inspired by a trip Kahn made to Tunisia, where he was influenced by the simple, eternal beauty of the local farm buildings.

BUILDING IN JERBA, TUNISIA
Pure, undecorated, geometrical forms – cylinders, cubes and pyramids – are used in the whitewashed houses and mosques to be found on the island of Jerba, Tunisia.

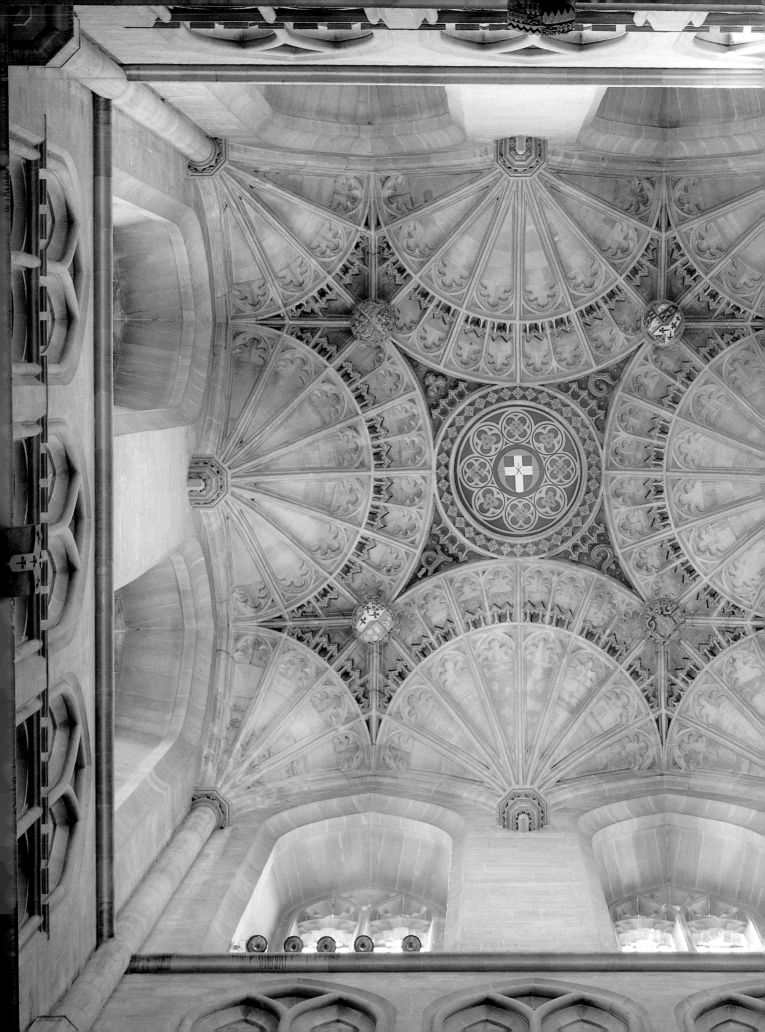

GOTHIC

Gothic architecture is one of the glories of European civilization, an attempt to lift our everyday life up to the heavens, to touch the face of God, in the highest stone vaults, towers, and steeples that contemporary technology allowed. Here were great buildings that owed as much to the grand vision of client and architect as to the hands of skilled masons. High above the naves of these shiplike structures, and often well out of the range of the human eye, we find expertly carved angels, demons, fronds, and finials, the work of individual craftsmen for whom nothing was to be hidden and nothing was too good for the all-seeing eye of the heavenly father. The style emerged in France at the time of the bloody crusades to the Holy Land. Its dark beginnings led to some of the most inspiring and daring buildings of all time.

BELL HARRY TOWER, CANTERBURY CATHEDRAL
After a fire in 1174, the monks at Canterbury commissioned William of Sens to rebuild the church. He was to design it in the French Gothic Style, making it the first Gothic church in England.

THE GOTHIC WORLD
THE AGE OF THE GREAT CATHEDRALS

INNOVATIONS IN GOTHIC ART

The assimilation of the Gothic style was slower in painting than in architecture or sculpture. Emerging in late 13th-century Italy, the new style in painting reached its zenith in the work of Florentine artist Giotto di Bondone (c.1267–1337). Recognized in his lifetime as an innovator, Giotto was responsible for introducing a greater naturalism into painting, freeing it from the stylized Byzantine tradition. His powerful sense of pictorial space is as evident in his famous fresco cycles as it is in this small panel, the *Madonna Enthroned* (c.1310).

"The pictures in the windows are primarily for the humble, who cannot read the Word, to show them what to believe"
ABBOT SUGER

BEAUVAIS CATHEDRAL was perhaps the medieval equivalent of the biblical Tower of Babel. It was designed to touch the face of God. Its nave – the highest ever built – rose 157 feet (48 meters) above the faithful and its spire topped 492 feet (150 meters). Yet, such was the ambition of this lofty place of worship that after 60 years work was halted, largely through lack of funds, before the nave could be built. Remarkably, the vast Gothic building you see today is only about a half of what was proposed in 1220 – the existing nave, dwarfed by medieval ambition, dates from the tenth century.

But, there were also signs (from God perhaps?) that this was a cathedral too far, or at least too high. In 1284 a part of the vertiginous choir vault

NORTH ROSE, CHARTRES CATHEDRAL, FRANCE, C.1235
Rose windows decorate the west front and two transept façades at Chartres. The vast walls of stained glass were made possible by a complex system of flying buttresses.

collapsed and in 1573 the spire fell. Beauvais marked the limits of medieval structural engineering. What survives is a dazzling achievement and in many ways is the apotheosis of a form of architecture that, emerging around Paris at the end of the twelfth century, was the first to detach itself entirely from precedent. Beauvais appears to owe nothing to the canons of Classical architecture and nothing to history. The Gothic style it champions was the first to challenge architectural orthodoxy. It was a way of building that was to develop its distinctive character in Europe for 400 years before finally giving way to the Classical revival ushered in by the Renaissance in Italy.

THE ILLUMINATED NAVE

The soaring choir and transepts of Beauvais display the key elements of Gothic architecture at their most extreme. The aim of the builders, clients, and architects of the new cathedrals (many of whose names have been lost), was to build as high and with as much glass as possible. They were to be caskets of light, light that shone through stained-glass windows and illuminated, richly decorated naves, aisles, and choirs. The most notable and daring buildings of their time, the great cathedrals were built not only to impress rival clergy and those who came to pray in them, but to symbolize the confidence of rival French cities that, until the Hundred Years War with England (1337–1453) and the Black Death of 1348 (which killed between a quarter and a third of the population of Europe), had been enjoying a long economic boom.

Later on, such ambitious cathedrals as Beauvais were simply too expensive to build. Most, although costly to maintain, are very much at work as places of worship and tourist magnets 700 years on. They retain the power, as Hadrian's Pantheon and Justinian's Hagia Sophia do, to take the first-time visitor's breath away. In the age of computer technology and visual overkill, this is a remarkable achievement.

The key to building as high as Beauvais was the flying buttress (see p.56), a device that allowed masons to carry as much weight as they could away from cathedral walls. The higher the walls, the greater the span of the buttresses. Flying

BEAUVAIS CATHEDRAL, FRANCE, BEGUN 1220

Beauvais was the last in a series of French cathedrals directly inspired by Chartres, and represents the culmination of French High Gothic. The emphasis on soaring height and light are qualities that were to be enthusiastically adopted across Europe.

buttresses can be seen to great effect looking at the choirs of the cathedrals of Notre Dame, Le Mans, Amiens, and, of course, Beauvais. By transferring the download away from the walls themselves, the builders were able to increase the size of the windows, until – as in the case of Chartres (1194 – 1220) – the windows appeared to take over from the wall. Filled with colored glass telling stories of the Old Testament, and of the lives of Christ, his apostles, and saints, these buttressed churches were the medieval world's version of color television or the movies.

The contrast between these extraordinarily ambitious and lavish structures and the hovels most of the peasantry lived in could not have been more extreme. Small wonder the church was able to keep most people in a state of awe.

SOARING SPIRES

If the French aimed high with the naves of their cathedrals, abetted by the flying buttress, the English and Germans reached for the sky in the guise of spires. The very tallest, although far from being the most elegant, is the spire of Ulm

GOTHIC FEATURES

TRACERY
The decorative stonework filling the upper part of a Gothic window may be either "plate" or "bar" tracery. In plate tracery, stone infilling occupies a larger area than the glass. Bar tracery, developing from plate tracery after the mid-13th century, is composed of thin stone elements, so that the glass dominates. The East window at York Minster is one of the finest examples of Perpendicular tracery.

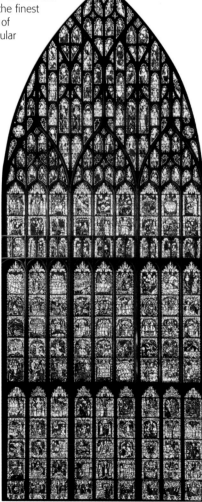

TRACERY, EAST WINDOW, YORK MINSTER, 1405–1408

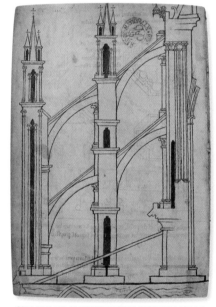

VILLARD DE HONNECOURT'S PATTERN BOOK, 1220–1230

FLYING BUTTRESSES, BOURGES CATHEDRAL, 1209–1214

THE FLYING BUTTRESS
The buttress is a mass of masonry or brickwork projecting from, or built against, a wall to resist the pressure of an arch, roof, or vault. The flying buttress is an arch or half-arch on the outside of a building that transmits the thrust of a vault or roof from the upper part of a wall to an outer support or buttress. The upper levels of the Romanesque cathedral of Bourges are supported by a double range of double-span, steeply angled flying buttresses.

The buttress came into its own after the 12th century, when galleries were dispensed with and the height of churches and the size of their windows could be massively increased. The innovative designs in this respect were the cathedrals of Bourges and Chartres, leading to the vast structures of Amiens, Beauvais, and Cologne.

Cathedral in Germany. Work began, probably, in the l380s, but there were several changes of plan and even by 1543 when the cathedral was entirely usable, the great tower and spire had yet to be built. It was only when rival authorities in Cologne decided to complete their cathedral from the 1840s, that those in Ulm finished the job its masons had embarked upon nearly half a millennium earlier. The tower and spire were finished to the preserved designs of Matthaus Boblinger who worked on the cathedral in the fifteenth century. The spire is 530 feet (160 meters) high, the peak of Gothic ambition. Cologne (begun 1284) boasts twin spires, completed in 1880, reaching up 492 feet (150 meters); inside it remains perhaps the most startling of all medieval cathedrals, a soaring cavern of colored glass, abstract, cold, and utterly magnificent.

The tallest spire outside Germany is that of Salisbury Cathedral in the south of England. The whole church, including the stone spire, was built in two stages between 1220 and 1266. The spire is 404 feet (123 meters) high and takes off from the second stage of the tower rising from above the central crossing. At the time it was thought unwise to build this high, but more than 700 years later, Salisbury Cathedral still soars majestically into the sky and appears to be almost as good as new, aside from a bend in the piers supporting the tower (you can see this by lying on the floor of the crossing and looking up; other visitors will think you are nuts – let them).

TRACERY

The greatest and most impressive decoration in medieval cathedrals was the stone tracery that fleshed out the windows. These grew increasingly in size and ambition between the beginning of

ULM CATHEDRAL, 14TH–16TH CENTURY, OCTAGON AND SPIRE 19TH CENTURY
The octagon and spire of Ulm Cathedral were not completed until 1890, when the building became the tallest medieval structure in Europe with a height of 530ft (160m). The overall width of the nave is a vast 147ft (45m).

Gothic architecture – seen in the choir of the abbey church of St. Denis, Paris from the 1140s – and the last great cathedrals that seemed more glass than stone. In simple terms, tracery became ever more complex, showing off the mason's skill in devising new ways of filling huge windows with as much glass as they could possibly hold.

Fashions came and went, but peaked in two periods, special again to England, the Decorative and the Perpendicular; the first belongs to the fourteenth and early fifteenth centuries, the latter to the fifteenth and sixteenth. The former is naturalistic and flowing, full of swoops and curves; the latter is geometric, refined,

that covered the stone vaults of naves, aisles, and choir — as if to frighten away unwelcome demons. The richness of imagination that went into the creation of these Gothic creatures remains one of the delights of medieval cathedrals, where it is clear that individual craftsmen were given some leeway in the otherwise mighty designs of architects and master masons.

VISIONS OF HEAVEN

Perhaps the most charming, if not the most rigorous, medieval cathedrals were built in England. Why? Because rather than build their cathedrals as single powerful statements as the French and Germans did, the English saw the cathedral as a sequence of related spaces: a plan of a typical English cathedral reveals a small galaxy of chapter houses, family, and other chapels. This meant that there were roofs to cover and English carpenters — among the world's best — were given license not just to explore new forms of roofs, both internally and externally, but to decorate them. The result was a proliferation of truly magnificent, show-off timber roofs that reached their peak in the great oak hammer-beam roofs of the late fourteenth and fifteenth centuries.

In fact the most ambitious does not cover the nave of a cathedral but St. Stephen's Hall, Westminster (1394–1400). This meeting hall, the English Gothic equivalent of a Classical Roman basilica, was crowned by a hammer-beam roof

ST. WENDREDA'S, MARCH, ENGLAND, EARLY 16TH CENTURY
Hammer-beam roofs were used only on buildings of the highest status. Timbers (hammer beams) stick out from the sides, supported by curved braces beneath. In this spectacular example, carved angels decorate the end of each beam.

and almost mechanical. Both are beautiful and enhance churches throughout England that owe more than their siblings in Germany and France to the skill of individual craftsmen than to the celestial visions of architects and master masons.

In reaching so high, it is easy to imagine medieval craftsmen and masons wondering if they were inviting a challenge from God or the Devil. Whatever, they ornamented their cathedrals with a bestiary of fantastic creatures — many of them, gargoyles, acted as waterspouts to drain water from the great pitched lead-over-timber roofs

designed and made by Hugh Hurland, the King's carpenter. Delightfully, Hurland carved great angels on the ends of his hammer-beams, raising the roof truly into the realm of celestial heights. Even then, there were more joyful roofs than this: a firm favorite of English parish church crawlers is that of St. Wendreda's parish church at March, Cambridgeshire. Here, there are no fewer than three tiers of angels, their wings spread, which appear to be flying from the walls and roof, while a fourth flies the length of the roof's apex. The other great exercise in bravura carpentry was the unique octagonal lantern covering the central crossing of Ely Cathedral in Cambridgeshire and dating from the mid-fourteenth century.

The English were also among the most entertaining wood and stone carvers elsewhere inside their cathedrals and parish churches. Pew ends and the undersides of misericords (tip-up seats used by monks and priests to lean back on while appearing to stand during the recitation of long prayers or the singing of interminable anthems) are often carved with quite riotous and plain crude carvings depicting scenes from contemporary life. As for the corbels (the keystones at the center of stone vaults) in the cloister of Norwich Cathedral, these are more enjoyable than a Disney cartoon, awash with terrifying seamonsters swallowing saints and all sorts of medieval entertainment. How people were meant to look at them it is hard to say; today, the cathedral provides mirrors mounted on trolleys for visitors to push around the cloister. This saves on osteopaths' bills.

TIMBER CONSTRUCTIONS
Much of the great architecture of the Gothic era was realized in stone, and some in brick where stone was not readily available as, for example, in the Low Countries. The one material that was used to spectacular effect inside such buildings was timber. Yet timber was rarely used for the construction of major buildings and for one very obvious reason: it was susceptible to fire. Even so, certain countries made a special contribution to the story of architecture with timber buildings, among these Norway, Sweden, and Transylvania, three lands covered by forest.

One of the best surviving and most famous of the Scandinavian timber churches is at Borgund on the Sogne Fjord. Built in about 1150, the church at first appears to have little

at all in common with Christian churches elsewhere; what visitors see first are the tiers of steep timber-tiled roofs, their topmost gables decorated with wild dragon heads. The result is a building that might come from the pages of a horror story aimed at frightening children, and certainly just as worrying as a contemporary Viking longship must have seemed to those living on the coasts of medieval Europe and faced with frequent raids by Norse warriors. In fact the church has a plan adopted from Byzantine and Roman basilicas, yet it is all – colonnades, capitals – realized in richly carved timber.

There are more highly decorated examples of such churches to be found elsewhere in Norway: at Urnes, also on the Sogne Fjord; at Lund in

BORGUND CHURCH, NORWAY, C.1150
Stave timber churches derive their name from the vertical posts (stav in Norwegian) that are used to construct the framework of the building. The upper gables of Borgund are decorated with carved dragons' heads.

Sweden, an early example (c.1020); and in an arc that takes the hardy traveler down to the borders of present-day Hungary and Romania.

SECULAR GOTHIC

Cathedrals and churches are not the only Gothic. Although most people shared poor and insanitary homes in medieval Europe, many superb civic palaces were built as symbols of the wealth of cities. The most inventive and noticeable of these buildings were town halls and cloth halls. Much of the wealth of the Low Countries was based on cloth as England's was on wool. Two of the greatest civic buildings of medieval Europe are the cloth halls of Ypres and Bruges, both in Belgium.

The Ypres building – astonishing for its size and thoroughly disciplined façades – was started in 1202 and erected over the next century. A regular design, it boasted a vast central clock tower and was the inspiration for many Victorian town halls built during the Gothic Revival of the nineteenth century (see pp.148–49). Sadly, this medieval masterpiece was destroyed during World War I; a lovingly detailed replica was built soon afterward. The Cloth Hall at Bruges survives essentially unharmed; it is renowned for its soaring brick tower, built in 1282, which rises 262 feet (80 meters) above the tightly woven streetscape of old Bruges.

Equally impressive are the towered and battlemented town halls of Italy; dating from the mid-thirteenth century, the town halls of Florence, Siena, Montepulciano, and Perugia in Italy mark the moment when defensive architecture was just on the point of retreat.

MARCO POLO

The Venetian merchant, traveler, and writer Marco Polo (c.1254–1324) came from a family of successful traders and merchants. Trade between Europe and China along the Silk Route had long been established by the time Marco Polo accompanied his father and uncle on a trading expedition that reached China in 1275. There, he became a favorite of the Mongol emperor and remained in China until 1292. He returned to Venice in 1295 and three years later he commanded a galley at the Battle of Curzolain in a war against the rival city of Genoa. He was captured during the fighting and spent a year in a Genoese prison until the summer of 1299, when a peace was concluded between the two cities. He remained in Venice until his death in 1324.

CLOTH HALL, YPRES, 1202–1304
The hall, which began as an exchange for the Flemish woollen textile industry, was one of the finest medieval buildings in Europe. It was destroyed in 1915, and the present building is a replica.

Perhaps the most assured and characterful secular Gothic building is one of the most photographed of all, the Palazzo Ducale (Doge's Palace, 1309–1424), which fronts the Grand Canal beside St. Mark's Square in Venice. Designed by Giovanni and Bartolomeo Buon, the palace was rebuilt and remodeled several times, partly as a result of fire.

It took on its present distinctive appearance in the sixteenth century when a new third story was built over the elaborate medieval arcades of the first and second floors. The result, especially because the ground floor columns appear to have sunk into the pavement (originally they were raised on a dais mounted on three steps) is a building that appears to be top-heavy. Like so many Venetian buildings it is simply idiosyncratic, and certainly so when you consider that much of the rest of Italy was building in the Classical styles of the Renaissance at the time. The building has an almost Islamic quality about it (look up at the roof); but then Venice was closely connected to the Byzantine empire, and its trade with countries as far overseas

DOGE'S PALACE, VENICE, 1309–1424
The 14th-century Doge's Palace has a façade that is almost 500ft (152m) in length. A network of arcades and open stonework supports the colorful façade, which is faced with pink and white marble.

as India and China – via the legendary Silk Route – was legion (Marco Polo was a Venetian). The style – long arcades of open, ogee-arched Gothic windows – was uniquely Venetian. It was rather laughingly revived in the late nineteenth century under the influence of the great Victorian critic, John Ruskin (see pp.154–55): "On the Nature of the Gothic" the opening chapter of his book, *The Stones of Venice*, however, is almost as magnificent as many of the buildings that inspired it.

SPANISH COURTYARD HOUSES

In Spain, the ever-increasing power of the soldier-courtiers – who would lead the last crusades against the Muslims under the banner of Ferdinand and Isabella of Castille – were building themselves noble stone courtyard houses. These were remarkably restrained compared to those erected by *conquistadores* returning from Spanish America a century later, but even then their essential austerity is offset by flamboyant flourishes: a perennial favorite is the Casa de las Conchas (1475–83) in Salamanca, home of Talavera Maldonado, Master of the Military Order of Santiago; the shells that decorate the walls of the house are the symbol of the order.

CASA DE LAS CONCHAS, SALAMANCA, 1475–83
This Spanish town palace has alternating rows of shells covering the exterior walls. The façade has a doorway with an escutcheon carved on it, with fleur-de-lys supported by two lions.

TIMBER CONSTRUCTION

Timber construction was used extensively throughout much of Europe for the building of houses and lesser buildings. In towns these were always in danger of burning down; survivors, however, are far greater in number than they appear to be because the structure of many houses, notably in England, had been covered at a later date by a façade of stone or stucco.

It is possible that church builders had some influence on one peculiar English form of timber construction, the cruck frame. This comprised inward or Gothic pointing wooden beams that met at the apex of a roof, in effect like the structure of a wooden rowing boat turned upside down. Most timber frames to be found to a lavish degree in German towns including Dresden and Nuremburg were of post-and-lintel construction: the cruck frame was a unique English contribution stemming possibly from England's distinguished shipbuilding tradition, which was also a major feature of medieval cathedral architecture.

DÜRER'S WIRE-DRAWING MILL, 1489–90, DETAIL

The cruck frame is shaped like an inverted V.

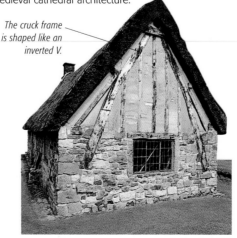

HUTTON-LE-HOLE, NORTH YORKSHIRE, ENGLAND

CRUCK FRAME TALE

The cruck frame has always been of interest to the English, if to no one else. Sir John Summerson, the distinguished architectural historian, liked to tell of the photograph of a supposedly cruck-framed house that used to appear in virtually every history of English architecture in the early part of the twentieth century. One day Summerson went to visit the house and discovered that it was quaint and interesting in every way, not least because the one thing it conspicuously lacked was a cruck frame.

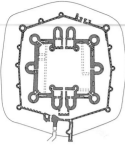

PLAN OF BEAUMARIS

The idea of concentric lines of defense is evident in the symmetrically composed plan of Beaumaris Castle (1283–1323). The inner ward – with its two large gatehouses and six towers – is surrounded by a lower outer fortification, which was reached only by crossing a wide moat fed by the sea.

CASTLES
FORTIFIED DWELLINGS

THE GOTHIC WORLD conjures up images not just of cathedrals but also of courtly love, chivalry, crusades, and castles. This was the age of mounted knights in suits of elaborate armor that cost their owners the equivalent of the price of a top-of-the-range Ferrari today. It was also the era of the bloody suppression of those, like the Celts, who lived on the fringe of mainstream European society, of the reconquest of Spain in the name of Christianity, and of the fight to win back the Holy Land to the Papal fold. It is hardly surprising, then, to learn that, cathedrals aside, the most expensive buildings of their time were castles.

The most spectacular, and effective, are to be found in Syria, the Welsh Marches, and Spain. The most dramatic of all is undoubtedly Krak des Chevaliers (1142–1200, and later), the castle mounted high on a rise in present-day Syria. It was given to the Knights Hospitallers, who protected pilgrims on their way to the Holy Land, by Raymond, Count of Tripoli in 1142. The main body of the castle is built up on a massive and sheer sloping wall, 82 feet (25 meters) deep at its base. This soars above the perimeter wall with its many round towers below. It must have been an extraordinary place to have been stationed when it was completed in the 13th century and made civilized with Gothic loggias and courtly interiors; it withstood sieges by Arab armies a dozen times before the knights were tricked out of their castle in 1271. The castle remains an unforgettable experience.

THE BRITISH ISLES

Some of the most sophisticated castles, and those that play in our childhood imaginations – reinforced at every turn by comics, adventure stories, and Hollywood movies – are those built the length of the Anglo-Welsh border by Edward I from 1277 onward to subdue the Celts. These were built in two waves, and although Conway (1283–89) is the most dramatically sited by the sea, Beaumaris (1283–1323) by James of St. George is the most sophisticated, a highly symmetrical design organized around a double skin of walls and easily defended. A much later generation of English castles – such as Deal and Walmer (c.1540) in Kent – were built as gun platforms for artillery on the lookout for would-be Spanish, French, or Dutch invaders.

As threat of invasion and civil war appeared to retreat, so did the castle itself. Small castles gave way to the fortified manor house in late 13th-century England. Stokesay Castle (1285–1305), Shropshire, is a justifiably famous example of the type, a charming home arranged around a high-roofed great hall and guarded by a tower and military gatehouse. Tattershall Castle (1436–46), Lincolnshire, a handsome five-story brick keep shows how the memory of the castle was kept alive in later, more luxurious houses. In Spain, castles

TATTERSHALL CASTLE, LINCOLNSHIRE, ENGLAND, 1436–46
More than 98ft (30m) high, Tattershall Castle – a fortified manor house – is built on the site of an earlier castle. The five-story tower resembles a 12th-century keep.

CARCASSONNE, FRANCE

Sited high on a hill, the medieval city of Carcassonne is enclosed within spectacular fortified walls. The inner rampart was built by the Visigoths and dates from AD 485. The outer walls were constructed in the reign of Louis IX (ruled 1226–70).

were conservative in the north and glamorous in the south. The 15th-century mudéjar (Spanish Moorish) castle of Coca, Segovia, built by Don Alonso de Fonseca, is a carnival of color and clearly built as much to be a pleasure palace as it was a defensive gesture. By the end of the 15th century, the great age of castle building had clearly come to an end. Many towns and cities, however, continued to huddle behind castle-like defenses and battlemented walls. A superb example is Carcassonne in the Languedoc

region of the south of France, although the fairy-tale sight you see today is largely a result of a major 19th-century restoration by the Gothic Revivalist Eugène-Emmanuel Viollet-le-Duc (see p.149).

(see p.149)

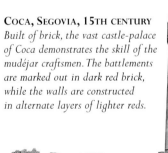

COCA, SEGOVIA, 15TH CENTURY
Built of brick, the vast castle-palace of Coca demonstrates the skill of the mudéjar craftsmen. The battlements are marked out in dark red brick, while the walls are constructed in alternate layers of lighter reds.

TAPESTRY

Used to adorn the walls of churches and castles, tapestries were considered the most luxurious form of decoration in the Middle Ages. The art of tapestry flourished in Europe from the beginning of the Gothic period in the 12th century, with major workshops in Flanders (Arras, Tournai, and Brussels) and France (Paris and Angers).

LATE GOTHIC
OPENING THE JEWEL BOX

THE GOTHIC STYLE continued to evolve – to spectacular effect in Britain and Spain – well into the 16th century, when the Italian Renaissance was already mature and taking European architecture down another path altogether. In fact, Gothic ways of working were to continue further into the 17th century, notably in the Cotswolds in the heart of England. By then, however, the days of great invention had long gone, as the most imaginative architects explored the possibilities of the Classical revival that connected architecture back to ancient Greece, Rome, and even Egypt.

PERPENDICULAR STYLE

The late flowering Gothic of 16th-century England gave us some of the most exquisite buildings of all time. Among these are King's College Chapel, Cambridge (1446–1515) and Henry VII's Chapel, Westminster (1503–19). These two buildings took the notion of the medieval church as a casket of glass to its furthest extreme. The walls of King's College Chapel seem to be made almost entirely of glass with little more than a spider's web of stone to support them.

The window area is prodigious and was made possible by the adoption here of fan vaulting by the chapel's architect, John Wastell. This looks like it sounds: ceilings made of elaborate fans carved from stone that, spreading out from each side of the chapel walls, touch in the middle of the high and seamless nave. The effect is extraordinary, rather like walking through an avenue of palm trees. And, yet, this

KING'S COLLEGE CHAPEL, CAMBRIDGE, ENGLAND, 1446–1515
The chapel, lit by giant Perpendicular windows, is notable for the magnificent fan vaulting by master mason John Wastell. The vaulting was completed between 1512 and 1515.

ultimate expression of the Perpendicular style was also very different from earlier incarnations of English Gothic. It was altogether more machinelike, regimented, and almost Classical in terms of rhythm and consistency. And what it lacked in terms of riotous hand-carving and the organic quality earlier English churches and cathedrals enjoyed, it made up for in terms of a purity of vision that had rarely been achieved in previous centuries.

A Tudor Jewel Box

Henry VII's Chapel at Westminster was even more extreme, taking English Gothic into the Renaissance in one last final flourish. An exotic stone and glass casket, it was as highly decorated outside as it was inside, rare for an English building of almost any period. The effect really is that of a jewel box, and it is hard to escape the feeling that no matter how a fine a building this is from a technical and craft point of view, it is a case of a style and a tradition being stretched to the point where it is in danger of tipping over

SEVILLE CATHEDRAL, SPAIN, 1402–1519
The sheer size of Seville Cathedral is astonishing. The whole rectangular ground-plan measures 118,620ft², making it the largest of all medieval cathedrals. The central nave rises to an impressive 130ft (40m). The altarpiece is one of the largest in the world and one of the finest examples of Gothic wood carving.

into the realm of kitsch. Significantly, the chapel contains the tomb of Henry VII, designed and made by the Florentine artist Pietro Torrigiani; dating from 1509, it is the first example of truly Renaissance work in England.

Spanish Gothic

Seville Cathedral (1402–1519) represents a very different version of Late Gothic. It is not at all delicate, but rather a willfully massive and almost absurdly broad-shouldered design that symbolized the might of the Catholic Church and the monarchy. The cathedral is as wide as it is because it was made to cover, and smother, the site of the Islamic mosque that stood there before the Catholic reconquest of Seville; as a result, the nave is flanked not by one but two spacious aisles.

This is the biggest of all the medieval cathedrals: it is bombastic, aggressive, and shows no real technical or artistic innovation. Its saving grace is its belltower – the Giralda – which is the slightly remodeled minaret of the 12th-century mosque built by Yusef I; however, even then size appeared to matter. The stair leading up the tower is designed for horses and riders.

HENRY VII'S CHAPEL, WESTMINSTER, ENGLAND, 1503–19
Henry VII, the first Tudor king, built this chapel for his private use. It has a particularly rich Perpendicular interior, with a fan-vaulted apse and sideaisles. The central section has intricate circular vaulting embellished with Tudor badges and carved pendants.

John Wastell

The master mason John Wastell (d. c.1515) probably started his career under the distinguished mason Simon Clerk. Wastell worked with Clerk both at the Abbey of Bury St. Edmunds and King's College Chapel, Cambridge. He was the last and perhaps most brilliant mason that worked at King's, one of four master masons responsible for the superb craftsmanship at the chapel. Wastell took charge in 1508 and was mason from 1512 to 1515, the years when the beautiful fan vault was built and the chapel completed. He was also the master mason of Canterbury Cathedral and was responsible for the East chapels of Peterborough Cathedral, begun in mid-15th century and completed in the first quarter of the 16th.

The RENAISSANCE

The rebirth of Classical values and of Classical architecture emerged not fully formed — as Minerva, Greek goddess of wisdom, did from the head of Zeus, father of the gods — but slowly, over a century or more in Italy. Painters, scientists, and architects began to see themselves not as pawns in the service of an unappeasable sky God, but as the measure of all things. They, not God, held the pairs of dividers that could set a compass on the face of the world and shape its towns, cities, and architecture. This new rationalism was matched by a rediscovery of Roman architecture, a fascination with the recently established laws of perspective, and a desire to recreate the glories of the ancient world.

THE LIBRARY, MELK MONASTERY, AUSTRIA
Founded in AD 976, the Benedictine abbey at Melk was rebuilt after fire in 1702. The library (1702–14), a masterpiece of Austrian Baroque, contains over 100,000 books and 1,100 manuscripts.

RENAISSANCE ITALY
THE BEGINNING OF THE MODERN

JOHANNES GUTENBERG
Born in the last decade of the 14th century, Gutenberg first worked as a metalsmith and craftsman. His enduring invention, however, was the movable blocks of type that made possible the production of printed books. Gutenberg s principal printed works were a Bible and a Psalter, but the invention of printing was one of the major engines behind the Renaissance and the dissemination of its ideas. Architectural treatises such as Alberti s spread throughout Europe, revolutionizing the way that architects built.

> *"Everything that nature produces is regulated by the law of harmony"*
>
> LEON BATTISTA ALBERTI

A WATERSHED in the story of architecture, the Renaissance marked the opening up of trade routes and banking, and the absorption of new and rediscovered knowledge. The invention of movable type, by Gutenberg in 1450, and thus printing, led to the rapid dissemination of the new knowledge, while the discovery of perspective drawing (very possibly by the architect Filippo Brunelleschi, c.1425) was to create major changes in architecture. It was a period in which books, literacy, and knowledge and ideas, spread beyond the clergy. This led to the challenge to Catholic orthodoxy that culminated in the Reformation and the creation of the Protestant churches.

If the Dark Ages had been the province of the Devil and the medieval world the realm of God, Renaissance Europe witnessed the ascent of man, who was now in the immortal phrase of the Greek philosopher Protagoras, "the measure of all things". Although Renaissance architecture is said to have begun with the work of Brunelleschi and in particular the dome he added to Florence Cathedral between 1420 and 1436, it really got a grip and spread fast across Europe with the publication of the first architectural treatises since those of ancient Rome. Leon Battista Alberti wrote the first of these in 1452, although *De re aedificatoria* was not printed until 1485; the first publication of Vitruvius, the first-century Roman architect (see p.32), followed the next year. Alberti's book was a revelation and hugely influential. He set out in mathematical

DE RE AEDIFICATORIA
Alberti's seminal architectural treatise adapted the principles of imperial Rome to the projects of 15th-century Florence.

detail the principal elements of architecture — square, cube, circle, and sphere — and the ideal proportions of a building that should follow on from them. These proportions were not only in harmony with music and nature, but with those of the idealized human body. As man was created in the image of God, so a building could represent the very image of the divine creator, if architects followed the logic of mathematical proportions.

This sacred geometry was absolutely key in the making of the Renaissance mind: man was no longer impotent in the face of an omnipotent God, but an independent agent of God able to carry out his will through the arts. The role and self-image of the architect was thus greatly enhanced. He was no longer the largely anonymous designer-mason of the Gothic world, but a stand-in for God himself. No wonder that since then so many architects have had impossibly big egos.

Other important books followed by, among others, Sebastiano Serlio in 1537 and Giacomo

Barozzi da Vignola in 1562, while the next most influential after Alberti and the printed translations of Vitruvius was *I quattro libri dell' architettura* (1570) by Andrea Palladio, one of the greatest of all architects (see pp.74–75). The first book of importance written in English was Sir John Shute's *First and Chief Groundes of Architecture* of 1563. With the invention of the printed book, architectural ideas could travel. With books came the desire to draw buildings to comparable scales and, as Alberti demonstrated, to show the plan, section, and elevation of a building. What this meant, of course, was that architectural ideas could travel independently of the architect himself and that the architect was no longer a slave to the building site. This was always, however, to prove as much a blessing as a curse.

THE RATIONAL AND THE HUMANE

Renaissance architecture and urban planning was intended to be rational and humane as the painting in the Palazzo Ducale in Urbino demonstrates. This is a famous image, possibly by Piero della Francesca, and is important in more ways than one. First, it shows a model of how the new architecture might look in an ideal setting. Second it is bereft of people, which is

PROPORTIONS OF THE HUMAN BODY
Leonardo Da Vinci's famous drawing of *Vitruvian Man* (c.1487) shows the human body in perfect balance. Its proportions became the measure of Renaissance architecture. While Da Vinci's influence on the architects of the High Renaissance was profound, and while he covered his notebooks with plans and elevations of buildings, as far as we know, none of his designs for buildings was ever realized.

PANEL FROM PALAZZO DUCALE, URBINO
This view of an ideal city, attributed to Piero della Francesca, shows the influence of Alberti's treatise. During the late 15th century, Federico da Montefeltro's ducal court at Urbino became a center of learning. His palace is a masterpiece of the period.

THE SPREAD OF RENAISSANCE STYLES

Architecturally, the Renaissance began in Florence around 1420 and in the following decades spread to the other urban centers in Italy. The vanguard of the movement relocated to Rome in the late 15th and early 16th centuries. By this point, Renaissance styles had reached most of Europe – even as far as Moscow, via Venice, and to Hungary, through the marriage of a Neapolitan princess. The Italian Wars (1491–1530) and the intrusion of the French kings and Habsburg emperors on to Italian soil led to a constant exportation of the new ideas and their proponents.

how architects have depicted their buildings ever since. This was not necessarily because people would have spoilt the view, but because of Alberti's belief – a fundamental of Renaissance architecture – that the buildings themselves represented both human and divine images. Human and divine proportions were part and parcel of these ideal buildings set in an ideal townscape. It is also an important image because it shows how architects and artists – they were often still one and the same person – had begun to think of planning cities on a rational basis: very soon the ideal city with its gridiron, radial, and star patterns would begin to

PALAZZO STROZZI, FLORENCE, 1489–1539

The rusticated stone façade is marked by horizontal banding and has divided two-arched windows along the upper floors and squarish ones on the lower. The main entrance leads to a central courtyard designed by the stonemason-architect Il Cronaca (Simone del Pollaiuolo).

emerge across the Italian landscape. Early ideal buildings turned into stone and marble included the Pazzi Chapel (1429–61) in the cloisters of the Franciscan church of Santa Croce, Florence, and the palazzi built for the Florentine families Pitti (by Brunelleschi and Fanelli, 1458–66), Riccardi (by Michelozzo, 1444 onward) and Strozzi (by Sagnello and Pollaiuolo, 1489 and later). The three houses are similar in spirit, the homes of merchant princes gathered around courtyards hidden behind forbidding façades. In one sense these fifteenth-century houses are still fortified and, as with many of Brunelleschi's designs, they are often as much Romanesque as Roman. Although they boasted details drawn from

PAZZI CHAPEL, FLORENCE, 1429–61

Brunelleschi's chapel for the Pazzi family, the chapter house of the church of Santa Croce in Florence, beautifully demonstrates the order and restraint of Renaissance architecture. The glazed terracotta roundels are by Luca della Robbia and others.

the Venetian Republic), and produced an early jewel in the much loved church of Santa Maria dei Miracoli (Pietro Lombardo, 1481–89), a marble-clad design in which a timber barrel-vault and dome ride over a simple nave and choir. Again, although the detail is more Romanesque than Roman, it is at the same time very different from a Gothic church of similar size and status. The Renaissance came relatively late to Venice – relative that is to Florence and Rome – it was not until the second quarter of the 15th century that the city became a center for the new style.

PORTA DELL'ARSENALE, VENICE, 1460
Antonio Gambello's entrance arch for the arsenal at Venice is based on a Roman model and has often been credited as representing the first Renaissance construction in the city.

antiquity – such as the superb cornice that divides stone façade from Florentine sky in the example of Palazzo Strozzi (modeled on one in Trajan's Forum, Rome) – they are not the models of reason and light that would emerge half a century later in the work of Bramante in Rome. Even so, the lovely rhythms of Brunelleschi's Pazzi Chapel – gray Corinthian columns against white plastered walls – were to become a hallmark of the great architecture that followed, spreading across the whole of Europe between 1500 and 1750.

VENICE

Florentine architects traveled, as did their books, and so their new architecture reached other parts of Italy very quickly. Renaissance architecture is detectable in Venice as early as 1460 (in the Porta dell'Arsenale, the gateway to the great shipyards of

SANTA MARIA DEI MIRACOLI, VENICE, 1481–89
Often likened to a jewel box, this remarkable church was built to house Nicolò di Pietro's painting, Virgin and Child (1408) believed to have miraculous powers. The church is now a favorite with Venetians as a place to get married.

HIGH RENAISSANCE
THE GRANDEUR OF ROME

BRAMANTE

Born in 1444, Donato Bramante was the first great architect of the High Renaissance. He created a number of designs in Milan for Ludovico Sforza, but with the French invasion, moved to Rome, where his new patron was Pope Julius II. He drew up a vast plan for St. Peter's and the Vatican, only part of which was used by Michelangelo. Other commissions included St. Maria del Popolo in Rome and the Santa Casa at Loreto. Bramante died in 1514.

RAPHAEL

Born in Urbino in 1483, Raphael first studied painting under Perugino. He moved to Rome in 1508 under the patronage of Pope Julius II, where he designed various palazzi and in 1515 was appointed Super-intendent of Roman Antiquities. The role was to have a profound effect on his designs. His work was influenced by Bramante, but extended the Classical repertoire. Along with Sangallo and Giocondo he was appointed architect of St. Peter's. Raphael died in 1520.

THE HIGH RENAISSANCE is the era when Italian architects, beginning with Donato Bramante (1444–1514) in Rome at the start of the 16th century, began to analyze and reinterpret ancient Roman architecture with exactitude and finesse. They did not attempt to copy past buildings but to learn from them; theirs was an age of great invention and resourcefulness. The architects themselves were the Renaissance men of legend, at once painters, sculptors, poets, military engineers, soldiers, and playwrights. Now was the time to let rip with a brave new architecture that looked back only in so far as it could leap forward.

Bramante's Tempietto (1502) is shoehorned into the cloister of the church of St. Pietro in Montorio. This is a small, perfectly formed building, based loosely on the Temple of Vesta

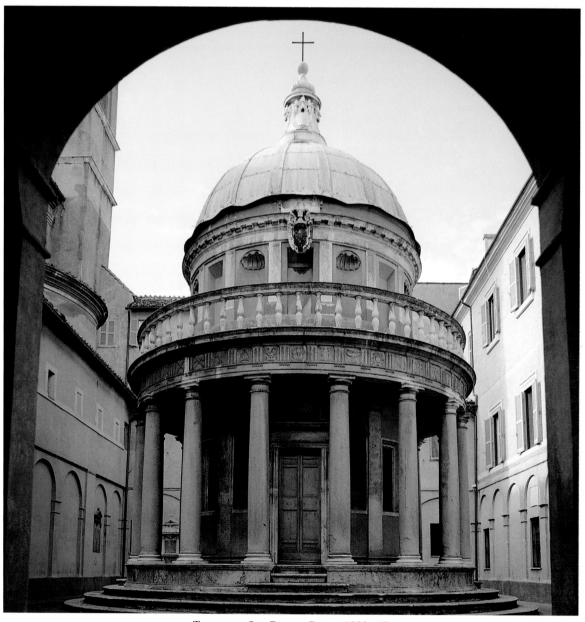

TEMPIETTO SAN PIETRO, ROME, 1502–10

Rather than simply repeat the motifs of Classical antiquity, Bramante employed his knowledge of perspective and volume to create an elegant and harmonious building. He also redesigned the surrounding courtyard, but his plan was never carried out.

ST. PETER'S, ROME, 1506–1626

Initially planned by Bramante and then revised by Sangallo, St. Peter's was then put in the hands of Michelangelo, who reverted to

Bramante's original centralized plan. The dome, the unifying element in Michelangelo's design, was executed by Della Porta.

at Tivoli; its influence has been incalculable, the inspiration not just for Michelangelo's dome that crowns nearby St. Peter's, but also the dome of Wren's St. Paul's, the dome of the US Capitol, Washington, D.C., Hawksmoor's mausoleum at Castle Howard, Yorkshire, the Pantheon in Paris, Gibb's Radcliffe Camera, Oxford – to list only the most famous from across 350 years.

The design of the Tempietto – its job is to mark and protect the site of the martyrdom of St. Peter, the first pope – is of a stepped circular plinth leading up through a Doric colonnade and up through a balustrade to a delightful drum and dome. Here at last – after many hundreds of years – one can enjoy the play of warm Italian sunlight through classical columns; here at last is a building that speaks of reason and civility rather than fear and religious domination. Of course religious intolerance continued, but the architecture did its best to point to a more civilized world than that ordered by the Church at the beginning of the 16th century. The 135-foot (42-meter) diameter dome of

St. Peter's, Rome, designed by Michelangelo in 1546 and built by Giacomo della Porta between 1588 and 1591, marked the pinnacle of High Renaissance architecture. The result is an overblown confection that is too big, too rich, and ultimately indigestible. Many visitors find it all too much to take in and remember only the café on the roof – cappuccinos served by nuns – and the gift shop alongside with its kitsch souvenirs. From the roof, though, visitors do have a superb view of the dome.

This is a masterly piece of sculpture verging on the Baroque and pulls the whole vast, marble-clad construction below it together. St. Peter's remains one of the biggest buildings in the world – St. Paul's, London could sit inside it with room to spare – and a monument to the ambition and wealth of Renaissance popes, particularly the great patron of the early 16th century, Pope Julius II. It represents the combined efforts of at least nine major architectural talents including those of Bramante, Raphael, and Michelangelo – and took 120 years to build.

MICHELANGELO

The dominating personality of the High Renaissance, Michelangelo Buonarroti's first architectural works were executed in his native Florence, but in 1534 he left for Rome, where his first commission was to reorganize the Capitol. His genius was to take the Classical influences of the Early Renaissance and then supersede them – for example in his use of the giant order, a column that ran through two floors of a building. At the time of his death in 1564, none of Michelangelo's major projects was complete, despite this, his influence has been enormous.

RENAISSANCE DOMES

Starting with Brunelleschi's dome in Florence, the architects of the Renaissance rediscovered methods of construction unknown since Roman times. Various techniques and features were used to buttress or support these large domes and resist the outward thrust of the cupola. With the exception of Les Invalides, each dome has become a symbol of the city where it stands and the dates of construction roughly reflect the point at which the Renaissance began to dominate architecture there.

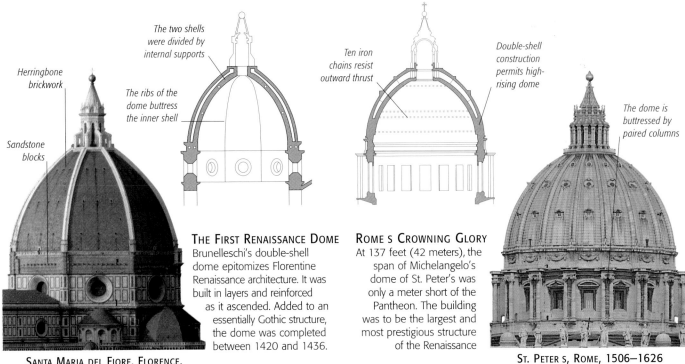

Herringbone brickwork

Sandstone blocks

The two shells were divided by internal supports

The ribs of the dome buttress the inner shell

Ten iron chains resist outward thrust

Double-shell construction permits high-rising dome

The dome is buttressed by paired columns

THE FIRST RENAISSANCE DOME
Brunelleschi's double-shell dome epitomizes Florentine Renaissance architecture. It was built in layers and reinforced as it ascended. Added to an essentially Gothic structure, the dome was completed between 1420 and 1436.

SANTA MARIA DEL FIORE, FLORENCE, c.1294–1462

ROME s CROWNING GLORY
At 137 feet (42 meters), the span of Michelangelo's dome of St. Peter's was only a meter short of the Pantheon. The building was to be the largest and most prestigious structure of the Renaissance

ST. PETER s, ROME, 1506–1626

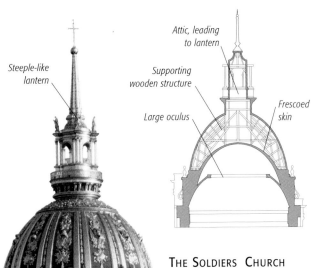

Steeple-like lantern

Attic, leading to lantern

Supporting wooden structure

Large oculus

Frescoed skin

Wood framing

Brick cone

Oculus

Brick inner dome

Peristyle

Outer cupola is supported by timber and covered in lead

THE SOLDIERS CHURCH
Designed by Libéral Bruant (1635–97) and modeled on St. Peter's, Les Invalides was originally intended as a hospital for disabled army veterans. Unlike the Roman church, however, Les Invalides has an attic above the dome.

LES INVALIDES, PARIS, 1670–1708

WREN s MASTERPIECE
Christopher Wren's St. Paul's has three shells: the external cupola and the lantern are supported by a brick cone, itself bound by iron chains. The oculus allows a view through into the space of the lantern.

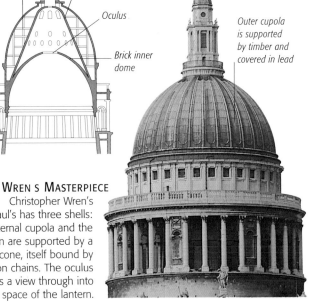

ST. PAUL s, LONDON, 1675–1710

STEPPED GARDENS, VILLA LANTE, BAGNAIA, 1566 ONWARD
Elaborately carved fountains were a feature of Rome in the 16th century, but in the villas of the wealthy, with their lavish cascades and intricate waterworks, they became models of sumptuousness.

It is a relief to get away from St. Peter's to some of the High Renaissance villas within a day's ride of Rome; what is so special about many of these grand palazzi is the way in which their gardens are an essential part of the composition. The best include the magnificent stepped gardens at Villa Lante, Bagnaia (Vignola, 1566 onward) where flowing water plays innumerable games with the architecture – as it does at the Villa d'Este, Tivoli (Ligorio, 1565–72). Here, aside from more fountains than you can confidently count, is the Rometta, a miniature reconstruction of ancient Rome with an equally miniature Tiber River flowing through it.

MANNERISM
The architects of the High Renaissance, and the princes, bishops, cardinals, popes, dukes, bankers, and merchants they served, had learned to enjoy themselves as the predecessors that they so admired had done 1,500 years earlier. In fact the architecture of this period and notably the work of Giacomo Vignola (1507–73) and Giulio Romano (1492–1546) is described as Mannerist.

At the time this was a put-down, but perhaps we can see it today as the equivalent of the Postmodernism, spawned in the US, that rocked world architecture from the 1960s to the 90s with its knowing games, visual tricks, and puns.

The Mannerists were illusionists who treated architecture as a high game, and there are few higher games than those Romano played at the Palazzo del Te, Mantua (1525 onward), where you will find Classical elements and details mixed up as, from a historically correct or Vitruvian point of view, they never should be. Architecture was moving from the civic and ecclesiastical realms into the private domain and as it did so it began to lighten up; from the mid-16th century you can see architects beginning to enjoy themselves.

PIAZZA D ITALIA, NEW ORLEANS, LOUISIANA, 1978
Charles Moore's, (1925–93) Postmodern circular piazza was built for the Italian community of New Orleans. It employs the grand Classical themes, but with ironic features, such as the metallic capitals of the Corinthian and Doric columns. The whole effect is one of gaudy playfulness.

PALAZZO DEL TE, MANTUA, ITALY, 1525 ONWARD
Built by Giulio Romano for the Gonzaga dukes, this extraordinary palace was the family's villa retreat. Romano was the Gonzaga's court painter and architect and the extravagant interior decoration, here in the Loggia di Davide, was carried out by his workshop.

ANDREA PALLADIO
THE MOST COPIED ARCHITECT

ANDREA PALLADIO (1508–80) was one of the greatest and most influential architects of all time. The magnificent yet practical farmhouses he built around Vicenza, the peerless churches he designed in Venice, and his book, *I quattro libri dell' architettura* (1570), which has been in print ever since, have had a profound effect on architectural design in countries as far apart as Russia, the United States, and Great Britain.

Palladio might also be considered to be the first modern architect. Neither a mason nor a dilettante, he was trained as a stonemason in Padua before being sent to Rome by a wealthy intellectual patron, Gian Giorgio Trissino. Here he made an in-depth study of the ancient monuments before returning to Vicenza. He was also able to read treatises on architecture by Alberti, Vitruvius, and others. When he came to design practical everyday farmhouses in the Veneto in the 1550s he was able to combine the skills of builder, craftsman, antiquarian, and scholar. Unlike the Renaissance men of myth – Michelangelo, Raphael, and Alberti – architecture was both his all-consuming passion and,

ANDREA PALLADIO
Palladio's name was given to him by his patron after Pallas Athene, goddess of wisdom and knowledge, poetry, drama, and the fine arts.

although this is a word that no one would have used at the time, his profession. The life and career of Andrea Palladio thus mark a turning point in architecture.

FARMHOUSES AND CHURCHES
His principal buildings fall into two categories, the farmhouses of the Veneto and the churches of Venice. He also built impressive and influential civic buildings such as the Basilica (Palazzo della Ragione, 1549) and the Teatro Olimpico (1580) – the first permanent theater since antiquity – both in Vicenza. His finest houses include the Villa Barbaro, Maser (1550s), in which he brought farm buildings together in one monumental composition with the family house and the hugely imitated Villa Capra (or Villa Rotonda, 1550–59) on the edge of Vicenza. A four-sided villa, each side faced with a Roman temple pediment, the whole building crowned with a dome

VILLA CAPRA, 1550–59
The Renaissance revived not only an interest in Classical forms, but also the concept of the villa surbana, an elegant retreat from city life.

"Beauty will result from the form and correspondence of the whole"

ANDREA PALLADIO

modeled on that of the Pantheon, Villa Capra was a new type of house altogether. It was never meant to be practical in the way Palladio's farmhouses were; instead, it was a retreat from the buzz of city life for a wealthy gentleman who could afford the time to come here, read, drink wines, and look at the stirring views from all four sides of his house.

The design was adapted by English architects – notably by Colen Campbell, author of *Vitruvius Britannicus* (1715), at Mereworth Castle (1722–25), Kent, and by Lord Burlington, spearhead of the English Palladian school at Chiswick House (1723–29), London. In the United States it was the model for Jefferson's Monticello (1770–1809), Charlottesville, Virginia (see p. 124).

In Venice, Palladio designed two considerable churches, San Giorgio Maggiore (1565 onwards) and Il Redentore (1577 onward). San Giorgio is the more picturesque; it rises from a small island of its own and is the heart of a Benedictine monastery. Cleverly, although the church draws brilliantly on ancient Roman sources, combining the body of a basilica and the façade composed of two intersecting and heroic pediments, the dome is a nod to the Byzantine exoticism of St. Mark's across the lagoon and the campanile is a salute to its freestanding counterpart in St. Mark's Square. Inside, the church is all reason, clarity, and light, its color scheme the gray and white that Brunelleschi introduced in the Pazzi Chapel, Florence a century earlier.

The church of the Redentore, built by the Venetian government in thanksgiving for the end of a terrible plague, is a masterwork. Sitting on the Giudecca and facing square on

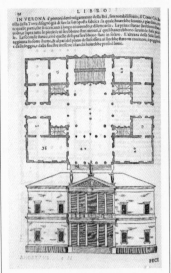

I QUATTRO LIBRI
Published in 1570, I quattro libri dell'architettura (The Four Books on Architecture) *drew on 20 years of experience as an architect.*

PALLADIO'S KEY WORKS
Basilica (Palazzo della Ragione), Vicenza *1549*
Villa Barbaro, Maser *1550s*
Villa Rotonda (Villa Capra), Vicenza *1550–59*
San Giorgio Maggiore, Venice *1565 onward*
Il Redentore, Venice *1577 onward*
Teatro Olimpico, Vicenza *1580*

to the canal, the impression one has is of a highly charged, highly compressed, and highly complex building that takes some while for the delighted eye to unravel. The front of the church appears to be constructed from no fewer than five intersecting Roman pediments; in lesser hands than Palladio's this would seem little more than a Mannerist trick; yet what the architect achieves is a depth of façade and spirit that draws us deep into the nave of this domed and turreted church.

A VENETIAN WARSHIP

The church is also, in the way the Parthenon can be read as Greek fighting ship represented in marble, a depiction through architectural means of a Venetian warship come to berth between the low houses of the Giudecca. The interior is more somber than that of San Giorgio. Behind the church is a monastery garden where the monks grow vegetables set out in Classical rows and raise chickens: Palladio's great city church, seen from the back, might be set in the countryside adorned by his farmhouses. Palladio was a master of fusing urban and rural values, the architecture of antiquity and that required by the Venice of his lifetime; the fact that his approach to architecture was to meet the needs of such diverse societies as aristocratic Britain, democratic America, and imperial Russia speaks volumes of the universal spirit that underlined this practical visionary.

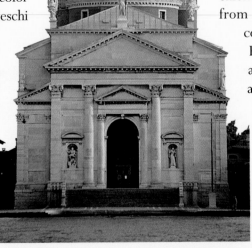

IL REDENTORE ("REDEEMER")
On the Day of the Redeemer in July, a causeway of barges enabled dignitaries to approach the church's virtuoso façade head-on.

FRANCESCO BORROMINI

Born in northern Italy, the architect Francesco Borromini (1599–1667), learned his craft in Milan. In 1620 he went to Rome and worked for the architects Carlo Maderno and Gian Lorenzo Bernini. An independent architect from 1633, Borromini's major buildings include St. Carlo alle Quattro Fontane and St. Ivo della Sapienza in Rome. He was particularly noted for his command of spatial effects and structural innovations. Although now considered one of the great Baroque architects, Borromini had little immediate influence during his lifetime.

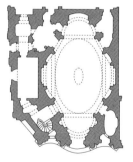

ST. CARLO ALLE QUATTRO FONTANE: PLAN

The plan of St. Carlo is basically an oval, with an entrance on the narrow side. The general plan started with two equilateral triangles forming a lozenge, and two circles inscribed in them so as to create an oval. Four chapels push out the oval so that the plan can be read as a Greek cross with convex corners. The most notable element is the sinuous periphery, with curves and counter-curves, so that the central oval nave overlaps with the four apsidal chapels.

ITALIAN BAROQUE
SENSUAL FORMS

A SPIRIT OF EXUBERANCE underlay Italian art and architecture at the beginning of the 17th century. It burst through in the 1630s in a style that its 19th century detractors labeled Baroque, which, via a rather complex play on words, meant deformed. And, at first glance, the extraordinary church of St. Carlo alle Quattro Fontane, Rome (1634–82) does seem perverse and even a little unhinged. Squeezed into a tight city center site, this gem was designed by Francesco Borromini (1599–1667). A stonemason who found fame if not fortune in Rome, he was considered more than a bit odd, and eventually committed suicide. The idiosyncratic exterior and willful curvaceous interior of St. Carlo have often been likened to the workings of Borromini's labyrinthine mind, his theatrical imagination. Certainly nothing like it had been seen before: it is hard to find a straight line here. The interior, a marriage of Greek cross and oval plan, the walls curving up to meet the dome, is as mesmerizing now as it was when the church was built.

THEATRICAL STYLE

What Borromini and his contemporary and rival Gian Lorenzo Bernini (1598–1680) did was to shape a new theatrical style of architecture that matched the spirit of a new era in which theater, opera, and an opulent street life had begun to emerge. The Church was quick to catch on to the message theater and opera sent out: if it was to win the souls of the Catholic masses and stem the tide of Protestantism, it must give the people the equivalent of opera and theater on Sundays and feast days. And so it did; through the Counter-Reformation — a quest to restore the dominance of Catholicism — the Church built lavishly in this new style. Now that architectural ideas were spread rapidly, the Baroque caught on through Catholic Europe and was even exported to Protestant Britain, although here it was to develop a special character very much its own (see pp.84–85).

ST. CARLO ALLE QUATTRO FONTANE, ROME, 1634–82
Borromini's church is one of the masterpieces of Roman Baroque architecture. The undulating façade, though designed in the 1630s, was not completed until after the architect's death.

CAPPELLA CORNARO, ST. MARIA DELLA VITTORIA, ROME, 1645–52

The Ecstasy of St. Theresa in the Cornaro family chapel is one of the great works of the Baroque period. Bernini places St. Theresa at the center of an oval altar experiencing an ecstatic vision as an angel pierces her heart with a golden arrow. Statues of the Cornaro family occupy two marble balconies set in recesses on either side of the chapel. Light from a hidden source dramatizes the scene.

Where Borromini was a mason by training, Bernini was a sculptor who also wrote operas and plays and designed the sets for them. His Baroque credentials were impeccable. He brought all his talents to bear in that sensual apogee of the Italian Baroque, the Cappella Cornaro in the church of St. Maria della Vittoria, Rome (1645–52). This is where you will find Bernini's famous statue of St. Theresa in the throws of ecstasy, watched on either side by sculpted members of the Cornaro family seated in balconies. Cinematic shafts of light shine down on the saint and to our modern eyes it is difficult, although this is sacrilegious, not to think of the shooting of a high-class erotic movie when faced

with this writhing scene. Was it meant to be sexy? It is impossible to say with any certainty, yet the Baroque style was without doubt the most sensual Western architecture has known.

BERNINI AND THE VATICAN

Bernini went on to create many superb theatrical spaces, including the Piazza of St. Peter's, Rome (1656 onwards), in which two maternal arms in the guise of curving Doric colonnades appear to pull the crowds into the womb of the Mother Church. The ceremonial stair he designed for Pope Alexander VII at the Vatican – the Scala Regia (1663–66) – is a wonderfully dextrous bit of scene management; the stairs appear to go

GIAN LORENZO BERNINI
The dominating figure in Roman Baroque art, Gian Lorenzo Bernini (1598–1680) was primarily a sculptor, but also a painter, poet, and architect. He spent the whole of his working life in Rome and in 1623 became the protégé of Pope Urban VIII. He was awarded the commission for the bronze baldacchino (canopy) in St. Peter's in 1624, and he continued to work on the cathedral and colonnade around the piazza as sculptor and architect until shortly before he died. His architectural commissions include the Palazzo Montecitorio and Palazzo Barberini in Rome. His buildings and sculpture express the grandeur and flamboyance of the Counter-Reformation.

on almost forever, but this is because the walls close in and the stairs get narrower as they rise; meanwhile an aperture half way up the staircase allows the sun to cast angled shafts of light across the stairs, changing angles during the day. Bernini was a master of the Baroque, but never as willful or extraordinary as Borromini. The balance he was able to make between the practical solution and the dramatic gesture was witnessed in the work of other Baroque architects in grand urban planning schemes such as the glorious Piazza del Popolo, Rome (1662–79) designed by Carlo Rainaldi (1611–91) for Alexander VII as a new northern gateway to the Eternal City. Rainaldi angled three streets into the square passing two new domed Baroque churches of his design on the way – St. Maria di Monte Santo and St. Maria dei Miracoli – and meeting at a point marked by an ancient Egyptian obelisk.

The Italian Baroque was to reach further heights of ambition and fantasy. In Venice, Baldassare Longhena (1598–1682) was commissioned to build the twin-domed St. Maria della

SCALA REGIA, VATICAN, ROME, 1663–66
The stairway between St. Peter's and the papal apartments is one of Bernini's finest achievements. Two rows of columns flanking the staircase converge and diminish in height as they rise, increasing the apparent length of the stair.

PIAZZA DEL POPOLO, ROME, 1662–79
The Piazza, designed by Carlo Rainaldi, lies just inside the northernmost gateway into Rome. This view, by Gaspar van Wittel, shows the square looking south, on the far side are the two domed churches of St. Maria di Monte Santo (left) and St. Maria de' Miracoli (right).

Salute to celebrate the passing of another dreadful plague. The church is an exuberant creation, entered through an octagonal lobby topped by a grand dome, its mighty drum supported from the outside by stone scrolls that mimic waves. As the church stands surrounded by water on all sides, this is an appropriate as well as stagey device.

GUARINO GUARINI

Apart from the work of Borromini, the most ingenious and extravagant Baroque experiments were made by the Theatine priest Guarino Guarini (1624–83), whose Chapel of the Holy Shroud (Il Sindone), Turin (1667–90) is a mind-bending structural and decorative *tour de force*. The chapel, gained by two long flights of stairs, is a circle housed in a square. It contains the Holy Shroud, the image of a man's body believed to be that of Christ as he lay in the tomb. Above it rises a kind of stepped dome that is almost impossible to recreate piece by

CHAPEL OF THE HOLY SHROUD, TURIN, 1667–90

Guarini's chapel was built to house the Turin Shroud. The upper stages of the dome are composed of diminishing tiers of arches, each framing a segmental window. The cone-shaped hexagon is surmounted by a lantern containing an image of the Holy Dove.

piece in the mind. Guarini was a renowned mathematician as well as philosopher and priest. It shows.

At its height the Baroque was a dazzling fusion of the geometric and the scenographic, wildly sensual and structurally sound. Remarkably, Guarani was able to capture this spirit even in such civic buildings as the Palazzo Carignano, Turin (1679), a building that seems unfinished and as much geological in inspiration as architectural. This was truly an architecture that puritanical minds would never understand.

BAROQUE BEYOND ITALY
HARMONY AND SPECTACLE

ST. JOHANNES NEPOMUK, MUNICH, 1733–46
*Paid for by the Asam brothers and attached to their residence, the church of St. Johannes Nepomuk is sometimes
referred to as the "Asamkirche." The brothers had control over all aspects of design and construction, and
the result is a perfect demonstration of the Baroque ideal of unity of the arts, where architecture, painting,
and sculpture work together to create a harmonious whole.*

THROUGH DYNASTIC marriages, wars, and increased travel, the Baroque insinuated its way across Europe with speed. Its curvaceous, daring forms flourished mostly in Catholic Europe and notably in southern Germany and Austria, where it was to take on some of its most fantastical guises. In Bavaria, the style grew with architectural studios that were inseparable from teams of expert craftsworkers.

The most spirited of these was the studio of the Asam brothers: Cosmas Damian (1686–1739) and Egid Quirin (1692–1750), whose masterpiece was the richly decorated church of St. Johannes Nepomuk (1733–46). shoehorned into a narrow site in the center of Munich. It takes some while to decipher this mysterious magic cave where no line seems straight and every surface that is not decorated with a peeping cherub (some with skeleton faces) is lavishly gilded or covered in silver and other rich materials. The façade is equally adventurous, rising from the pavement like some fantastic geological outcrop.

ARCHITECTURE FOR THE SENSES
Bavarian Baroque was a deeply sensual and pleasurable architecture. The intriguingly complex and joyously decorative pilgrimage church of Vierzehnheiligen (1743–72) by the great Balthasar Neumann (1687–1753) is as heady as ecclesiastical Baroque gets. Baroque's zenith, however, was appropriately enough not reached in the design of a church but in the Zwinger, Dresden (1709 onward), a pleasure palace comprising a number of fantasmagorical pavilions designed by Mathaes Daniel Pöppelmann (1662–1736). It is impossible not to hear the music of Bach and his contemporaries trilling through these sublime and multilayered buildings.

BENEDICTINE MONASTERY, MELK, AUSTRIA, 1702–14
At Melk, Prandtauer created a masterpiece of Baroque grandeur, setting the twin-towered façade of the abbey behind the projecting arms of the monastic buildings, which stretch forward to embrace a courtyard.

A FUSION OF THE ARTS
In Baroque design the individual elements were secondary to the overall effect. A good example of this principle is the architectural studio of the Asam brothers; both were architects, but Cosmas Damian was also a fresco painter and Egid Quirin a sculptor and stuccoist. As a team, they were responsible for the design and construction of several Bavarian churches, including the Benedictine abbey church at Rohr. The breathtaking altar, by Egid Quirin, depicts a life-size Virgin Mary ascending into Heaven.

climbs up and away from the rocky promontory on which it stands, ascending into a heavenly climax of domes and turrets. The interior of the church is as joyous as it is magisterial.

Equally impressive is the Karlskirche, Vienna (1716 onward) by Johann Bernhard Fischer von Erlach (1656–1723), a supreme example of Baroque urban set design. The church sits behind a façade – twice as wide as the nave and aisles – comprising a grand Corinthian portico set between two highly decorated Roman columns based on those of Trajan and Marcus Aurelius in Rome. The columns are, in turn, flanked by a pair of triumphal towers, and the whole stirring composition crowned with a lofty dome. Von Erlach's decision to recreate imperial Roman columns in archaeologically correct fashion was a hint of the Classical Revival that was to supersede Baroque and Rococo architecture in

Austria was also home to some magnificent Baroque buildings. High on the banks of the Danube, passengers on the hydrofoils that ply between Vienna and Budapest catch sight of the mighty Benedictine monastery at Melk (1702–14), the masterpiece of Jakob Prandtauer (1660–1726). The monastery

KARLSKIRCHE, VIENNA, 1716 ONWARDS
Commissioned by the Emperor Charles VI, the Karlskirche is an unprecedented combination of Baroque Roman elements with features of Classical Rome. The column reliefs, like those on the Roman columns of Trajan and Marcus Aurelius, symbolize a victory – here, a victory of faith over the 1713 plague. The life of the plague saint Charles Borromeo is illustrated in the reliefs.

LATE BAROQUE MUSIC
The music of the late Baroque period is exemplified in the work of Johann Sebastian Bach (1685–1750) and George Frideric Handel (1685–1759). They were born in the same part of Germany and both Lutheran by religion, but musically their careers diverged. Bach was profoundly influenced by the church and composed mainly sacred works – over 200 cantatas. Handel, by contrast, drew inspiration from his time in Italy and wrote primarily opera and secular pieces, mostly after his move to England in 1712.

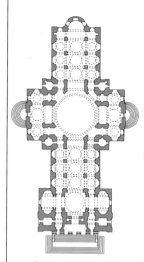

PLAN OF ST. PAUL'S
Wren's initial plan for the new St. Paul's was a centrally planned Greek cross crowned by an octagonal dome. However, the Dean and Chapter wanted a more traditional Latin cross. Thus in 1673 Wren produced the "warrant design" with a long nave, choir, and transepts. This was executed with the exception of the spire, which Wren replaced with a dome echoing that of his original plan. The weight of the dome is borne by a ring of arches supported on piers and by the corners of the central crossing.

" Si monumentum requiris, circumspice
[If you seek for a monument, gaze around]*"*

INSCRIPTION IN ST. PAUL'S, ATTRIBUTED TO WREN'S SON

ST. PAUL'S CATHEDRAL, LONDON, 1675–1710
This view of the west façade of St. Paul's shows the paired, freestanding columns of the portico. Statues are placed prominently at elevated positions: St. Paul stands above the central portico, flanked by St. Peter (left) and St. John (right). The portico pediment depicts the scene of St. Paul's conversion to Christianity.

Here, he raised perhaps the most elegant of all domes – cool, serene, watchful – but placed over the crossing of what had to be, to meet with the demands of a conservative clergy – a long, cruciform building following in the tradition of English medieval cathedrals. Wren's design was thus a compromise, but a brilliant one nevertheless and his perfect dome compensated for any fundamental artistic flaw in the building considered all of a piece. Wren's principal building material at St. Paul's was the brilliant white Portland stone successfully used by his successors. Notable among these was Nicholas Hawksmoor (1661–1736) who built a number of outstanding churches including St. Mary Woolnoth (1716–27) in the City of London. Here, Hawksmoor proved himself to be the Borromini of English architecture, with straight lines replacing curves. His Christ Church, Spitalfields (1714–29) is fronted by what looks like a giant Palladian "Venetian" window topped with a belfry and sky-piercing tower.

Wren, Hawksmoor, and John Vanbrugh (1664–1726) – the latter a soldier (taken for a spy and imprisoned in the Bastille), playwright (*The Provok'd Wife*, *The Relapse*), traveler (he spent some while in India as a merchant), and architect on a whim – designed a considerable number of fine palaces, country houses, and civic buildings. Compared to their counterparts in Catholic Europe, these were chaste and gently crafted, bringing a domestic note into the operatic score of Baroque design. Although dramatic, a large domed and winged house like Castle Howard, North Yorkshire (Vanbrugh and Hawksmoor, 1699–1712) sits happily in the rolling, cloudy, sheep-studded English countryside. English Baroque worked well on a less than heroic scale – as such delightful houses as Chettle, Dorset (1710–20) by Thomas Archer

Europe within the following half century. For almost a century afterward, the exact study and reproduction of ancient Roman and Greek prototypes was to become an obsession.

ENGLISH BAROQUE

In Britain, the Baroque developed into a style, if not entirely independently, then quite differently from that of Italy, Germany, and Austria. The key difference was that Britain was a Protestant country, and the Baroque was widely considered to be a three-dimensional weapon of papal propaganda. In the hands of Sir Christopher Wren (1632–1723), an English Baroque emerged after the restoration of the monarchy in 1660 that was more subdued than its continental counterpart but no less distinguished. Wren, a brilliant mathematician and astronomer, was commissioned to build the new St. Paul's Cathedral (1675–1710) in the City of London.

CHETTLE HOUSE, DORSET, ENGLAND, 1710–20
The English Baroque architect Thomas Archer was commissioned by the MP George Chaffin in 1710 to build this redbrick Queen Anne manor house in the English Baroque style. The house is set in five acres of gardens.

ST. MARTIN-IN-THE-FIELDS, LONDON, 1721–26
Gibbs' church was one the most influential designs of the 18th century. The exterior has recessed columns marking the side-entrances and a pedimented portico. The steeple emerges through the roof, tapering from a square base to a concave-sided spire.

(1688–1743) demonstrate. More significantly, the monumental yet restrained elegance of Wren's Royal Hospital, Chelsea (1682–89) and the church of St. Martin's-in-the-Fields (1721–26) by the Scottish architect James Gibbs (1682–1754), a Catholic who studied under Carlo Fontana in Rome (Wren traveled only as far as France; Hawksmoor never left England), was taken up enthusiastically in the American colonies and the fledgling United States; replicas of St. Martin's can be seen throughout New England.

Wren's further genius was in showing that the essentially grand and often grandiloquent Baroque style could be translated into a small, yet effective scale. The numerous churches he rebuilt in the City of London after the Great Fire of 1666 are some of the quiet gems of late Renaissance European architecture. Not to be missed are St. Stephen Walbrook (1672–87), a trial in miniature for the ideal interior arrangement of St Paul's, and St. Mary Abchurch

(1681–86), the polar opposite in spirit to the Asam brothers' St. Johannes Nepomuk, Munich.

Equally, Hawksmoor proved in the design of the Mausoleum (1729) at Castle Howard – a deeply moving rotunda – that a powerful and monumental architecture could be realized on a less than heroic scale, a sensibility that seems to have eluded his European contemporaries.

SIR JOHN VANBRUGH
The playwright and Baroque architect Sir John Vanbrugh (1664–1726) was born in London. He directed his attention to architecture following a career as a soldier and as the author of Restoration comedies, such as *The Provok'd Wife* (1697). He was made Comptroller at the Office of Works in 1702, and the commissions for Castle Howard and Blenheim Palace established his reputation.

MAUSOLEUM, CASTLE HOWARD, YORKSHIRE, 1729
Designed by Nicholas Hawksmoor, the Mausoleum at Castle Howard was begun in 1729. Inside there is a chapel, below which is a vaulted crypt encircled by 64 niches for the dead.

ABSOLUTISM
PALATIAL GRANDEUR

PHILIP II OF SPAIN

The son of Holy Roman emperor Charles V and Isabella of Portugal, Philip (1527–98) became king of Spain and the Spanish empire in 1556. After his return to Spain from the Netherlands in 1559, he conducted his 42-year reign from Madrid and the Escorial. Under his rule the empire suffered setbacks in its relations with the Protestant countries of Europe, including rebellion in the Netherlands (1568–1609). In 1588, his desire to return the English to Catholicism led to war and the destruction of the Spanish Armada.

RENAISSANCE ARCHITECTURE spread quickly through Europe south of the Alps, but was slower to reach up to France, the Low Countries, and Britain. In the sixteenth century, Italian Renaissance styles emerged in these countries in the form of a rag-bag of half-digested details as witnessed in the French chateaux and Jacobean and Elizabethan country houses of this period. Many of these houses were magnificent, notably the chateaux built along the Loire – Chenonceaux (1515–23) and Chambord (1519–47) – and, in England, Wollaton Hall, Nottingham (1580–85) and Hardwick Hall, Derbyshire (1590–97) by Robert Smythson.

SPANISH RENAISSANCE
In Spain, the Renaissance style also filtered through patchily, although it reached new heights quite early on in the Palace of Charles V at Grenada (1527–68). Influenced by Raphael and Bramante, the palace was designed by Pedro Machua (dates uncertain; active 1517–50) and his son Luis. The highlight of the palace, heavily rusticated on the outside, is the magnificent circular patio in the center of the block, which comes as a complete surprise. The patio comprises circular colonnades, Ionic above Doric, and is a wonderful, contemplative place to while away time.

The Spanish Renaissance, however, took on a unique aspect with the rise and rise of the absolute monarchy of the ascetic Philip II. Although Philip ruled over an ever-growing empire stretching as far as Chile, he more or less led the life of a monk. The monastery-palace he built beyond Madrid under a baking sun is one of the most imposing and perhaps frightening buildings in the world. The Escorial (1562–82) by Juan Bautista de Toledo (d.1567) and Juan de Herrara (c.1530–97) is a colossus, its prisonlike walls bereft of decoration. Behind them is an enclosed world in which, grouped around more than a dozen courtyards, loom monastery,

THE ESCORIAL, NEAR MADRID, 1562–82
This austere and monumental building, built from yellow-gray granite, was intended to commemorate Spanish victory over the French at the battle of St. Quentin in 1557. The vast complex includes a palace, monastery, college, and a domed church.

college, palace, and the towered and domed church dedicated to St. Lawrence. The Escorial imbued Spain with a monumental approach to architecture that remains one of the most striking characteristics of a country that was at once sensuous and puritanical, highly expressive, and deeply conservative at heart.

FRENCH CLASSICAL ARCHITECTURE

The French took up Renaissance architecture fully as the power of the monarchy increased to an unprecedented degree during the long and resplendent reign of Louis XIV, the "Sun King" (1638–1715), which began in 1642. France was now under the thumb of an absolute monarchy – "*L'Etat c'est moi*" ("I am the State") said the King. The only architecture suitable for such a powerful egomaniac was that of imperial Rome reflected in a seventeenth-century French mirror. Just before Louis' architects set to work on Versailles, the greatest of all European palaces in size if nothing else, Paris had been introduced to the grandeur of Italian Renaissance architecture in the guise of the church of Val-de-Grace (1645–47) by Jacques Lemercier (c.1580–1654): this beefy design was crowned by a muscular dome copied from that of St. Peter's itself.

Versailles (1661–1756), however, was a thing apart. The palace was colossal and set in an apparently infinite and regimented landscape shaped by André Le Nôtre (1613–1700). The main buildings of the palace itself, set back immediately from the town center, were principally the work of Louis Le Vau (1612–70) and Jules Hardouin Mansart, and to a lesser extent (the Petit Trianon, for example) of Ange-Jacques Gabriel. What began as an almost impossibly ambitious palace – the French court moved to Versailles in 1668 – ended its glory days in the model farm built for Marie-Antoinette who played games of milkmaids and shepherdesses a century later.

Utterly unlovable, at its height Versailles was the uncomfortable home to thousands of toadying courtiers who crammed into lodgings even in its rafters so as to be close to the king and grace

PIERRE PATEL, CHÂTEAU AND GARDENS OF VERSAILLES, FROM THE AVENUE DE PARIS, 1668
Louis XIV's famous palace complex was constructed around a château built in 1624 as a hunting lodge by his father. In the 1660s Louis Le Vau encased and extended the building, adding two service wings, while the landscape architect André Le Nôtre laid out vast, formal gardens with geometrically arranged avenues, woods, and canals.

and favor. It is significant, perhaps, that the famous Hall of Mirrors was copied by Albert Speer, Hitler's architect, in his design for the German Fuhrer's Reich Chancellery, Berlin in the late 1930s (see pp.180–81). Versailles had established itself as the house style of absolute monarchs and power-crazed dictators.

The Louis XIV style in all its cold, monotonous manner was perhaps perfected in the initially impressive, if ultimately yawn-inducing, east façade of the Palais du Louvre, Paris (1667 onwards) by Le Vau in collaboration with Claude Perrault (a doctor and dilettante) and the painter Charles Le Brun. The pairs of Corinthian columns that marched repetitively along the pedimented façade were to become a hallmark of much French classical architecture over the next century. In little more than half a century, French court architecture had moved a long way from the delightfully humane arcaded civic style of the Place Royale (now the Place des Vosges) commissioned by Henry IV. He lived in one of the apartments there set under a variegated roofline over a uniform, yet intimate, brick and stone arcade. The arcade stood around a garden square which remains one of the most delightful anywhere.

CHARLES LE BRUN

The French painter, designer, and art theorist Charles Le Brun (1619–90) dominated French art during Louis XIV's reign. After training in Paris, he went to Rome in 1642 where he worked under Nicolas Poussin. In 1648 he helped to found France's Academy of Painting and Sculpture and was made the first director of the Gobelins tapestry works in 1663. In 1667 the Gobelins royal furniture manufactory was founded under his direction. From 1668 to 1683 he was employed by Louis XIV to manage the decoration of Versailles. Le Brun's talents lay in the direction of grandiose decorative effects. Among his most outstanding works at Versailles were the Hall of Mirrors (1679–84) and the Great Staircase (1671–78, destroyed in 1752).

ROCOCO
THE FLOWERING OF LATE BAROQUE

RENAISSANCE ARCHITECTURE had begun with an elegant solution – a feat of engineering and construction as much as it was a work of art – with Brunelleschi covering the crossing of Florence Cathedral with a dome. It had moved on through the mathematical perfection of Palladio to the dramatic structural and decorative heights of the Baroque. Now in the eighteenth century it looked to be either floundering or luxuriating, depending upon your point of view, in an exuberant and ultimately decadent flourish of decoration. A dreamy, creamy extension of Baroque at its most sugar-candyish, Rococo was the final flourish of an increasingly fantastic and whimsical architecture that was to be nailed on the head with the academically correct hammer of Neo-classicism, a new purism that revolutionized European architecture while retaining the Classical orders and paying even more respect to the perceived spirit of the Greeks and Romans at their noble best.

However, there should be little doubt that Roman architecture in the heady days of Nero and Caligula was Rococo in spirit. Decoration became increasingly fussy in the first century, and perhaps it was only because it reached the limits of decorators' skills that Nero felt forced to hang literally tons of rose petals from the ceilings of the dining rooms of his Golden House (crushing unfortunate guests to a sweetly scented death) and to light his gardens with flaming and living human torches. Yet the serious-minded Neo-classicists who effectively put an end to Rococo design may well have regarded the decadence of this pretty style as on a par with Nero's architecturally and morally incorrect approach to interior and garden décor.

THE BIRTH OF ROCOCO

Rococo – the terms derives from *rocaille*, the French decorative trend for inverted plaster scallop and seashells – emerged at the court of Louis XIV, a sunny style for the Sun King. The first agreed example of this essentially interior style was a room decorated in a light-hearted fantasia of birds, monkeys, ribbons, tendrils, masks, and other playfulness by the painter Claude Andran in a room in the Château de la Menagerie for the thirteen-year-old fiancée of one of Louis' grandsons. This was in the 1690s, although the style really only got under way some years later in the salons, royal and otherwise, of eighteenth-century Paris. Lots of decorative and

HALL OF MIRRORS, AMALIENBURG PAVILION, MUNICH, 1734–39
This single-story hunting lodge is one of the most perfect examples of secular Rococo. The circular room at the center is lined with mirrors, which heighten the sense of lightness and movement.

ABBEY CHURCH, OTTOBEUREN, GERMANY, BEGUN 1737
The rich interior of Fischer's church at Ottobeuren is countered by its structural simplicity. The nave is made up of three domed bays, the central one forming the crossing. The domes were spectacularly decorated with illusionistic frescoes.

(1745–54; see p.2) by Dominikus Zimmermann (1685–1766). The latter is awash with light and looks its best on sunny winter days when the fields surrounding it lie deep in snow.

SPAIN AND PORTUGAL

Rococo found its own forms in both Spain and Portugal. In Spain, the lavish style – known as Churrigueresque after the family of architects who brought it into prominence – was, in part, a reaction against the severities of the reign of Philip II, and was to last through at least three more or less distinctive phases from roughly 1680 to 1780. In Portugal, otherwise simple buildings – churches and palaces – were smothered in licentious decoration after the arrival of galleon-loads of gold and diamonds from Brazil. Interiors of churches like São Francisco, Oporto (a reworking of a medieval design) are for those of a strong aesthetic constitution.

ROCOCO DECORATION
Ornamental motifs were commonly used for door and window surrounds and to enclose the decorative schemes of walls and ceilings. Usually made of wood or stucco, typical Rococo motifs include C- and S-scrolls, shells, flowers, ferns, and coral forms. This example, from a house in Prague, shows a stylized shell.

gilded plaster and mirrors everywhere – the style enlivened otherwise simple rooms: few architectural tricks were needed when decorative devices could do the job.

This chocolate-box style reached its peak not in France, however, but in Bavaria. One of the most light and waltzy interiors of all is that of the Amalienburg Pavilion (1734–39) at Schloss Nymphenburg, near Munich, built for the Elector Max Emmanuel by his court dwarf François Cuvilliés (1695–1768) who had been sent to Paris in 1720 to train as an architect. Cuvilliés worked on the decoration with Johann Baptist Zimmermann. Scalloped windows alternate with gilded mirrors; above them wonderfully wavy gilded plants grow up through the cornice line (Palladio would have turned in his grave), while gilded birds fly up from them into the rounded white skies of the pavilion's ceilings.

GERMAN ROCOCO

While the French thought Rococo over the top for church decoration, the Bavarians had no such scruples. Two of the finest Rococo interiors are those of the Benedictine abbey church at Ottobeuren (1737 onward) by Johann Fischer (1692–1766) and the Wieskirche, Steinhausen

SÃO FRANCISCO, OPORTO, PORTUGAL, 18TH CENTURY
A magnificent example of the Portuguese Rococo style, over 450lbs (200kg) of gold was used in the richly carved and gilded interior of São Francisco.

THE DECORATIVE ARTS
The spirit of Rococo is exemplified in the various branches of the decorative arts. It was not unusual for painters and sculptors to produce tapestry and porcelain designs. The French artist François Boucher (1703–70), a favorite of Mme de Pompadour, is a good example. Court painter to Louis XV and director of the Gobelins tapestry factory from 1755, he also completed various commissions from the interior decoration of the châteaux of Marly and Fontainebleau to stage settings for the opera and designs for domestic objects.

LOW COUNTRIES
THE DOMESTIC IDYLL

DELFTWARE

Delftware is the name given to tin-glazed earthenware first made in the early 17th century at Delft, Holland. Artisans had migrated to the Netherlands and Belgium from Italy in the 16th century, settling in several Dutch cities. Dutch ceramics were strongly influenced by the tin-glazing techniques these artists had brought with them. Trading by the Dutch East India Company in the early 17th century led to the importation of Chinese blue-and-white *Wan-Li* porcelain into Holland. This influenced Dutch ceramics, resulting in the blue-and-white style we associate with Delft today.

HOLLAND BEGAN TO develop what can be described as a distinctive Protestant architecture of its own in the seventeenth century. At heart this was a domestic architecture. If quietly elegant, it was also to be rather flat, appropriate perhaps in a country that has few hills. Not only was there little in the way of hierarchy – a palace was little more than a much-enlarged merchant's house – but there was also little in the way of the animation found in the High Renaissance or Baroque in Catholic climes south of the Alps. The flat pilaster set against a simple, if handsome, brick wall was the norm, while colonnades and bravura pediments and porticoes were rarely seen. This chasteness was not simply the result of a homely temperament and iconoclastic religion, but also that of a lack of stone: brick was and remains the standard building material in Holland.

Nevertheless, decorative flourishes abound in the inventive and often exotic steeples of the Baroque churches of Hendrik de Keyser (1565–1621) and Jacob van Campen (the "Dutch Palladio," 1595–1657). Climbing into the watery skies above Leyden and Haarlem, the spires of these Dutch parish churches are animated with obelisks and finials, pedimented windows, ogee arches, and onion domes. They were to have a direct effect on the spires and towers of the City of London churches designed by Sir Christopher Wren. Equally, in the gables of the tall, thin merchants' houses that surround the canals in the heart of seventeenth-century Amsterdam, one sees a desire for decoration and individuality trying its best to break free from the near uniformity below.

HOMELY ARCHITECTURE

Even then, the underlying quality of this archetypal Dutch architecture is its homeliness. The houses are light and bright, and it is here in Holland that we see the emergence of the idea of the modern family home – neat, ordered, and as clean as a new pin. They inspired contemporary Dutch painters – Vermeer only the most famous – to capture and to an extent create a domestic ideal or idyll that continues to affect us today.

JOHANNES VERMEER, *VIEW OF DELFT* (DETAIL), 1660–61

Vermeer's masterpiece shows the domestic appeal of Dutch architecture and suggests something of its quiet order. The city was a major center for artists, who became particularly famous for the study of perspective and the effects of light and color.

GUILD HOUSES, GRAND' PLACE, BRUSSELS, 1690s ONWARD
The fronts of these gabled façades on Brussels' main square have been decorated with Baroque detailing, each is quite distinct from the other. However, the relatively uniform height of the building, and the use of relief ornament creates a cohesive effect.

This style was mixed with Palladianism, as can be seen in the designs of Van Campen – a good example is the Mauritshuis in The Hague, built for a general in 1633. It was also a fusion of styles that led to the classic English Georgian terraced house, which set a new standard in city housing that was to be widely copied.

A far more exuberant tradition existed in Belgium. In the gloriously rich façades of the Baroque houses that line the Grand' Place, Brussels (1690s onward), with their coats of carved animals, swags, deities, medallions, and cartouches, it is hard not to see a culture that has long made a great play of its skills in the arts of lacemaking and confectionery. These buildings are the architectural equivalent of a box of Belgian chocolates.

INFLUENCES ABROAD

The Dutch influence pervaded at least some of the early colonial architecture in the United States, although it was to have a much deeper and lasting effect in South Africa. In New Jersey and New York, there are several memorable houses in the Dutch style. The earliest is the Abraham Ackerman House, Hackensack, New Jersey (1704, demolished, 1865), and, among the latest, the Vreeland House, Englewood, New Jersey (1818).

In South Africa, the distinctive white Dutch colonial style began to develop once the castle at Cape Town had been completed in 1679 and settlers began to feel secure. The first public building was the Burgher Watch House of 1716, although this was rebuilt in 1755–61 (architects unknown).

But the true glory of Dutch South African architecture lies in the beautiful and simple white farmhouses, many at the heart of the country's famous vineyards today, seen at their best in Stellenbosch. These remain some of the most liveable and covetable houses to be found anywhere in the world and because they are simple, light, and airy they appear as modern today as they were when built.

STELLENBOSCH, CAPE TOWN, EARLY 19TH CENTURY
Dutch South African farmsteads built in the early 19th century almost always had a central front door and two half-windows, with two or four full-width windows flanking the space on either side.

The
AMERICAS

THE MOST POWERFUL CIVILIZATIONS OF
THE PRE-HISPANIC AMERICAS WERE THOSE
OF THE MAYA, AZTECS, AND INCAS. EACH
DEVELOPED A STRONG, SIMPLE, AND OFTEN MASSIVE
ARCHITECTURE BASED ON SIMPLE FORMS, NOTABLY
THE PYRAMID. FOR THE AZTECS, WHO BUILT
PYRAMIDS AT ALL SCALES, THESE SACRED STRUCTURES
FORMED CHAINS OF ARTIFICIAL MOUNTAINS
CONNECTING HUMANS, NATURE, AND THE COSMOS.
IF THE MONUMENTS OF CENTRAL AND SOUTH
AMERICA SOMETIMES FEEL SINISTER AND REMOTE
TO OUTSIDERS, PERHAPS THIS IS BECAUSE THEY
ARE ASSOCIATED WITH BLOODY SACRIFICES
AND INEFFABLE RITUALS AND BELIEFS. THE SPANISH
AND PORTUGUESE INVADERS BROUGHT A FLORID
BAROQUE ARCHITECTURE TO THE AMERICAS
THAT FLOURISHED FROM SANTIAGO DE CUBA TO
SANTIAGO DE CHILE. THE RITUALS AND CUSTOMS
THAT ACCOMPANIED THEM WERE OFTEN NO LESS
BLOODY THAN THOSE THEY ATTEMPTED TO REPLACE.

MACHU PICCHU, PERU
*The magnificent setting high in the Peruvian Andes must
have overshadowed the original palace fortress that stood here.*

ANCIENT MESOAMERICA
A MONUMENTAL ARCHITECTURE

CHALCHIUHTLICUE

This Aztec goddess was invoked for the protection of newborn children and marriages. She was the goddess of running water, springs, and streams, and the wife or sister of Tlaloc, the god of mountains, rain, and springs. Aztec society was agricultural, so there were numerous deities associated with weather and the earth's products who had to be appeased. Tlaloc, for example, received the sacrifice of newborn children.

MAYAN WRITING AND TECHNOLOGY

The Maya were the only truly literate people of the pre-Colombian Americas. Their hieroglyphic inscriptions remained impenetrable until the second half of the 20th century, since when the purpose of many Mayan buildings has been discovered. Much of the Mayan script that we can now read is on buildings because only three Mayan codices are known to survive – the others having been destroyed by the Spanish as "pagan." Writing enabled the Maya to keep records and plan their agriculture, and they were accomplished farmers and astronomers Modern anthropologists believe that the reason the Mesoamericans did not use the wheel was from a lack of domesticable animals that could be used to pull wheeled vehicles.

WHEN THE SPANISH *conquistadores* literally burned their boats and fought their way in a spirit of death or glory into the heart of Mexico, they were astonished to find architecture and cities on such a monumental scale. Teotihuacán was planned around grand avenues leading to and from capacious plazas. The city was dominated, though, by vast stepped pyramids topped by temple platforms. These had a purpose that even the cutthroat Spaniards found revolting: they were for the daily human sacrifices demanded by the gods. Unless a fresh, still-beating heart was held up to the sun, and then hurled from the top of the pyramid temples, together with the young body it was pried from, the sun would sulk and refuse to rise the following day. According to the architect and historian Patrick Nuttgens, five years before the arrival of the *conquistadores*, the Great Temple of Teotihuacán was consecrated with "the sacrifice of a great many victims, variously estimated at 10,000 and at 80,000, ritually slaughtered four at a time, from sunrise to sundown, for four days." Worse things were to happen in twentieth-century Europe, but it was terrifying stuff all the same.

THE PYRAMIDS

Teotihuacán's most impressive monument is the Pyramid of the Sun (c. AD 50), erected to the immediate east of the Avenue of the Dead, the principal avenue running through this city

THE AVENUE OF THE DEAD, TEOTIHUACÁN, MEXICO
The city of Teotihuacán is laid out on a grid system, and was irrigated by canals fed by the Rio San Juan. On the left of the Avenue of the Dead is the massive Pyramid of the Sun, measuring 187ft (57m) in height.

of canals, bridges, and great meeting places. The pyramid form is, of course, familiar from Egypt, but whether ideas traveled by sea in the Bronze Age from North Africa to Mesoamerica, or whether the Aztec, Olmec, Maya, Zapotec, and Toltec pyramids emerged independently remains a matter of speculation. The Pyramid of the Sun is certainly impressive, measuring 712 feet (217 meters) at its base, rising to a surviving height of 187 feet (57 meters). It overlays at least two earlier pyramids and was originally topped with a temple building. The sheer scale of the Pyramid of the Sun and its numerous attendant temples mean that it dominates the central avenue.

The pyramid form appeared in both North and Central America in approximately 200 BC, although dates are a little sketchy. Pyramids were built in the region for a period of at least 800 years. The earliest designs were those of the Mayans. These stepped up steeply in numerous tiers and were crowned with temple buildings adorned with curious stone plumes, rather like the combs of roosters or, more likely, the headpieces of priests or warriors. Poking up over the treetops, in more recent times these were a sign for several teams of archaeologists that, beneath rampant vegetation, ancient temples were waiting to be discovered. All temples were aligned with the heavenly bodies, whether the sun, moon, or stars. The Mayan calendar remains famous for its accuracy. What still seems strange to us is that none of these peoples ever employed the wheel. Building sites must have been exhausting places.

The temples of the whole region are largely built in stone: very often this was plastered and then polished to a shine. The color chosen was always red, not just because it was readily available in ocher form, but because it represented blood in cultures that could never have enough of the stuff spilling down the walls and long stairways of these stern temples.

UNIQUE STRUCTURES

Much of daily life in the America of the Aztecs and Mayans would have been lived in the open air. As a result, Mesoamerican architecture features little in the way of windows. Most buildings appear to have been lit from doorways. There is no evidence of sophisticated interior decoration of any sort. We know little of the Aztecs' architecture beyond a few key types. Among these are the temple, governors' palaces, and the fascinating ballcourts, a kind of indoor football field dating back to the eighth century AD and possibly earlier. Two of the latter are more or less

THE CALENDARS
Both the Maya and the Aztecs had complex calendars that share many similarities. The Mayan calendar consisted of a year of 365 days and ritual cycle of 260 named days; 52 years constituted a Calendar Round. There were 18 named months of 20 days and five additional "unlucky" days. All of these features were shared with the Aztec calendar. Years did not begin at the same point in all regions. To correlate all historical records there existed a Long Count, a continuous count of time from a fixed date calendar. The Aztec calendar consisted of a cycle of numerals from 1 through 13, and a cycle of 20 day names. Deities were associated with the numerals, in addition there were nine deities of the night. The calendar was used to decide auspicious days for beginning projects and for reading the importance of natural signs and events such as births. At the end of each 52-year cycle for example, household utensils were discarded and replaced, and temples renovated.

well preserved, at Copán in Honduras just over the Guatemalan border and at Chichén Itzá in Yucatán, Mexico. The walls of the latter boast murals which suggest that members of losing teams were scarified in games played out as some form of religious ritual. Today's silk-clad footballers are merely "sick as parrots" (there are plenty of these in Honduras) when they lose.

The ancient ruined Mayan city of Uxmal, Yucatán, is typical of Mayan architecture around the period AD 600–900. In addition to the residential quarter, important buildings here include the Governor's House, the Temple of the Magician, which sits atop a large pyramid, and the Nunnery Quadrangle, four rectangular buildings set around a central courtyard and probably used to house priests. Rooms in these ancient American buildings do not seem to connect, but as the climate is normally hot, there was no great discomfort involved in walking outside from one room or chamber into another. The Governor's House at Uxmal is decorated in distinctive molded panels; originally these would have been inlaid with relief sculptures carved into stone mosaic. The effect of the sun on these would, doubtless, have been spectacular. The molded panels were, a thousand years later, adopted as a decorative concrete structure in some of the houses and religious buildings designed by the famous North American architect Frank Lloyd Wright.

MACHU PICCHU

The most dramatically sited of the pre-conquest American monuments is Machu Picchu, the stone-walled fortress city located high between two mountain peaks overlooking the Urubamba River far below. Completed in about 1500, Machu Picchu is more glorious for its setting than for the quality of its architecture.

Rising on a complex series of terraces are the ruins of houses, palaces, stores, temples, and graveyards. These are solidly built in stone. There appear to be few decorative or structural flourishes, although it is hard to ascertain just how this Andean citadel appeared 500 years ago.

BALL COURT, CHICHÉN ITZÁ
An important religious center during both the Mayan and Toltec periods, old Chichén was built in the Mayan style. Remains include a stepped temple pyramid and a 479-ft- (145-meter-) long ball court.

HOLLYHOCK HOUSE, LOS ANGELES, 1917

Built for the oil heiress Aline Barnsdall, Frank Lloyd Wright's stunning house is clearly influenced by Mayan architecture, both in the Hollyhock friezes around the exterior walls and in the building's pyramidal structure. The house is built around a central courtyard.

We do know that many of the buildings have windows, unlike their distant northern relatives, and that life beneath the snow-capped peaks here may have been more civilized than we can fairly

judge. In any event, Machu Picchu remains one of the wonders of the world, a ghost city in which the works of man and nature have been almost seamlessly united.

THE END OF THE ANCIENTS

Very little of the earth pyramid architecture of North America survives, although there was a substantial temple complex known as Monks Mound at Cahokia in the Mississippi Valley – an area where there were many early settlements. We also know of Pueblo sites in the southwest United States, but effectively the ancient architecture of the Americas belongs to Mexico, Guatemala and, in South America, the Peru of the Incas. The cities, architecture, peoples, and cultures of the regions were largely destroyed by accident or design by the Spaniards. Today, the poorest and most abused people in Mexico are the descendants of the Aztecs who, under the banner of the Zapatista National Liberation Army, began to reassert their rights in a very unbloody fashion after an uprising in Chiapas in 1994. They live in huts. They have no temples.

THE INCA

The Incan Empire stretched from the northern border of modern-day Ecuador to the Rio Maule in Central Chile. The Inca established their capital at Cuzco in the 12th century and began to conquer other peoples in the early 15th century. They developed a complex form of government ruled by an emperor with the aid of an aristocratic bureaucracy. The majority of the people were farmers, and they were particularly skilled at metalworking and stonecutting, the latter particularly evident in the complex forms of Incan walls such as those at Cuzco. The Incan civilization was destroyed by the Spanish invasion, its people and empire then becoming a colony of Spain.

TEMPLE OF THE THREE WINDOWS, SACRED PLAZA, MACHU PICCHU. PERU, C. 1500

This temple is meant to represent the three-windowed cave which the Inca believed was their place of origin. As at other Incan sites, what is remarkable about the architecture here is not the form of the buildings, but their intricate, close-fitting stonework.

COLONIAL AMERICAS
NEW-FOUND LAND

CRISTÓBAL COLÓN
Born in Genoa, Italy Cristóbal Colón (Christopher Columbus; 1451–1506) was one of the world's greatest navigators. His voyages opened the way for exploration and colonization of the New World. Believing he would reach the East by sailing west, he set sail in 1492 financed by Queen Isabella and King Ferdinand of Spain. His flotilla of three ships led by the Santa Maria reached the Bahamas in 33 days and went on to visit Cuba and Haiti. His third voyage, begun in 1498, resulted in the discovery of the South American mainland.

THE AMERICAS were settled over many thousands of years. Cristóbal Colón (Christopher Columbus) did not "discover" America when he sailed to the Caribbean in 1492, but the Genoese navigator did open up the Americas to European colonial exploitation. At the cost of great suffering, disease, slavery, and deep cruelty, the Americas were rewarded with some fine architecture and towns that flourished in response to tropical, mountain, and rain forest climates.

FORTIFICATIONS

Some of the earliest colonial architecture was in the form of impressive fortresses and other fortifications. These were needed to keep the navies and armies of rival European powers and pirates at bay. This is how Havana, the one great Caribbean city, developed from its foundation in 1519. The great Spanish fortresses give Old Havana much of its special charm nearly five hundred years on. These are the Castillo de la Real Fuerza, 1558–82, by Bartolome Sanchez, the Fortaleza de San Salvador de la Punta (completed 1600), the Castillo del Morro (1587–1630), both by Giovanni Battista Antonelli (father and son of

the same name) and Cristóbal de Roda, and the Castillo de San Carlos de la Cabana (begun 1763, after the surprise conquest of Havana by the British the year before, completed in 1773). Once these problems were put behind them, the Spanish built magnificently. The Palacio de los Capitanes-Generales (1772–76), now the Museum of the City, in Plaza de Armas, is one of the finest buildings in the Americas. Built of heavy coral limestone, arcaded and gathered around a large courtyard, it forms a city block. Behind a façade of impressive stone coats of arms, Corinthian columns, and huge barred window openings, the courtyard is graced with birdsong and magnificent trumpetwood and yagruma trees. Home to the City Historian today, the palace has been at the center (together with the restoration work carried out at the Covento de Santa Clara) of Havana's impressive renovation program.

RESTORATION

Other major restoration works in Cuba from the 1970s included the subtle renovation of the whole of Trinidad, a delightful Spanish Colonial town that had survived intact through years of poverty, neglect, and revolution. Trinidad was one of several towns and places of major architectural and historical interest that was declared a World Heritage Site by UNESCO, the education arm of the United Nations Organisation, who put up much of the capital to restore Trinidad and Old Havana.

CASTILLO DE LA REAL FUERZA, HAVANA, CUBA, 1558–82
Built by Bartolomé Sanchez, this military fortification is an early example of the forts built to guard Spanish possessions against pirates. The basic plan is square with triangular bastions in the corners.

OPERA HOUSE, MANAUS, BRAZIL, 1888—96

One of the most important monuments of the rubber trade, the opera house in Manaus has an interior decorated with murals *depicting exotic flora and fauna and a frieze painted to give the viewer the impression of standing beneath the Eiffel Tower.*

In Mexico and down into Central and South America, the Spaniards, led by Hernan Cortes who landed in the Aztec world on a brief voyage from Havana in 1519, developed a form of massive Baroque architecture that depended for much of its effect on florid doorways and porches. This is witnessed for example in the highly exaggerated Zacatecas Cathedral, Mexico (from 1612) by Francisco Jimenez or the encrusted entrance and twin western towers of the church of San Sebastian and Santa Prisca, Taxco (1751—81). This love of fecund ornament was endemic to many American cultures. In rural Mexico, whether in Hidalgo, Puebla, or Tlaxcala, Indians still build wooden houses, thatched earth to rooftop in complex and deliciously decorative layers of sun-dried rye, the stalks of maguey plants, palm, grass, or cactus.

THE OPERA HOUSE AT MANAUS

Flamboyant Baroque architecture traveled with Spanish and Portuguese explorers, traders, and other ambitious colonialists throughout South America. One of the greatest architectural surprises at the time it was built was the Opera House at Manaus in the very heart of the Amazonian

rain forest in Brazil. Manaus, named after the local indigenous Manau tribe, was founded by Francisco do Motta Falco in the early seventeenth century. It was raised on the banks of Rio Negro that flows into the Amazon some six miles downstream. The climate is one of intense humidity and torrential rain for half the year. Termites, damp, and other bugs devour buildings with relish — so much so that the world's most unlikely opera house, today the Teatro Amazonas, (Lisbon architects, 1888—96), has had to be rebuilt no fewer than four times since in 1929, 1960, 1974, and again in 1990.

Designed in a voluptuous Italianate style, its wrought-iron frame was shipped from Scotland, stone and marble cladding and chandeliers from Italy, tiles and bronze fittings from France. The restoration of 1990 saw the building rendered pink as it has been when it opened. In its heyday at the beginning of the twentieth century, the Ballet Russe danced here, Jenny Lind sang under its 246-foot (75-meter) dome, while the great tenor Enrico Caruso, fearing disease, refused to disembark from his ship. The Manaus opera house is a dreamlike symbol of a dramatic and decidedly baroque land.

QUEBEC CITY

In North America, the colonial legacy was remarkably frugal. Architecture in what was to become the United States and Canada was essentially the work of settlers with their own beliefs and ways of doing things. In Canada, the one distinctive historic settlement is the fortified Quebec City, a French colonial outpost until taken by General James Wolfe for the British in 1759. Fort Chambly (1709–11) was designed and built by Josué Boisberthelot de Beaucourt, the chief engineer in Canada. Built of stone, the fort was designed along the lines of fortifications in France built by Sébastien Le Prestre de Vauban, Louis XIV's military architect and siege engineer.

CHINA
And JAPAN

THE GREAT WALL THAT STRADDLES CHINA IS PERHAPS THE COUNTRY'S MOST REMARKABLE STRUCTURE, BUT A STRONG ARCHITECTURAL TRADITION HAD EXISTED LONG BEFORE IT WAS BUILT. ISOLATED FROM OTHER CULTURES, THE CHINESE HAD FOUND THEIR OWN INDIVIDUAL STYLE. THIS SPREAD TO JAPAN AND SOUTHEAST ASIA, BUT NEVER FAR WESTWARD UNTIL SILK AND SPICE TRADE ROUTES OPENED UP RELIABLY IN THE 17TH AND 18TH CENTURIES. METHODS OF CONSTRUCTION WERE TRIED AND TESTED OVER MANY HUNDREDS OF YEARS AND, WITHOUT EXTERNAL INFLUENCES, THE DESIGN OF BUILDINGS BECAME HIGHLY RITUALIZED, GREAT SIGNIFICANCE BEING GIVEN TO COLOR AND TO TIMBER JOINTS OF EVER-INCREASING SOPHISTICATION. IN THE 20TH CENTURY IT WAS THE ZENLIKE SIMPLICITY OF THE MOST REFINED JAPANESE ARCHITECTURE THAT WAS TO HAVE A SIGNIFICANT EFFECT ON MODERN ARCHITECTURE IN EUROPE AND THE US.

KINKAKUJI GOLDEN PAVILION, KYOTO, JAPAN
This Zen Buddhist temple was founded toward the end of the 14th century. It was destroyed by arson in 1950 and later rebuilt exactly as the original, a fact symbolized by the golden phoenix on the roof.

CLASSICAL CHINA
BALANCE AND CONTINUITY

PLAN OF THE FORBIDDEN CITY

The buildings of the Forbidden City are set within a walled compound and arranged on a north-south axis that stretches 5 miles (8km). The Meridian Gate (bottom, center), is the entrance to the city, north of this five marble bridges span the moat that crosses the next great court. Ahead is the Gate of Great Peace, the entrance pavilion to the main precinct. At the center is the Hall of Supreme Harmony.

THE FORBIDDEN CITY (1406–20) was the home of 24 Chinese emperors over a period of nearly 500 years. Built like a giant Chinese puzzle – boxes within boxes – it dominates Beijing today. Its great courtyards and colorful halls cover 180 acres (73 hectares), bounded by a wall that measures 3,149 feet (960 meters) by 2,493 feet (760 meters). It is a remarkable place and the heart of traditional Chinese architecture. Given the iconoclastic political and social upheavals that tore China apart throughout much of the 20th century its survival is almost miraculous.

The walls that surround the imperial complex echo China's long isolation from the rest of the world. Although Indian, Persian, and even Greek influences did seep into China from the third century AD, this was also the time when the Great Wall was built to keep not only warring Mongol horsemen, but the outside world, at bay. China developed independently of the Western world. Her architecture developed slowly over very long periods and, although there were regional differences, especially in the design

and construction of housing, courtly architecture was always something of a house style, especially after it had been codified by Li Jie in *The Methods of Design and Architecture* (see opposite), which was published in 1103.

THE PALACE COMPLEX

The Forbidden City conforms to all the rules of *feng shui* ("wind and water"), the "science" by which buildings must be laid out if the gods are to be appeased and good fortune follow. The great halls – imperial apartments, harem, lodgings for courtiers, reception rooms – are arranged in two rows on either side of a grand axis, five miles (eight kilometers) long, that runs north to south through Beijing. They are grouped in eight courtyards and gilded, painted in rich reds, greens, yellows, and blues, beneath swooping roofs animated with dragons, and covered in glazed tiles, which make a colorful and dramatic sight. The timber halls are raised on terraces of up to 26 feet (eight meters) and set behind impressive marble balustrades. Inside, their ceilings are richly carved and gilded, held up by columns supporting extremely complex capitals or brackets that are supreme examples of the

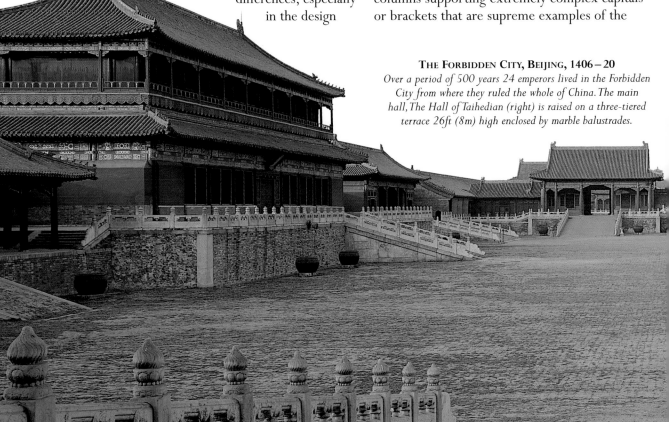

THE FORBIDDEN CITY, BEIJING, 1406–20
Over a period of 500 years 24 emperors lived in the Forbidden City from where they ruled the whole of China. The main hall, The Hall of Taihedian (right) is raised on a three-tiered terrace 26ft (8m) high enclosed by marble balustrades.

carpenters' art. The Chinese did not lack stone or other building materials nor the ability to construct arches and vaults. They simply chose not to, delighting in timber and, in the process, chopping down much of the ancient forests that once covered what became empty plains.

To the northwest of the city, later emperors of the Ming and Qing dynasties created the delightful Summer Palace (from 1750), reports of which helped to fuel a passion for Chinese decoration – chinoiserie – in Europe at the time. The Summer Palace with its pleasure pavilions and intricate gardens enclosed 7,165 acres (2,900 hectares), three-quarters of this water. The various parts of this dreamy escape from the Forbidden City were linked by a gloriously decorated gallery that stretches 2,493 feet (760 meters). All the buildings, as with those of the Forbidden City, were designed to be pretty much earthquake-proof.

Common sense was matched in imperial Chinese society by a commitment to ancient ritual. The gods and ancestors must be kept happy. In Beijing they were surely happy looking down on the perfect form of the Hall of Prayer at the Tiantan Shrine, a vast religious complex covering 691 acres (280

QINIANDIAN HALL OF PRAYER, TIANTAN SHRINE, BEIJING, 1420
Part of a group of buildings built for emperors of the Ming and Qing dynasties, the Qiniandian Hall was designed for prayers for good harvest. It has a triple, conical roof of deep-blue glazed tiles.

THE MODULAR SYSTEM

In his illustrated book *The Methods of Design and Architecture* (1103) the architect Li Jie formulated the modular system – a system of proportions, derived from the vertical breadth of a bracket arm, to govern the size and spacing of columns and beams. It became a standard text and established the modular system across the whole empire.

hectares) built during the Ming and Qing dynasties. This circular wooden prayer hall is 105 feet (32 meters) high and 78 feet (24 meters) in diameter. It is gloriously colorful, the deep blue glazed tiled roofs spinning out from the hub of the

THE GREAT WALL OF CHINA, C.210 BC

One of the great architectural projects of the ancient world, the Great Wall was built by Qin Shih Huang Ti, the first emperor of

the Qin Dynasty, to protect China from its enemies. The existing wall was restored and reinforced by the Ming dynasty.

TERRA-COTTA ARMY

The first Chinese emperor, Qin Shih Huang Ti, designed his own tomb, a vast underground palace that attempted to recreate the magnificence of his empire. Ten thousand life-size terra-cotta warriors with real weapons guarded the approach to the tomb. Discovered in 1974, the warriors represent every rank in the army, including archers, infantrymen, and charioteers. The terra-cotta army represents the power of the great Qin dynasty.

tower with its red doors, columns, and window frames and its dark green beams. This lovely structure stands on top of three circular platforms surrounded by white marble balustrades. The ball on top of the concave, conical roof is gold-plated. Visitors now, as those centuries ago, are struck by the huge spaces in which these Chinese buildings are set and the extent to which everything appears to be part of a hugely grand plan, each element of a particular building related to the city or to the religious or palace complex itself. China's intense national homogeneity is surely reflected in the architecture of its emperors.

QIN DYNASTY

Like the Romans, of whom they knew little or nothing, the imperial Chinese were supremely competent builders of roads, bridges, and other structures that enabled Beijing to command even its most distant subjects – as Rome did. But where the two great ancient empires differed was

in the way they protected their boundaries. Rome did this through the supremacy of its legions. The Chinese did it by building a wall that reached from one end of the empire to the other, the 9656 miles (6,000 kilometers) separating the Gulf of Pohai from Chia-yu-Khan in Kansu province. Hadrian's Wall, which stretched from the Irish to the North Seas to keep the warring Picts out of Britannia, is a mere fence in comparison. The Great Wall was completed in around 210 BC by Qin Shih Huang Ti, the first emperor of China, whose tomb, complete with 600 and more lifelike and life-sized terra-cotta warriors was uncovered in the 1970s. It has long been the stuff of legend and remains not just a remarkable achievement, but in parts a thing of architectural beauty. The wall was completely refaced and adorned in stone in the 15th and 16th centuries during the Ming dynasty. For much of its length the Wall is 26 feet (seven to eight meters) high rising to a maximum of

46 feet (14 meters); it is between 20–23 feet (six and seven meters) deep at its base, 16 feet (five meters) at its top.

In Chinese the very word "wall" came to mean "city": civilization depended upon walls and everyone, save far-flung peasantry, lived to some degree behind walls: walls of towns, cities, and monasteries. Town houses were often designed as a number of different pavilions gathered around courts hidden behind faceless walls.

THE POTALA PALACE

The Great Wall apart, perhaps the most formidable structures elsewhere in the new Communist empire are the sheer, mountainous walls of the Potala Palace, Lhasa (1645–95) in occupied Tibet. Rising from a high ridge looking out over a vast plain fringed by mountains, the Potala Palace commands one of the most dramatic sites of any building or complex of buildings in the world. The architecture is not complex, but the sheer scale of the Palace with its white, red, and gold leaf makes for an imposing sight. Here is an architecture designed to make

its mark on a colossal and forbidding landscape in a part of the world that has always been mysterious and all too often forgotten.

The Chinese were also great bridge builders. These vary from the whimsical, such as those spanning lakes in the grounds of the Summer Palace, Beijing, to more demanding structures like the Anji Bridge (AD 605–17), Zhaoxian in Hebei province. Built during the Sui dynasty, this is the oldest bridge of its type – arched with open spandrels – constructed at least 700 years before the first example of this type in Europe. The bridge has 28 stone arches and spans 121 feet (37 meters). Not only is the bridge a superb piece of structural engineering, but it is also sparingly yet elegantly decorated, as much a thing of beauty as a functional tool. It proves, like so many ancient Chinese structures, that the Chinese appeared to pull the stops out only when they needed and for the rest of the time were happy to live with a very slowly developing architectural tradition. The tradition survived only to be shattered by war, invasion (by the Japanese), and revolution in the 20th century.

MING DYNASTY

Major achievements were made in painting and pottery during the Ming dynasty (1368–1644). In pottery there were many new developments as well as the continuation of old traditions. In general, porcelain replaced stoneware. The Ming dynasty was the golden age of white porcelain with cobalt-blue underglaze decoration. There were further experiments during this period and the ensuing Qin dynasty with various decorative techniques using enameled glazes.

POTALA PALACE, LHASA, TIBET, 1645–94
Built as the residence for the Dalai Lama and as a monastery, the palace rises 660ft (200m) against a hillside. Inside, the palace has nine stories.

JAPAN
RITUAL AND REFINEMENT

SAMURAI

For much of the period between the 12th and the 19th centuries Japan was dominated by *daimyos* (military barons). As leaders of the *samurai* (warriors), they established a military dictatorship in 1192 under a *shogun* (great general). The *samurai* were a privileged élite who gave absolute loyalty to the *daimyo*. The *samurai* wore two swords, one short the other long, and followed a rigid code of ethics known as *Bushido* – founded upon loyalty, honor, and the willingness to face death. From the 17th century their military duties became largely ceremonial. In 1867 the last *shogun* resigned and Meiji reformers abolished their rank in the 1870s.

HIMEJI CASTLE, Himeji City (1601–14) is a feature of as many calendars in Japan as Neuschwanstein is in Germany and Windsor Castle is in Britain. Not only is it a particularly beautiful building, and remarkably serene for a castle, but in the Japanese mind it represents an important period in recent history, the reunification of the country in the sixteenth century by Nobunaga and Hideyoshi. It is also an image of oriental architecture that once seen is never forgotten and somehow captures the spirit of a way of building that developed independently and very differently from that of the West. Agriculture was introduced to Japan in the third century BC. Its early architecture was temporary or rebuildable. It was not until remarkably late – by Western standards – that solid, permanent buildings appeared realized in stone rather than timber.

The castle was one of the principal types of permanent buildings. Constant fighting between rival clans and tribes prompted the most powerful warlords of twelfth-century Japan to create the Shogunate, with influence passing from the emperor to powerful military commanders –

shoguns – who established law and order through their highly trained *samurai* warriors. Under the Shogunate, which lasted until the nineteenth century, Samurai created great fortresses like Himeji that commanded distant views across the rice fields and mountains. Townships huddled beneath them.

FORTIFIED RESIDENCE

The remarkable thing about Himeji and other Japanese castles is its whiteness and, to Western eyes, its fairy-tale rather than Gothic-horror-story beauty. Equally, the armor, weapons, and rituals of the Samurai seem very beautiful. Himeji Castle is the only Japanese castle to survive in its complete state. Its magnificent six-storey *donjon* or keep, with its white plastered-timber walls rises above a rocky base, the wings of its gables reflected in the moat below. Although a substantial structure, the castle looks as if it might

HIMEJI CASTLE, DONJON, HIMEJI CITY, 1601–14
The donjon of Himeji Castle is the most impressive of the fortified residencies of the 16th and early 17th centuries. It has six stories, with pent roofs and curving eaves.

suddenly flap its great gables and take majestically to the air, which is why the Japanese know it as the White Heron. The keep is at the heart of a maze of courtyards, designed to baffle intruders and is as different from the medieval European castles of, say, Edward I in the Welsh Marches as sashimi is from roast beef.

Japanese architecture came to the islands from Korea on the way from China. Although Chinese architecture can be traced back to c.1000 BC, it is Japanese architecture that has had a far more considerable influence in Western culture. Until very recently, however, Japan was a closed book to the West. Although missionaries and merchants from Portugal, Spain, and the Netherlands reached Japan in the 16th century, all foreigners – "hairy devils" – were banned in the 1630s on pain of death. Japan's isolation led not to decline but to the flourishing of its indigenous culture. The period between the ban on foreigners and Japan's restoration of links with the outside world in the 1850s witnessed the perfection of Noh theater, Haiku poetry, and a domestic architecture that was surely among the most refined and civilized of all. When Japan opened its doors again, the culture it offered the world had grown quite differently from that of China, long the dominant power in the East.

SHINTO SHRINES

The indigenous religion of Japan is Shinto. Its earliest places of worship were temporary shrines. The gods came to Earth for brief visits at a time and so there was no need to build them permanent homes. Temporary shrines appeared only after a large shrine dedicated to the sun goddess Amaterasu was erected for the imperial family in the seventh century AD, although the court itself continued to travel around the country until it settled at Nara in AD 710. Amaterasu, meanwhile, became a national goddess and her wooden shrine in Ujiyamada City has been rebuilt every 20 years since it was first dedicated.

In general, Shinto shrines are rebuilt completely every 20 years: Japanese views regarding conservation can be very different from those held so dearly in the West. It would be considered completely the wrong thing to do, for example, to rebuild the Parthenon in all its fifth-century BC glory. Yet the Ise shrine is very much as it would have appeared 1,300 years ago. It is a simple

ISE INNER SHRINE, MAIN SHRINE, UJIYAMADA, 8TH CENTURY
The Shinto Imperial Shrine at Ise is dedicated to Amaterasu Omikami, the sun goddess. The shrine, destroyed and rebuilt on alternating sites at 20-year intervals, contains objects belonging to the emperor, including a comb and a mirror.

timber structure and represents a storehouse. Local people would have prayed to Ise to fill their storehouses with rice and other crops, and this is presumably how the architectural form of the Shinto shrine was derived. It is also, like a storehouse, raised on pillars above the ground. The roof is thatched in reeds; bargeboards at either end project up from the roof and cross to form a pair of forked finials, a characteristic of Shinto shrines after Ise. The temple precinct is entered through a simple, symbolic gateway or *torii,* now copied for the entrances of bars and burger joints. It comprises a pair of timber pillars crossed and topped by a pair of timber beams. Originally straight, as in the Ise shrine, the beams were later curved upward as we have come to expect of traditional roofs throughout Asia.

The shrines developed gradually over a long time. One of the oldest surviving is the Izumo Shrine, Shimane Prefecture, last rebuilt in 1744. It shows the modest changes made to the initial design over a period of 1,000 years. The most

NOH THEATRE

One of the most traditional theatrical forms of Japan, Noh theatre is a form of drama characterized by rigidly stylized speech and movement – using dance, mime, masks, and minimal scenery. Subjects include gods, warriors, and supernatural beings. Noh began as a festival drama at shrines and temples in the 12th and 13th century; however, most of the Noh plays performed today date from the Muromachi period (1338–1513).

SYMBOLIC GATEWAY

In Kamakura, Japan, a *torii* has been used to mark the entrance to a pedestrianized shopping area, illustrating how this traditional feature continues to appear in contemporary architecture.

KIYOMIZUDERA KONDO, KYOTO, 1633

This Buddhist prayer hall was built on a sloping site on a mountainside east of Kyoto. The stiltlike foundations enabled the *builders to leave much of the surrounding vegetation. The wings and stage are supported by a structure of posts and tie-beams.*

AMIDA BUDDHISM

This massive representation of the Buddha, under the name of Amida, is considered the finest of its type in Japan. Amida Buddhism was oriented around the figure of Amida Buddha and stressed that man is powerless to save himself and must rely on the compassion of the Buddha. Cast in bronze by Ono Goroemon in 1252, it is almost 38ft (11m) in height, and weighs 450 tons. The third eye signifies spiritual insight.

ambitious and the largest is the Kibitsu Shrine, Okayama Prefecture (1425). This is characterized by its intricate gabled roofs, deep eaves, and complex flow of ceiling and roof heights inside. Even here though, there remains the powerful echo of a way of building that not only dated back to the time when the court and the gods themselves were peripatetic creatures, but reflected a tradition in which it was wise to build in modular timber components: Japan is riven through with seismic faults. Timber buildings could not only be dismantled and transported from site to site but they were reasonably earthquake-proof and, if they did collapse, could be quickly rebuilt.

THE ARCHITECTURE OF ZEN

The arrival of Buddhism in Japan from between the first and fifth centuries AD was formalized in the construction of the first Buddhist temple in Horyuji (the world's oldest surviving wooden buildings) in the seventh century. Unlike Shinto shrines, Buddhist temples were complex groups of monastic buildings. Among the most important component buildings were the pagoda (reliquary), the kodo (lecture hall) and the kondo (image hall). Monks lived in dormitories served by detached refectories and bath houses. The tradition of bathing was to become an important part of Japanese culture, its ritualistic bath houses matched only by the hammams of Islamic society in Turkey, North Africa, and southern Spain. Buddhist temples became increasingly complex

and ambitious over the next 1,000 years, reaching their zenith in the sixteenth and early seventeenth centuries. The kondo at Kiyomizudera (1633) set high on the mountainous eastern slopes above Kyoto (the gridded city famously set about with temples was founded in 794) is perhaps one of the finest of the buildings of this period. It is designed in what is known as the Wayo style. By the time of Kiyomizudera the kondo had become a prayer hall with outer and inner shrines gathered under vast hipped and gabled roofs. The Kiyomizudera kondo is particularly impressive because it stands on the top of a tall post-and-lintel timber tower; the building is set closely into the landscape with architecture and nature flowing one into the other.

This harmony between the natural and the man-made world was something Japanese architects tried increasingly to achieve as the influence of Zen Buddhism spread. Zen Buddhists sought a simplicity, harmony, and order that was enthusiastically taken up not only by the priests and intellectuals but by cultured Samurai warriors. This desire for simplicity and harmony was finally established in a sequence of standardized measurement decreed in 1615 when the Japanese capital moved for the final time to Edo (modern-day Tokyo). The height of refinement was now to live in houses that combined the best of ancient Japanese tradition and the influence of Zen.

TRANQUILITY AND RETREAT

This spirit was expressed at its most sophisticated in the tiny and uncluttered rooms designed for *cha-no-yu*, the tea ceremony. A tea room measured between two and four and a half *tatami* in the standardized Edo system of measurements. A *tatami* is a traditional rice-straw mat measuring six feet (1.8 meters) by three feet (0.9 meters). The tea ceremony had been invented by Zen Buddhist monks: drinking tea kept them awake during long prayer vigils. The idea was to make a ritual ceremony of drinking tea in a room lit ideally by sunlight filtering through translucent paper screens (the moveable walls that characterized Japanese houses from early on). There was no decoration, no ostentatious furniture, and no single focus point in the room such as a grand fireplace – as there was in a contemporary European home, for example – to distract attention. This approach to interior architecture was to have a huge influence on Modern European and American design in the twentieth century when a small proportion of the educated middle classes reacted against, first, Victorian clutter, and then the rampant excesses of consumerism. Japan seemed to have the answers. In the seventeenth century, the Japanese "country

TEA ROOM, KINKAKU-JI TEMPLE, KYOTO, 14TH CENTURY
The tea ceremony demands tranquility. In the tea room there is no ostentatious decoration to distract attention and the wood is left plain.

KATSURA PALACE, KYOTO, 1620–58
Katsura Palace is an open, timber-framed building with verandas from which to view the gardens. The gardens feature a lake, bridges, stone pathways, clipped plant displays, and artificial hills.

house" was perfected. Fine examples are the houses that make up the Katsura Palace (1620–58), Kyoto. These were villas for aristocrats and warriors, characterized by asymmetrical exteriors concealing sequences of rooms divided by paper screens that could be slid back to extend living spaces as required or opened back in summer to let maximum sunlight and air into the house. Each house looks over ornamental gardens, so important to the Japanese for whom the garden was a representation of nature in miniature and designed for contemplation from inside the house and not for walking through.

What is clear is that at this stage in its history, Japan had not only developed an architecture very much of its own, but it was one that, until modern industry and Western influences invaded the country from the mid-nineteenth century, had little need to change. Where the history of Western architecture had been one of continual change, a combination of ritual and the rigours of nature – precious little land to build on and even that threatened by earthquakes – had made Japan an architectural landscape apart.

TEA CEREMONY
Tea drinking started in China around 1191, but was developed as a ceremony in Japan between the 14th and 16th centuries. Hardly any other institution has influenced the culture of Japan during the last few centuries more than the tea ceremony (*cha-no-yu*). Introduced by priests who found that drinking tea kept them awake during long prayer vigils, it was heavily influenced by Zen Buddhism. The ceremony is based on simplicity and economy of action and places an emphasis on harmony and purity. This is reflected in the traditional arts and architecture of Japan.

ASIA

THE HOT AND STEAMY CLIMATE OF MUCH OF
INDIA AND SOUTHEAST ASIA MEANT THAT LIFE
COULD BE LED AS FAR AS POSSIBLE IN THE OPEN.
SHELTER WAS NEEDED PRIMARILY TO SHADE PEOPLE
FROM A FIERCE SUN AND TO KEEP THEM DRY
DURING MONSOONS. TEMPLES AROSE, NOTABLY IN
INDIA, THAT WERE ESSENTIALLY GREAT SCULPTURAL
MONUMENTS RICHLY AND EVEN VOLUPTUOUSLY
CARVED. UPON THEIR SURFACES WERE
REPRESENTATIONS OF PLANT LIFE, ANIMALS, GODS,
AND AT THEIR MOST SENSUAL, HUMANS
COPULATING IN EVERY CONCEIVABLE POSITION.
THESE WERE BUILDINGS TO BE SEEN FROM THE
OUTSIDE; INTERIORS, ALTHOUGH OFTEN GILDED
OR OTHERWISE FILLED WITH RICH FURNISHINGS
AND STATUARY, WERE FOR THE MOST PART SIMPLE,
ELEMENTAL SPACES. THE EXOTICISM OF INDIAN
DECORATION WAS RENEWED BY THE MUGHAL
INVASION OF INDIA AND THEN TEMPERED BY THE
CULTURES OF WESTERN EMPIRES AS THEY TOOK
OVER SOUTH ASIA IN THE NINETEENTH CENTURY,
CHANGING ITS ARCHITECTURE FOREVER.

ROOM IN THE AMBER FORT, JAIPUR, INDIA
*Jaipur is called the Rose Pink City because of the soft hue of its
walls. Commissioned by Man Singh I in 1592, the interior of
the Amber Fort is a beautiful fusion of Hindu and Mughal styles.*

INDIA
SACRED ARCHITECTURE

THE PALLAVA TEMPLES and monuments at Mahabalipuram, south of Madras, are the exquisite remains of Hindu architecture dating from the seventh and eighth centuries. Such is their positioning here by the sea, and the tenderness of the relief carvings which decorate the attendant shrines, that surely no one can fail to be moved by the warmth and sensual nature of the culture that inspired these lovely ruins. Here, in the cave temples, are sacred cows suckling their young, and protecting the Shore Temple are Shiva's Nandi bulls.

To Western eyes, temple complexes like those at Mahabalipuram are confusing. Where is the center? What are you meant to look at? Why is everything so richly decorated? The answers lie in understanding the religious culture. Hinduism grew out of the ancient Indian Brahmanism. Buddhism was the first religion on the subcontinent to erect shrines in durable materials, stone, in the third century BC. Before that, Indian shrines and temples would have been made of mud, timber, or bamboo. In Hinduism, there are very many gods and everything, every creature, every inanimate object

is connected to them in a binding relationship. In short, all things are divine. So, the tall, stepped *sikharas* at Mahabalipuram — multitiered temples that rise up to the heavens — are alive with depictions of all things sacred, from bulls to kings and gods.

TEMPLE SCULPTURE

This trend to decorate temples was to reach its zenith 300 or 500 years after those erected here on the Bay of Bengal. Indian temples like these seem so encrusted with sculpture that it is difficult to understand their structure. But their architects had no intention of expressing the structural elements. They are designed first and foremost as sculpture and are best experienced and understood from the outside. Interiors are often little more than dark caverns and can be disappointing to those expecting more. The joy is to watch the sun trace shadows across the rich sculpture and to feel that the structure is somehow joyously alive. Hindu temples could hardly be more different in structure and purpose from medieval

NATURE SPIRITS

In addition to the main religions in India, there are various cults dedicated to the worship of nature spirits. Demonstrated in the worship of male and female divinities – *yaksa* and *yaksi* – these fertility cults found their greatest expression in the sculpture of the Kushan period (1st – 3rd centuries AD). The distinctive imagery adopted for these male and female figures was important in the development of iconographic types such as the Buddha and other divinities. The tree goddess, above, is a *yaksi* from a stupa at Mathura (2nd century AD).

SHORE TEMPLE, MAHABALIPURAM, 8TH CENTURY
Consisting of a complex of three shrines, the Shore Temple was built up of stone blocks. It was originally covered with relief sculptures, but many have since been eroded by the sea.

cathedrals; they are about a joyful expression of divinity and not a form of penitence written large in oppressive, if impressive, vaulted masonry. Where we look up inside a Gothic cathedral to see the stonework soar toward heaven, at Mahabalipuram, we stand outside and see the stepped tiers of the *sikhara* representing the six levels of existence from that of mankind to the 27 heavens of the gods at the top.

THE STUPA

The earliest surviving heroic architectural monument of India is the Great Stupa at Sanchi, Central India. This Buddhist shrine was built by the Mauryan emperor Asoka at some time between 273 and 236 BC, although only the core of the original structure, hidden behind later work, survives. What stands today dates mostly from the first century BC. Even then, during their long occupation of India, the British took the Stupa to pieces out of curiosity and so we are left with a nineteenth-century reconstruction of a shrine that nevertheless spirits us back to the origins of permanent Indian architecture.

The hugely distinctive Stupa comprises a shallow brick dome raised on a circular platform 131 feet (40 meters) in diameter. This is surrounded by stone railings, as is the enclosed sacred platform at the top of the Stupa, and is reached through four richly carved gateways, or *toranas* (these would become the *torii* of Japanese temples exported there via Nepal, China, and Korea over many years). A superb sculptural monument, the Stupa is solid throughout. It represents the world and is designed both as a stimulus to prayer and as a representation of the path that leads to Nirvana or divine understanding. A mast, representing the axis of the world, rises from the center of the dome bearing a three-tiered umbrella (symbolizing the Three Jewels of Buddhism: the Buddha, the Law, and the community of monks). Stupas were also built in Nepal, Sri Lanka, and Burma. Asoka is said to have built 84,000 stupas and other shrines in the course of just three years, but presumably no matter how many he actually built, few would have been as impressive as the one at Sanchi.

In addition to the stupas, there was also a long tradition of building temples into rock faces as in ancient Egypt. Other temples were built of wood and if they were replaced in stone, masons mimicked the work of carpenters and so the rich layered tiers of later Hindu temples often echo more ancient structures. This development can

KESHAVA TEMPLE, SOMNATHPUR, 1268
Dedicated to Vishnu, the Keshava Temple consists of three shrines within a walled compound. The low towers and elaborate carving conceal the architectural form, giving the temple a squat appearance.

be seen clearly in the extravagant decorative spire (*shikhara*) of the Ghateshvara Temple, Badoli, in Rajasthan (tenth century). Long before this, Buddhism had declined in India and Hinduism had become the leading religion. From now on, although there were many regional differences, it is possible to see the Hindu temple develop in a more or less single, if immensely rich, idiom, covered in ever more intricate, lavish, and even erotic sculpture. This reached successive orgasmic peaks in such almost impossibly rich designs as the 13th-century Keshava Temple at Somnathpur in southern India.

> *" It is forbidden to descry other sects; the true believer gives honor to whatever in them is worthy of honor"*
> EMPEROR ASOKA

THE GREAT STUPA, SANCHI, 3RD CENTURY BC – 1ST CENTURY BC
The gateways (toranas), added in the first century BC, correspond to the four quarters of the universe. Pilgrims enter via the east gate and walking in a clockwise direction keep the shrine on their right.

MUGHAL PAINTING
A distinctive form of art evolved in India under the Mughal dynasty (16th–19th centuries). Essentially a court art, the style was initiated by Humayun and at first showed Persian influence. Comprised mainly of book illustrations and miniatures, Mughal painting reached a peak during the reign of Akbar (1556–1605). This miniature from the *Akbar-nama* of Abul Fazl (c.1595) depicts Akbar crossing the Jumna River on an elephant. The red sandstone walls of the palace enclosure are visible in the background.

In the south, temple complexes grew to include schoolrooms, dormitories, dining halls, water tanks, granaries, and storehouses. As they expanded so did the need to make the towers ever bigger and more expressive, dominating the more worldly buildings gathered about them; a fine example can be seen in the Ekambareshvara Temple, Kanchipuram (1509 onward). In the north, a further layer of complexity was the gradual assimilation and accretion of Islamic details during Mughal rule in India. As early as the thirteenth and fourteenth centuries, domes and pointed arches began to appear in the design of Hindu temples, adding to the richness of the Indian architectural experience.

An exceptionally elegant and very successful example of typical principles of indigenous town planning can be seen in the construction of the city of Jaipur in Rajasthan. The building of this gridded city was ordered by Rajput King Jai Singh of Amber (1699–1743) who moved his capital here from nearby Amber in 1727. The rich, pink architecture is highly theatrical yet uniquely disciplined. Shops are uniformly arcaded with viewing terraces above and the city is built of just one material, pink rendered rubble intended to imitate sandstone. The king's palace sits at the heart of the city which, remarkably, has changed little over the ensuing 275 years.

MUGHAL STYLE

When Babur Shah marched from Afghanistan and defeated Ibrahim, Sultan of Delhi, in 1526, he established a golden age of Muslim architecture in India. In northern India and what today is Pakistan, the Mughal rulers built some of the most inspiring and beautiful architecture of all time, including the world-famous Taj Mahal. The Taj Mahal's predecessor, the Tomb of Humayun, Delhi (begun 1564) was the first of these great Mughal monuments. It was commissioned by Humayun's son Akbar.

Standing in a superb formal water garden, the tomb is a massive structure, its handsome red sandstone bulk offset by white marble detailing. The double-skinned dome rises from a drum that appears between four octagonal towers that in' turn stand on a magnificent arcaded, red

TAJ MAHAL, AGRA, 1630–53
Built as a mausoleum for Queen Mumtaz Mahal, the Taj Mahal is the architectural gem of Shah Jahan's reign. The shimmering white marble façades conceal the heavy brick and rubble construction within.

podium. The power of the architecture is only magnified by the fact that, tombs aside, the cavernous spaces inside the building are quite empty. The axes of the building are echoed in the lines traced by the paths and canals of the garden. The tomb remains a welcome retreat from the frenetic and superheated bustle of Old Delhi.

Akbar also built the well-preserved hilltop town of Fatehpur Sikri (c.1569–80) with its wonderfully airy palace, the Panch Mahal, and the Great Mosque with its triple domes. The decoration in the remains of the palace complex shows how rapidly the Mughal rulers were able to abstract Muslim architecture to represent the spirit and needs of a new dynasty. Akbar was buried in a magnificent tomb at Sikandara, near Agra (1602–13), a building that combines gravitas and a sense of the ethereal: a masterpiece.

BIRD'S-EYE VIEW OF THE RED FORT, DELHI
This painting (c.1820) by a Delhi artist shows how the Red Fort may have looked during Shah Jahan's reign. The palace-fortress (1639–48) was one element of Shah Jahan's new city, Shahjahanabad (Old Delhi), and derives it name from the sandstone walls that enclose it.

ARCHITECTURE UNDER SHAH JAHAN

The most celebrated Mughal monuments, however, are those commissioned by the legendary Shah Jahan. These include the awe-inspiring Red Fort, Delhi (1639–48 and later), the Great Mosque, Delhi (1644–58), and, most famous of all, the Taj Mahal, Agra (1630–53).

The Red Fort, which backed onto the Jumna River (since moved), covers an area measuring 1,608 feet (490 meters) by 3,215 feet (980 meters). It is surrounded by high, red walls interspersed with tapering towers and is entered via a gate that takes visitors through a glorious bazaar and then out to the gardens and pavilions of the palace beyond. The palace buildings are a brilliant meeting of enclosed, semienclosed, and open spaces set between arcades and colonnades under deep eaves that act like eyelids. These are ideal for Delhi's climate which is all but impossibly hot in summer months. The pavilions all feature sculptural devices through which water flows, while the gardens are lined with canals and

adorned with fountains. On one pool stands a summer pavilion. This is the Garden of Eden idyll that Islamic rulers tried in different ways to recreate over many centuries.

The Great Mosque is notable mostly for its commanding scale. Its appearance, however, is slightly forbidding. This could never be said of Shah Jahan's masterpiece, the Taj Mahal. One of the world's most celebrated and photographed buildings, this stunning tomb stands on an axis at the end of a canal running through a walled garden. It rests on a plinth surrounded by four minarets, scaled down to exaggerate the pregnant form of the dome. The core of the building is a development of the theme set by Humayun's tomb, but here the towers surrounding the dome are closely coupled to the core of the building, increasing the sense of unity and oneness the tomb expresses – the love that Shah Jahan felt for his dead wife.

The loveliness of the light that shimmers from the white marble is hard to express, a wonderful sensation to experience. Inside, and under the 200-foot (61-meter) dome, the royal tombs are set behind elaborately carved marble screens inlaid with precious stones. The effect in a light just the right side of dim is very moving.

SHAH JAHAN
The reign of Mughal emperor Shah Jahan (1628–58) is notable chiefly for its architectural achievements. Among other projects, he built the city of Shahjahanabad and the Taj Mahal, the magnificent tomb for his wife, Mumtaz Mahal, at Agra. Inscribed "a good portrait of me in my 40th year," this portrait of the emperor was painted in about 1632 by Bichitr, one of the court painters.

SOUTHEAST ASIA
HINDU AND BUDDHIST ARCHITECTURE

HINDU TEMPLE SYMBOLISM

Hindu temples are centered on a primary shrine crowned by a roof tower representing the sacred Mount Meru of Indian mythology. Meru was conceived of as the axis of the world, reaching far below the ground into the nether regions and extending high into the heavens. As Indian traditions spread through Southeast Asia, the mountain symbolism was readily adopted in the construction of temples, as the people of Southeast Asia also believed mountain-tops to be the sacred abode of spirits and gods.

" …it was grander than anything left to us by Greece or Rome"

HENRI MOUHOT

IT WAS THROUGH HINDUISM and Buddhism that Indian traditions were introduced to Southeast Asia, so much so, that by the 13th century, the architecture of the stupa, the stepped pyramid, and the lotus bud tower stretched right down through Burma (Myanmar), Cambodia, and Thailand to Indonesia. Of the abundant religious and palace architecture in this region, much of it fell into a ruinous state after the decline of the civilizations that built it 500 years ago. In many cases, it remained so until its rediscovery and conservation in the 19th and 20th centuries.

In fact, the forest had completely covered Southeast Asia's supreme architectural achievement, the temple mountain of Angkor Wat in Angkor, Cambodia, until its chance rediscovery by the French naturalist, Henri Mouhot, in 1858. Angkor Wat is a massive conception by any standards. The temple, crowned with five lotus bud towers, rises on a series of colonnaded platforms set behind tiers of walls fronted by a moat 2½ miles (four kilometers) long. The complex is approached across the water, via a causeway bordered on either side by giant balustrades in the form of serpents associated with the Hindu myth of creation. It was built by

Suryavarman II (ruled 1113–50), king of the Khmer Empire, as a temple dedicated nominally to the Hindu deity Vishnu, as a monument to the king's power, and, as with the pyramids of the pharaohs, his sepulcher. It is impressive, beautiful in silhouette and in the delicate detail of the reliefs carved into its sandstone blocks. The way the temple changes as one approaches is unforgettable. The walls of the lower terraces are rich in relief sculpture. All 2,625 feet (800 meters) of these carvings tell the tales of the legendary Indian epics the *Mahabharata* and the *Ramayana*.

TEMPLE MOUNTAINS

Symbolically, the architecture of Angkor Wat represents the cosmic Indian mountain, Meru, and although a forceful monument, construction is very simple. Here, as in nearby Angkor Thom, the colossal moated and ruined city built by Jayavarman VII (ruled 1181–1215), the construction of classical Khmer architecture proved to be elementary but technically perfect. Stones were piled without mortar on stones, the sheer mass of the structure keeping the whole stable and, because there was no development of

ANGKOR WAT, ANGKOR, CAMBODIA, 12TH CENTURY
At 5,085ft (1,550m) long and 4,593ft (1,400m) wide, the Hindu temple of Angkor Wat is the largest temple complex in the colossal Khmer city of Angkor.

STUPA OF BOROBUDUR, JAVA, 8TH–9TH CENTURY
Borobudur, "Temple of the Countless Buddhas", is the largest Buddhist shrine in the world.
It was built under the ruling Sailendra dynasty (AD 775–864) and completed in about AD 850
to the original design, with only one later addition – the lower processional terrace.

the highest order. The whole composition is at once a holy mountain set against the spectacular backdrop of live volcanoes and rain forest, and a representation in stone of the soul's journey toward nirvana reached through nine stages of understanding. These nine stages are given shape in the guise of stone terraces. The first five are rectangular and have enclosed galleries; the next three are circular and open, surrounded by 72 bell-shaped stupas (some missing) shrouding statues of the meditating Buddha. The final stage is the central stupa leading the eye and soul toward nirvana. Inside, the galleries are decorated with more than 1,200 sculpted panels that tell stories from the life and legends of the Buddha. The example of Borobudur was never to be repeated in Java, or indeed in the rest of Southeast Asia. Scholars continue to ponder the meaning of Borobudur and the rituals that were carried out there.

BUDDHIST SHRINES

The Buddhist tjandis (shrines) of Central Java were more than simple places of worship, they were conceived as expressions of complex metaphysical theories. At Borobudur, for example, the five square terraces correspond to the vajra-dhatu or earthly realm; above this, the three circular levels represent the garbha-dhatu, various incomplete states of understanding, through which the pilgrim must travel to reach the ultimate condition of spiritual enlightenment at the summit. The walls of Buddhist shrines were usually lined with figurative and symbolic reliefs to be read in series from right to left.

the brick or stone vault as in ancient Rome or medieval Europe, the corbelled arch was used instead. This suited the ritual needs of the Khmer kings, creating many small ceremonial areas within the massive structure. As with much Indian architecture, the climate meant that even such ambitious projects as Angkor Wat and Angkor Thom were meant to be experienced first and foremost from the outside.

BUDDHIST ARCHITECTURE

In Burma, the architecture of the stupa reached gloriously decorative peaks as witnessed in the unforgettable Shwe Dagon pagoda, Rangoon (Yangon), traditionally dated to the time of the Buddha in the sixth century BC, and the enormous and symmetrical Ananda temple at Pagan (twelfth century). The Ananda temple represents the zenith of classical Burmese architecture. Built of massed-up tiers of white brick, it has what a Western observer would call a Greek cross plan – complete with four entrance porticoes placed on the principal points of the compass – and is topped with a gold spire that rises from a central stupa, itself rearing its long, tapering neck from a cluster of lesser stupas. Inside are two dark ambulatories in one of which visitors meet four Buddhas 30 feet (nine meters) high.

Perhaps, though, the high point of historic architecture in the region is Borobudur in Java (eighth to ninth century). This Mahayanist Buddhist temple or shrine is a combination of architecture, sculpture, and landscape design of

ANANDA TEMPLE, PAGAN, BURMA, 12TH CENTURY
The most notable example of the cetiya – a building combining the features of stupa and shrine –
the Ananda temple derives its basic form from the Indian stupa, but the terraced plinths supporting
the dome are elaborated with stairways and the solid base opened up to create a roofed temple.

NEO-CLASSICAL

THE POWER, MIGHT, AND LEARNING OF WESTERN EUROPE WAS REPRESENTED IN THE EIGHTEENTH AND THE FIRST HALF OF THE NINETEENTH CENTURIES BY THE NEO-CLASSICAL ARCHITECTURE OF ANCIENT GREECE AND ROME BROUGHT UP TO DATE WITH NEW PURPOSE AND TECHNOLOGY. THE INVENTION OF EARLY AND HIGH RENAISSANCE DESIGN GAVE WAY TO A MORE ARCHAEOLOGICALLY CORRECT ARCHITECTURE AS THE CULTURE OF THE ANCIENT WORLD WAS INCREASINGLY REVEALED, DOCUMENTED, AND DISSEMINATED. THIS NEW CLASSICISM WAS SEEN AS AN IDEAL MATCH FOR THE AMBITION OF BOTH THE POWERFUL EUROPEAN STATES, WHETHER AUTOCRATIC OR WITNESSING THE BIRTH PANGS OF DEMOCRACY, AND OF THE YOUNG UNITED STATES OF AMERICA, FOR WHICH IT SYMBOLIZED A CONNECTION WITH THE REPUBLICAN IDEALS OF PRE-AUGUSTAN ROME AND THE DEMOCRACY OF ATHENS AND THE GREEK STATES. NEO-CLASSICISM WAS ABLE TO SERVE EVERY CONCEIVABLE PURPOSE, A NOBLE CLOAK FOR COUNTRY HOUSES, TOWN HALLS, RAILWAY STATIONS, AND IN NORTH YORKSHIRE, ENGLAND, EVEN A PIGSTY.

THE MADELEINE, PARIS
The history of the Madeleine is an example of how the Neo-classical style could be adapted to different purposes. Designated a temple to his Grande Armée by Napoleon in 1806, in 1837 it was proposed as Paris' first railway station before finally being consecrated as a church in 1842.

NEO-CLASSICAL
THE INFLUENCE OF GREECE AND ROME

PIRANESI

Born in Venice, Giovanni Battista Piranesi (1720–78) was trained as an architect and engineer. His engravings of Roman antiquities and reconstructions of ancient Rome had a profound influence upon the development of Neo-classical and Romantic architecture, including the work of John Soane (1753–1837) one of England's greatest architects, who met him while on a traveling scholarship to Italy. Piranesi was also an architectural theorist, but as an architect completed only one building.

CHANGES IN EUROPE

The 18th century saw fundamental changes in the political geography of Europe. Italy and Spain were in decline, Britain, France, and Prussia (northern Germany) were on the rise. Protestant Europe was about to flourish, while before the end of the century, the Bourbon monarchy of Le Roi Soleil was to end with the storming of the Bastille and the declaration of the revolutionary republic.

THE TEMPLE OF GLORY, or Madeleine, Paris (1804–09, see pp.118–119) shows just how far French architecture had moved a century on from the birth of Rococo. The Napoleonic temple was designed by Pierre Vignon (1762–1828), who in 1793 had been appointed Inspecteur General des Batiments de la République and his model (probably the Temple of Castor) was the temple architecture of first-century Imperial Rome.

THE GRAND TOUR

What the Madeleine also showed was the extent to which architects of the new Classical world had come to study that of the ancient civilizations of Greece and Rome. Throughout the 18th century, a small army of architects, artists, and their clients toured the ruins and monuments of Rome and then Greece on what was known as the Grand Tour. They were tourists, and from the middle of the 18th century, architects began to act more and more like tourists who have taken note of famous buildings through history and want to recreate them back home. Where we only show snapshots and videos of Greek and Roman temples, European and American architects of the 18th and early 19th century actually built them.

In Britain, a reaction to what were perceived as the excesses of Baroque (and what little Rococo design there was) was led by a group of young purists under Lord Burlington (1694–1753). Because of their coolly passionate enthusiasm for the work of Andrea Palladio they came to be known as Palladians. Their practical bibles were Palladio's *Quattro libri* and *Vitruvius Britannicus* (1715), the guide to a correct new British architecture written and illustrated by the Scottish architect Colen Campbell (d.1729). The style was adopted by the Whig government of Sir Robert Walpole; Campbell designed his country house – Houghton Hall, Norfolk (1722–26). He also designed Mereworth Castle, Kent (1722–25) as a homage to Palladio's Villa Rotonda (see p.74), as did Burlington with Chiswick House, London (1723–29).

The chaste new style (interiors were gorgeous yet disciplined) was also adopted by influential landowners such as Thomas Coke, Earl of Leicester (owner of Holkham Hall, Norfolk) who had radical ideas concerning agriculture and the landscape. With inspiration and help from Burlington and his protégé William Kent, Matthew Brettingham (1699–1769) created the

HOLKHAM HALL, NORFOLK, ENGLAND, 1734–65
The central block of Holkham Hall with its corner towers is surrounded by the four wings (chapel, kitchen, library, and guest rooms), each demarcated by separate roofing, which is lower than that of the main building.

VIEW OF BATH, ENGLAND
By the time that the Roman baths were rediscovered in 1755, Bath was already a fashionable spa town. Its elegant Georgian crescents are seen here from the rolling Mendip Hills.

about every town and city in Britain. Highlights include the Royal Circus (1754) and Royal Crescent (1767–75), Bath, by John Wood (1705–54) and John Wood II (1728–81), Bedford Square, London (1776–86) by Robert Palmer, and Edinburgh New Town (1766–) by James Craig.

A further refinement was the fusion of Palladian design with the latest research into Roman and Etruscan decoration. This manifested itself in the work of Robert Adam (1728–92), a Scottish architect whose work generated legions of imitators and which has endured, in bastardized forms, in the interior décor of bourgeois homes around the world. His finest designs include the interiors of Kedleston Hall, Derbyshire (1760s), Culzean Castle, Ayrshire (1777–92) and Syon House, London (1762–69).

DUBLIN FEATURES
Neo-classicism developed its own refinements across the Irish Sea in Dublin, where rows of elegant, unostentatious houses were enlivened with particularly fine doorcases, fanlights, and decorative plasterwork in noble hallways. An interesting development in Dublin was the fusion of Palladian correctness with monumental Baroque elements drawn from the work of Wren.

magnificent designs for Holkham. A paradigm of Palladian design, the house comprises four wings connected to a central towered and pedimented block, all but unadorned on the outside and built in a yellow Roman brick. The severity and relentless geometry of Holkham were new to the essentially pragmatic English.

PALLADIAN INFLUENCES

The Palladian influence was all pervading and for much of the 18th century became the house style of British and Irish, as well as to an extent North American, architecture. In a less correct, though still chaste form, it gave us the deeply civilized Classical squares, crescents, and circuses of Bath and Edinburgh, and, interpreted by housebuilders and developers, not only the much-loved streets and squares of Georgian London, but those of just

The genius of the Palladian style was its adaptability. Although its proponents would not have seen it as style for mass-produced urban housing, that is what in effect it became. It was possible to produce copy books, as many British builders did, that provided easy-to-copy designs for houses great and small. Ultimately it is possible to trace the Palladian influence down to small and cheap houses in the poorest parts of industrial suburbs. These, however, were a long way from the elegant escapism of Chiswick House and the radical self-confidence of Holkham Hall.

THE MARBLE HALL, KEDLESTONE HALL, 1757–70
James Paine's marble hall includes all the paraphernalia of the Neo-classical stately home: vast marble columns, Classical friezes, ornate motifs, and the obligatory copy of the Apollo Belvedere.

THE CLASSICAL LANDSCAPE
THE PICTURESQUE MOVEMENT

> *"Nature abhors a straight line"*
>
> HORACE WALPOLE

IF THE PALLADIAN movement set the tone for the British town and country house for much of the rest of the eighteenth century and beyond, it was also happily responsible for the Picturesque Movement in landscape gardening and design. Where voluptuous Baroque houses were matched to formal gardens, coolly elegant Palladian houses had their rolling, romantic landscapes. Each was a perfect match.

The idea of setting a country house in an idealized rural landscape was first put into practice by William Kent and then with great success by the omnipresent and evergreen Lancelot "Capability" Brown (1716–83). Up and down the country, Brown dug up farmland and unsatisfactory natural landscapes and turned them into the gentlest of all Classical landscapes. These were characterized by lakes and clumps of carefully placed trees and by the occasional bridge, obelisk, or other folly. Follies caught on in a big way from the 1720s. Charles Bridgeman (d.1738) is credited with having invented the ha-ha, and introduced it in the gardens at Stowe, Buckinghamshire. This clever ditch appears not to exist from the windows and parterres of country houses and so allows the garden to merge into the distant fields but it also prevents cows and sheep wandering from adjacent farms into expensively designed grottoes and ornamental lakes. The gardens at Stowe boast temples, grottoes, and bridges in a variety of styles and were much admired. Colen Campbell developed the theme in the allegorical gardens of the Hoare family seat at Stourhead, Wiltshire. These were laid out as a passage through life, a kind of horticultural *Aeneid*.

THE HEIGHT OF FOLLY

The idea was taken further in two directions, the development of the folly into a distinctive building type and the nurturing of the Picturesque Movement in town and city centers. The height of the folly in Britain was undoubtedly the remarkable Gothick house James Wyatt (1747–1813) built for the millionaire dilettante

GARDENS AT STOWE, BUCKINGHAMSHIRE, ENGLAND
Created by Bridgeman, the vast landscaped park at Stowe was refined over the following decades with the addition of temples, grottoes, and bridges by Kent, Vanbrugh, and Gibbs.

ARTIST'S IMPRESSION OF FONTHILL ABBEY, WILTSHIRE, ENGLAND
This engraving from John Rutter's Delineations of Fonthill (1823) shows Beckford's extraordinary residence shortly before the tower collapsed in 1825.

and author William Beckford. In the spirit of the burgeoning Gothic Revival – the serious revival of the Gothic style that followed the more romantic Gothick – Wyatt designed a lofty sham abbey complete with a sky-piercing tower that rose from an octagonal crossing itself adopted from Ely Cathedral. Fonthill Abbey (1796–1812) was characterized by its impossibly long flights of stairs, relentless internal vistas, and the vertigo-inducing properties of its central tower. Here, Beckford lived out a fantastic, if ultimately sad and lonely, life, holding parties attended by the fashionable, decorous, mad, and outcast. He moved to a second and less lofty tower just in time – Wyatt's tower, a folly in every sense, collapsed in 1825. Fonthill showed just how far the taste for the Picturesque had developed by the late eighteenth century.

JOHN NASH

A far more usable interpretation of the Picturesque Movement was perfected by John Nash (1752–1835), a hugely successful architect who acted as a developer and builder and was certainly no gentleman. What he did, though, was to bring the Picturesque into town with the design and layout of his masterpiece, Regent's Park, London (1811–30). Nash built a ring of

glorious set-piece terraced houses around the park in the guise of vast, noble, white Classical palaces. The fronts of these houses were faced in gleaming white stucco; the backs were simple stock brick affairs and generally rather badly built. Although the terraces were rushed up hastily, they were a magnificent foil to the park itself. Threatened with demolition in the 1950s, the Nash terraces have since been rebuilt to a much higher standard than they were in the first place and remain one of the architectural glories of London.

From a Picturesque point of view, the finest pseudo-palace is Cumberland Terrace (1827 onward). From the point of view of urban planning, Park Crescent (1812), a grand semicircle of stucco-fronted Ionic terraced houses, is a fine achievement, linking Regent's Park to Portland Place – a wide avenue by Nash – and to the existing section of the Palladian-inspired streetscape leading east and west of it. Nash also built some of the most delightful full-scale follies in England, notably the Royal Pavilion, Brighton (1815–21), a Hindu pleasure dome for his major client the Prince Regent, later King George IV.

LE JARDIN ANGLAIS

In France, the most notable designer of Picturesque landscape and follies was Richard Mique (1728–94), best known for his design of the gardens of the Petit Trianon at Versailles. The millions of visitors who come this way today will find the saccharine-sweet Temple de l'Amour and, of course, Le Hameau, Marie-Antoinette's life-sized toy farm where she liked to play at being a peasant – although she had cake at teatime while the peasants had no bread. Today, Le Hameau looks like the backdrop to a Walt Disney cartoon. If tragic, Marie-Antoinette's life was lived as if it were a kind of 18th-century cartoon.

NEO-CLASSICAL SCULPTURE
Classically inspired sculptures were greatly sought after by the wealthy, who used them to enliven their homes and gardens. One of the greatest sculptors of the period was the Italian Antonio Canova (1757–1822). Trained in Venice, Canova settled in Rome in 1781, where he gained instant recognition for his tomb for Pope Clement XIV. In reaction to the frivolous Rococo style, Canova sought a greater simplicity and grandeur in his work, drawing inspiration for many of his subjects from ancient Rome, such as in the *Italic Venus*, above (1804–12).

CUMBERLAND TERRACE, REGENT'S PARK, LONDON, 1827 ONWARD
At the heart of Nash's design for Regent's Park was the desire to reintroduce nature into the urban landscape: rus in urbe. *By lining the roads that bordered the park with palatial terraces, he created a perfect marriage of Classical and Picturesque elements.*

AMERICAN CLASSICAL

THE RESPECTABLE FAÇADE

THOMAS JEFFERSON (1743–1826) established what can almost be labeled as the official architectural style of the United States of America for the best part of a century or more: Classicism. As the principal author of the Declaration of Independence and one of the new republic's first presidents, Jefferson's influence was inevitably great. He had developed his architectural ideas while living in France as ambassador to the court at Versailles in the 1780s. There, he caught up on the Palladian style that had swept Britain half a century earlier and was considered chic in France when Jefferson arrived. The style was to leave its mark in Monticello, the ingenious house he designed for himself, near Charlottesville, Virginia (1770–1809), a homage to Palladio's Villa Rotonda (see p.74). He journeyed to Nîmes in the south of France to see the

Maison Carrée. This inspired his design of the State Capitol, Richmond, Virginia (1789–98), a grand Ionic temple into which offices and other administrative functions were somehow squeezed. The Capitol set the tone for numerous official buildings throughout the United States and ultimately beyond. The factories, concrete housing developments, and speculative offices you see lining the new streets of the inexorably expanding new towns of China's Guandong province, heart of the country's astonishing economic growth, are influenced (as if through the wrong end of a telescope) by this early US civic temple. Ever since these first American buildings were erected, new societies – ones trying to present a respectable façade to the world – have borrowed the Jefferson look.

Jefferson was also much impressed by the stirrings of the Greek Revival in revolutionary Paris, and was to incorporate Grecian ideas and motifs into Monticello as he developed and expanded his house over many years.

MAISON CARRÉE, NÎMES, AD 1–10

The design Thomas Jefferson sent from France for the State Capitol, Virginia was inspired by the Maison Carrée at Nîmes. Classical temple forms were adapted for other buildings, such as schools and banks.

PALLADIAN STYLE

The Palladian style was adopted for the president's official house, the White House, Washington, D.C. (1792–1829), originally designed by the Irish architect James Hoban (1762–1831). Damaged during the War of 1812, the White House was rebuilt and extended, although the curved porticoes had been added by Benjamin H. Latrobe in 1807–08. Beneath its famous 224-foot (68-meter) cast-iron dome, added much later on, the US Capitol, Washington, D.C., was also a Palladian country house at heart. This is still clear if the eye ignores both the dome and the wings added to either side of the original house. The Capitol was originally designed by William Thornton (1759–1828), with help from the French architect E. S. Hallet (1755–1825), and was very much

THE STATE CAPITOL, RICHMOND, VIRGINIA, 1789–98

The building follows the Maison Carrée, but varies from the original by magnifying its scale and not replicating the temple's fluted columns. Its central section was the first structure to combine both legislative houses under one roof.

in keeping with the style introduced and encouraged by Jefferson.

LINCOLN MEMORIAL, WASHINGTON DC, 1911–22

The Lincoln Memorial, designed by Henry Bacon, honors Abraham Lincoln, the 16th president of the United States. The interior is *divided into three chambers. In the central chamber is the famous white marble statue of Lincoln by Daniel Chester French.*

THOMAS JEFFERSON

Thomas Jefferson (1743–1826), third President of the United States (1801–09), was the principal author of the Declaration of Independence. He received no formal training in architecture, but was greatly influenced by Palladio's theories and the buildings of ancient Rome in his efforts to create and promote a new national architecture. He retired to Monticello in 1809 where he devoted himself to the establishment of the University of Virginia.

Jefferson was keen to spread the message of modern Classical architecture throughout the United States. One way of doing this was to design the new University of Virginia, Charlottesville (1817–26), as an exemplar of building designs to be copied or modeled from. In this spirit, the Library – the core of the campus – stands proudly at the end of a long, raised rectangular lawn, it was designed to resemble the Pantheon, Rome. It is flanked by two rows of student houses set back behind colonnades that recall Wren's arrangement at the Royal Hospital in Greenwich, London. Behind this inspiring quadrangle are houses originally built for the students' slaves. It is interesting to note that Jefferson, author of the finest opening sentence of any political tract – "We hold these truths to be self-evident, that all men are created equal, that they are endowed by their Creator with certain unalienable Rights, that among these are Life, Liberty and the pursuit of Happiness" – was a lifelong slave owner.

JEFFERSON'S LEGACY

Jefferson's Classical instincts were to inform official US architecture for a long time to come. Only in 1922 were the finishing touches put to the Lincoln Memorial, a grand Doric temple by Henry Bacon (1866–1942), designed not just to commemorate the life of Abraham Lincoln, the president who saw an end to slavery at the conclusion of the Civil War in 1865, but also to terminate The Mall, the grand avenue that runs to the Washington Memorial (the world's highest obelisk) and the US Capitol. In turn, The Mall was a reworking by a team, led by Daniel Burnham

(1846–1912), of the grand Classical street plan first proposed for the city in 1791 by the French architect Pierre Charles L'Enfant (1754–1825).

The grandness of Jefferson's vision, Classicism in the service of democracy, was matched by a homespun Classical way of building that had been developing throughout the original United States since the days that the Settlers had first really settled. The clapboard Classicism that can be found across New England and beyond is one of the glories of domestic architecture, at once elegant, high-minded, easy to achieve, and for everyman.

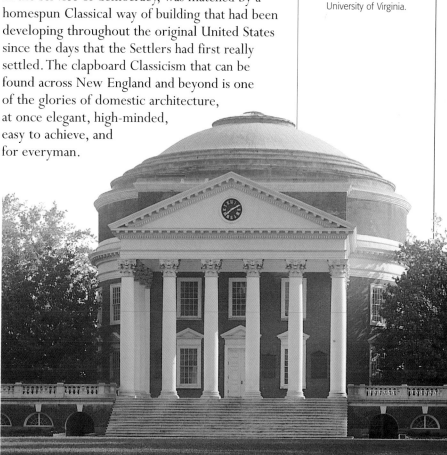

UNIVERSITY OF VIRGINIA, CHARLOTTESVILLE, 1817–26

At the University of Virginia, the first state university in the country, arcades connect buildings around a central lawn. The rotunda housed the library and was modelled on the Pantheon in Rome.

THE FRENCH REVOLUTION

VISIONARY SCHEMES

JACQUES-LOUIS DAVID
The artist most closely associated with Neo-classicism during the Revolutionary period in France was Jacques-Louis David (1748–1825). Influenced by Classical Rome and the work of Raphael, he was first a successful society painter, then an active supporter of the French Revolution. He used a realistic style to depict contemporary scenes of the Revolution, as in *The Death of Marat* (above, 1793) his celebrated painting of the murdered revolutionary.

THE FRENCH REVOLUTION was a turning point in European history. Not only did it mark the end of absolute government by royalty in Europe, it also undermined the power of the aristocracy and saw the slow rise of democracy, individualism, and the bourgeoisie. These are sweeping statements, but at the time of the Terror anyone who fell out with the uncertain new authorities was likely to be sent to the guillotine. This uncertainty led to Napoleon Bonaparte not just seizing power, but crowning himself emperor. There were to be many more equally dramatic episodes before France got on an even republican keel. Napoleon himself developed a powerful style or what we would now call corporate image for his court; the architect Charles Percier (1764–1838) was the Emperor's favorite and played a key role in the Empire Style for which, battles aside, we remember Bonaparte's reign (1804–15).

Nevertheless, it can be said that there was a style, or perhaps more accurately, a spirit that framed the Revolution, even though at least one of those who developed the monumental and bombastic style of late eighteenth-century France was imprisoned and very nearly executed. This was Claude-Nicolas Ledoux (1736–1806) who became Architecte du Roi in 1773 and designed some of the most heroic European buildings of his time. Undoubtedly he was a source of inspiration for those who followed him in the service of the Republic and then the Empire, particularly after he published his visionary designs in his *L'architecture considérée* (1804), many of which remained unbuilt or less than half built.

GRAND ASPIRATIONS

Ledoux's grandest work is that portion of the Royal Saltworks he built at Arc-et-Senans (1774–79), an almost impossibly imposing factory faced in the heaviest duty Doric order imaginable. The building, which was to have been at the heart of Chaux, the ideal early industrial city Ledoux hoped to build here, is at once a rockface and a cavern conjured into architecture.

This was a time of great scientific, mathematical, and philosophical enquiry. The most imaginative architects responded by trying to envisage an ideal new world inhabited by rational Man. The most extravagant fantasies of all were those of Etienne-Louis Boullée (1728–99) who built little, but whose mind-stretching designs have

ROYAL SALTWORKS, ARC-ET-SENANS, 1774–79
Planned as a circular complex at the heart of Ledoux's proposed city of Chaux, only one hall of the saltworks was completed. The entrance portico has unfluted Greek Doric columns fronting a rusticated voussoir arch beyond which lies a simple grotto.

ETIENNE-LOUIS BOULLÉE, *MONUMENT TO NEWTON*, 1784
Boullée intended to pierce the upper half of the 500-ft- (150-m-) high sphere of Newton's memorial with hundreds of small holes, giving the illusion of stars and allowing the interior to "sparkle with light and banish all shadows."

haunted the architectural imagination ever since (most notably those of Adolf Hitler and Albert Speer). What Boullée realized, on paper, was an architecture that matched the scale and ambition not of the greatness of new discoveries – with Newton's discovery of gravity and his Laws of Motion, surely Man was now truly the Measure of All Things? – but of the ambitions of politicians like Napoleon who dreamed of an empire stretching from Calais to Moscow.

Boullée's two most famous visionary schemes are those for a National Library and his Monument to Newton. The former shows readers the size of ants (literate ants) inside colonnaded halls of such immensity that the human spirit would surely be crushed, not elevated, were such a project ever to be realized. The Monument to Newton (1784) was in the form of a gigantic sphere rising from a two-tiered cube. The sphere represented the universe and Newton's sarcophagus was, in Boullée's mind at least, to have rested inside this huge and terrifying space.

NAPOLEON'S PARIS

Were such dreams realized? In part, yes. Aside from the Madeleine (see pp.118–19), a pupil of Boullée's, J. F. T. Chalgrin (1739–1811) was commissioned to design the Arc de Triomphe de L'Etoile, Paris. Work started on this formidable victory arch in 1808. It is famous for being (a) big and (b) there. Today, however, it has an offspring, the Arche de la Défense, one of the *Grands Travaux* commissioned by President François Mitterand in the 1980s. These two heroic, if vacant, monuments stand in line with one another and look directly along the Champs Elysées to the Place de la Concorde. This is the great square laid out for Louis XV between 1753 and 1775. To one side and across the River Seine stands Napoleon's Chambre des Députés (1807) by B. Poyet, an

imposing Roman temple fronted by a portico of ten Corinthian columns. Napoleon was also responsible for the look and the construction of the long Classical ranges of arcaded apartments and shops that appear to march if not quite to Moscow then a very long way. The architects were Percier and Pierre François Léonard Fontaine (1762–1853).

Does all this add up to a style? No, not a single style, but a feeling about architecture perhaps that could now be tuned to serve the needs of political regimes. There was nothing revolutionary about the structure of most of these buildings. For the most part Classical architecture was complex stylistically but structurally fairly straightforward to believe. The real experiments were happening elsewhere, in small-scale engineering works in England where the Industrial Revolution was under way and in early industrial buildings that, although not yet in the public eye, were to do more to revolutionize architecture worldwide as the nineteenth century got into its stride than all of Napoleon's monuments put together.

THE *ENCYCLOPEDIA*
Originally intended as a simple translation of the Chambers *Cyclopedia*, the first volume of Denis Diderot's massive work was published in 1751. Under Diderot's editorship it attempted to classify the new knowledge of the Enlightenment, providing a rational – as opposed to theological – explanation of its subjects. The complete work ran to 35 volumes; its contributors included Voltaire, Montesquieu, and Rousseau.

ARC DE TRIOMPHE DE L'ETOILE, PARIS, 1808 ONWARDS
This aerial view of Paris shows the Champs Elysées dominated by Napoleon's triumphal arch. The Tuileries, laid out in 1667 by André Le Nôtre, are visible at the head of the thoroughfare.

GREEK REVIVAL

THE ATHENIAN IDEAL

JOHANN WINCKELMANN
The "father of modern archaeology," Winckelmann was born in Prussia in 1717. He read Greek literature, studied theology and medicine before becoming librarian of the Vatican. His writings on Classical art and particularly ancient Greece inspired much of the Neo-classical movement. He maintained that "the only way for us to become great, or even inimitable if possible, is to imitate the Greeks." Winckelmann died in 1768.

GREECE WAS RIGHTLY SEEN as the historic frontier, the root of Western architecture. Its ancient architecture came to be regarded in the mid-eighteenth century as a kind of Holy Grail. No architecture was more perfect than that of fifth-century Athens and this surely was the pure, noble, and powerful aesthetic that would best represent the aspirations of the newly organised European states. The first influential treatise written on the roots of Western architecture was *Essai sur l'architecture* (1753) by the Abbé Laugier (1713–69). Laugier set out to prove that the first and fundamental architecture was that of the "primitive hut," which, illustrated in his book, is what looks to be a prototype of a Greek temple made of timbers and branches. What was the Parthenon, the Holy of Holies to the Greek Revivalists, but a development in stone and through great artistry of this ancestor? The most perfect architecture of all was thus rational and natural.

Less than a decade later, James "Athenian" Stuart (1713–88) and Nicholas Revett published the *Antiquities of Athens* (1762) after their long study tour of Greece. By then, Stuart had already built a Greek temple in the grounds of Hagley Hall, Birmingham (1758). The style was taken up with great enthusiasm. In Britain it proves suitable for the design not only of imitations of Greek monuments – an attempt was made to recreate the Parthenon as a monument to the fallen of the Napoleonic wars on the top of Edinburgh's Calton Hill – but also of churches, country houses, museums, galleries, universities, and even the earliest railway stations. At Euston Station, London (1835–37), Philip Hardwick (1792–1870) designed a giant entrance in the form of a Doric propylaeum, a colossal gateway demolished after a famous fight by conservationists in 1961.

ERECHTHEION, ATHENS, C.421–406 BC
Built to house the shrine of the legendary Athenian king Erechtheus, the Erechtheion is located on the north of the Acropolis. The "Maidens" of the caryatid porch represented young serving women who performed cleansing rituals.

Across the road from what was known as the Euston Arch, William Inwood and his son Henry built the new St. Pancras Church (1819–22) in the guise of a Greek temple, flanked on either side of its east end by caryatid porches adopted from the Erechtheion, Athens. Quite what the caryatids – scantily-clad Greek maidens carrying a pediment on their heads – think of hanging out in the damp, gray, and heavily polluted Euston Road is anyone's guess. Artfully, the church was topped with a tower based on the Temple of the Winds, Athens. In other words, the Inwoods had rearranged parts of famous Greek monuments to build an English parish church.

SCOTTISH CLASSICISM

This pick-and-mix approach to the architecture of ancient Greece was popular in England; the story was rather different north of the border, where the Scots embraced Greece with a warmth that their climate lacked. So much so that Edinburgh came to be known as the Athens of the North and the Greek Revival style here endured late into the nineteenth century, unlike in England where it had long given way to the Gothic Revival and a freestyle free for all. The most notable Edinburgh monument in the Greek style was the Royal High School (1825–29) by Thomas Hamilton (1784–1858). This scholarly building was superbly sited on a commanding hillside

ST. PANCRAS CHURCH, LONDON, 1819–22
The two caryatid porches at either end of the church were inspired by the Erechtheion in Athens (see above right). The set on the northern wall were originally larger but each figure had to have a section removed to fit under the porch.

overlooking the city in much the same way as the temples of the Acropolis do in Athens.

In Glasgow, the Greek style was pursued with great vigour and originality by Alexander "Greek" Thomson (1817–75) who never left his native Scotland except in his vivid imagination. Thomson built rows of handsome terraced housing, villas, warehouses, and above all two curious and haunting churches, St. Vincent Street (1857–59) and Caledonian Road Free Church (1856–67) that are serious adventures in a Greek idiom by way of Mesopotamia. His was a singular talent and, after decades of neglect, he has been restored to the pantheon – or should that be Parthenon? – of Architecture's greats.

THE PRUSSIAN STATE

It was in Prussia, though, that the Greek Revival was at its most assured. Under the firm, yet largely benevolent, military rule of Frederick the Great, Greek architecture became a symbol of this newly powerful state. The gateway to Frederick's capital, Berlin, is the famous Brandenburg Gate (1789–93), a Greek screen by C. G. Langhans (1733–1808). Friedrich Gilly (1772–1800) set the tone magisterially with his unrealized project for a giant monument to the king (1797). This was to have been an imposing Doric temple set on a massive podium in the heart of Berlin. Gilly died before the project could be realized, although its design was taken up by the future Ludwig II of Bavaria when he built the exquisite and deeply romantic Walhalla overlooking the Danube River near Regensburg (1829–42; see p.27). If you ever want to know what a Greek temple looked like in all its glory, here you have it.

ST. VINCENT ST CHURCH, GLASGOW, 1857–59
The idiosyncratic design here places the tower at the corner of the building. Thomson's confident use of the Greek idiom was a major factor in Scotland's largely resisting the Gothic Revival.

Leo von Klenze (1784–1864), a fellow pupil of Gilly's took the style to Munich. However, in his Glyptothek (1816–30), a collection of Greek and Roman sculpture, and Propylaea (1846–60), or gateway, to Konigsplatz, he mixed Roman and Greek forms and thus paved the way for a style – a fusion we would call it today – that became popular in much of Europe in the mid-nineteenth century. One of the finest examples is in England, the Ashmolean Museum, Oxford (1841–5) by C. R. Cockerell.

The Greek Revival made itself felt in Austria, Poland, and Hungary, and as far north as Sweden and Finland, far from the warm and sunny skies of Athens and Delphi. It made its way into Italy too – no one should miss having a coffee in the wonderful Caffè Pedrocchi in Padua (1816–31), a curiosity by Giuseppe Japelli (1783–1852) – and eventually back to Greece through the influence of German rule.

NEO-CLASSICAL MOTIFS
Examples of Roman, Greek, and even Egyptian motifs were published in books on the subject during the eighteenth century. These influenced architects and craftsworkers alike. The revival of Classical motifs was closely linked to the admiration for Classical learning, and such decorations were taken as an indication of good taste. The above design is from a drawing by Piranesi.

BRANDENBURG GATE, BERLIN, 1789–93
This imposing Doric doorway, based on the Propylaea on the Acropolis in Athens served as the architectural completion of the boulevard Unter den Linden and as a customs port. More recently it has been a symbol of German division and reunification.

KARL FRIEDRICH SCHINKEL
THE FIRST FUNCTIONALIST

THE GREATEST ARCHITECT of the Greek Revival was the Prussian Karl Friedrich Schinkel (1781–1841). Schinkel took the architecture of ancient Greece and translated, rather than copied it; he was never slavish in his approach to antiquity, nor was he eclectic in the sense of juggling styles together for the sake of novelty. What characterizes his buildings is not simply their often profound and elemental beauty, but their rigor. For as well as being a brilliant Greek revivalist, Schinkel was also perhaps the first true functionalist. His buildings are not simply perfect for the tasks set them, but express their structure clearly. More than this they make use of new technology and materials where appropriate; Schinkel traveled through Britain and what fascinated him most were not the set-piece buildings, but the handsome new industrial warehouses that made extensive use of iron. Nor was Schinkel a slave to one style. He prefigures the

KARL FRIEDRICH SCHINKEL
The greatest German architect of the 19th century, Schinkel was also a painter, craftsman, and stage designer.

eclecticism of the second half of the 19th century, although his own ventures into Gothic are highly disciplined – as one might expect of a man who from 1830 was head of the Prussian State Public Works Department. Schinkel, a pupil of Gilly's, had worked for the department since 1810. In other words he was a new type of architect in another way too: he was a civil servant supported by a government office. A very efficient civil servant, it must be added.

In the person of this precise and erudite Prussian, then, we see the emergence of a new figure in the story of architecture, that of the architect-administrator. The times had truly changed since Palladio. Where the great Renaissance master had trained as a stonemason, learned by studying the monuments of Rome firsthand and practiced very much on his own with a team of builders and craftsmen, Schinkel was trained academically and worked his way up through the quasi-military ranks of a state bureau.

ALTES MUSEUM, BERLIN, 1823–30
Schinkel felt that the site – among Berlin's principal civic buildings – required a monumental building. The museum has a colonnade with 18 Ionic columns running the full length of the façade, an imposing flight of steps, and equestrian statues framing the entrance.

He proved to be adept at whatever task came his way from charming and romantic villas such as the Court Gardener's House at the Charlottenhof, Potsdam (1829–31) to the moving severity of the Neue Wache guardhouse, Berlin (1816–18), now the monument to those killed in twentieth-century Germany by war and oppression. In between these extremes he designed the grand Schauspielhaus (opera house), Berlin (1819–21), the functional Academy of Architecture, Berlin (1831–36), and the superb Altes Museum, Berlin (1823–30).

A SYMBOL OF THE PRUSSIAN STATE

The Altes Museum was as influential in its way as Palladio's Villa Rotonda. It has two functions, first as a magnificent symbol of the Prussian state and, second, as museum and art gallery. Its genius is severalfold. The first thing a visitor sees is a long colonnade – 18 exquisitely executed Ionic columns – beneath an entablature patrolled by 18 fierce eagles, looking left and right in turn. The colonnade is mounted on a high podium. Close up, the entrance to the building proves to be set well back and gained only by ascending one of two flights of matching stairs. Top-lit

STAGE DECORATION (DETAIL) FOR *THE MAGIC FLUTE*
From 1816, Schinkel designed 42 productions for the stage. This aquatint, by C. F. Thiele, shows Schinkel's set design for Act II, scene 7 of Mozart's The Magic Flute, *performed in Berlin in 1816.*

galleries – they feel very modern – lead off to left and right. But, in the center is a wonderful surprise, a glorious two-story colonnaded rotunda under a graceful, undecorated dome. One of the world's most beautiful rooms, the rotunda is set with a box that rises as an attic above the colonnade, although this is invisible to the person standing in the square in front of the museum. What Schinkel has created here, then, are the basic elements of all architecture: the rotunda can be read as a sphere set within a cube and this cube is further set within a rectangle – the main body of the museum as defined by the reach of the colonnade – the proportions of which are taken from that of the sphere and cube. The Altes Museum is at once a rational and a romantic monument to the spirit of not just Greek but to all architecture. Those approaching the building from its back comment on the plainness of its rear and side elevations, yet the idea of the building is that it should be both a proud monument and a well-mannered companion, in a crisp, military-minded way, to its neighbors.

> *"Architectural detailing and design – the art of architecture – must never hide the larger structural forms"*
>
> KARL FRIEDRICH SCHINKEL

COURT GARDENER'S HOUSE, CHARLOTTENHOF, POTSDAM, 1829–31
Part of a group of buildings erected in the grounds of Schloss Charlottenhoff (built for the Crown Prince), the Court Gardener's house has low-pitched roofs, overhanging eaves, and an Italianate tower.

IMPERIAL RUSSIA
INTERNATIONAL CLASSICISM

CATHERINE THE GREAT

Catherine (1729–96) was born in Stettin in the Prussian province of Pomerania (now Szczecin, Poland). In 1745 she married Peter, Grand Duke and heir to the Russian throne. Peter was dethroned by a conspiracy and Catherine made empress (1762–96). Her rule was one of the most prosperous periods of the Russian empire. Catherine was renowned for her intelligence and learning. She promoted French culture in Russia, and corresponded with Voltaire and Diderot. She also commissioned buildings all over Russia, and started a royal art collection, which later became the Hermitage.

AT THE BEGINNING of the eighteenth century, Peter the Great (1682–1725) decided to build a new city, St. Petersburg. Although architects from other parts of Europe, notably Italy, had worked in Russia at the invitations of Tsars since Ivan the Great (1440–1505), Peter's heroic initiative not only changed the face of Russian architecture but gave the world some of its most fantastic and monumental buildings. In fact, it was not Peter, but Catherine the Great (at last, a woman in our story) who gave Russia buildings not simply to compare with those in Western Europe, but which exceeded them, mostly in scale and ambition, but some of the Empress' buildings are as original as they are breathtaking.

If Peter gave Russia the impetus to build adventurously in Western styles adapted to Russian tastes and weather, it was Napoleon Bonaparte who prompted the taste for truly gargantuan buildings. This might seem odd given

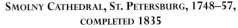

SMOLNY CATHEDRAL, ST. PETERSBURG, 1748–57, COMPLETED 1835

The blue-and-white cathedral is laid out as a Greek cross and forms the centrepiece of a convent complex begun by Rastrelli for Empress Elizabeth.

the fact that Napoleon invaded Moscow and, famously, was driven back after a month by the terrifying Russian winter. However, long before Napoleon the Russian court was hooked on all things French and this was the language spoken in smart circles. It was, in fact, after Napoleon's defeat that Imperial Russian architecture reached its climax. There were several important and ambitious building projects before Catherine, among them the astonishing Smolny cathedral and monastery complex (1748–57, completed 1835) built by the Italian architect Count Bartolomeo Rastrelli (1700–71) for the Empress Elizabeth; the Great Palace at Tsarkoe Selo (1749–52), a Rococo version in blue, white, and lashings of gold leaf for Elizabeth by Rastrelli; and of course

GREAT PALACE, TSARKOE SELO, 1749–52

The palace façade, designed by Rastrelli, stretches 978ft (298m). It combines various decorative elements such as columns, statues, and pilasters. In the second half of the 18th century, the palace became the favorite home of Catherine II.

the numbingly big Winter Palace (the Hermitage art gallery today) – Rastrelli for Elizabeth again. But Catherine's projects finally fused Russian ambition with Classical forms.

Important designs of Russian architecture include Tauride Palace, St. Petersburg (1783–89; rebuilt since), a superficially severe and relentless Doric job, but in fact the sumptuous home built by Catherine for her lover Grigory Potemkin. Behind the façade – which would have seemed uncomfortably plain to contemporary Russian taste – lay an opulent domed rotunda based on the Pantheon, Rome – and a vast Grecian hall at the back of the palace that extended into projecting apses at either side. The architect was Ivan Yegorovich Starov (1744–1808), who trained in Paris and also designed the imposing church at Nikolskoye (1773–76). This domed Doric structure borrowed from ancient Athens (the Tower of the Winds again) and from the febrile imaginations of Boullée and Ledoux.

NEO-CLASSICAL MONUMENTS

Catherine was generous in her patronage. She employed not just Italians and Russians, but French and even a Scottish architect too. This was Charles Cameron (1746–1812) who was invited to St. Petersburg by Catherine in 1779; to him we owe the tremendous colonnaded Cameron Gallery in the Great Palace (now the Catherine Palace) at Tsarkoe Selo and the handsome Pavlosk Palace (1782–86). Humble birth was no hindrance as the monumental Cathedral of the Virgin of Kazan, St. Petersburg (1800–11) proves; it was designed by the serf A. N. Voronikhin (1760–1814) who had been sent to Paris and Rome to be educated.

The greatest of these Neo-classical monuments, however, are the Ledoux- and Boullée-inspired General Staff Headquarters, St. Petersburg (1819–29), by Karl Ivanovich Rossi (1775–1849) and, above all, perhaps, the New Admiralty also in St. Petersburg (1806–23). Here Adrian Dmitrievitch Zakharov (1761–1811; also trained in Paris and Rome) shaped a building that was truly Russian in spirit. It was big – the façade stretches a staggering 1,575 feet (480 meters), broken up by 12-columned Doric temple fronts – and is centered on the sort of arched gateway Boullée would have died for.

CATHEDRAL OF THE VIRGIN OF KAZAN, ST. PETERSBURG, 1801–11
A. N. Voronikhin's vast cathedral faces Nevsky Prospect and was built to house the icon of Our Lady of Kazan. Constructed in the Classical style and inspired by both St. Peter's, Rome and Palladio's Villa Badoer, the cathedral has a semicircle of 96 Corinthian columns and a porticoed entrance.

Above this titanic archway rises an exotic tower composed of a sensational medley of the ancient Greek mausoleum of Halicarnassus, a Baroque dome crowned with a lantern from which shoots a needle-like Gothic spire. It sounds crazy, but it works superbly. Here, a new Russian architecture far from the onion domes of a Byzantine past had truly come of age.

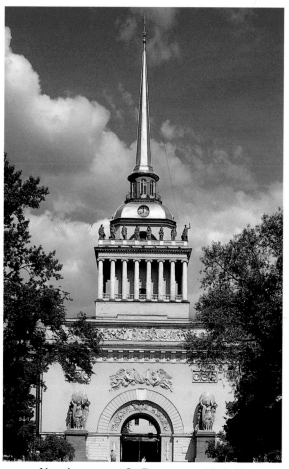

NEW ADMIRALTY, ST. PETERSBERG, 1806–23
The masterpiece of Adrian Zakharov, the leading Russian Neo-classicist, this vast building has a massive columned tower supporting a gilded spire over the central gate.

THE HERMITAGE

The 18th century saw the evolution and birth of public collections in Europe. In Russia, under Catherine the Great s patronage, science and the arts flourished. During her reign Catherine ordered the construction of a large number of public buildings, such as the Russian Academy of Sciences, the Academy of Fine Arts, and the first public library. Catherine the Great s personal museum — the Little Hermitage, designed by Vallin de la Mothe — was founded in 1764 when she purchased 255 paintings from Berlin, the collection of Johann Ernest Gotzowski. Under Nicholas I the Hermitage was reconstructed (1840–52), and the museum was opened to the public in 1852.

The
INDUSTRIAL
SOCIETY

WITH THE COMING OF THE INDUSTRIAL Revolution the role of the architect was challenged for the first time in centuries. Steam power, first successfully devised in England by Newcomen, Watt, Trevithick, and other inventors (but posited by Hero the Greek 2,000 years earlier) meant factory production, the extrusion and mass production of new materials, and new ways of making things — from bridges to buildings. In many ways this suited the skill of the engineer better than the art of the architect. The Crystal Palace, designed by Joseph Paxton and built in a matter of weeks for the Great Exhibition of 1851, was perhaps the most radical building of all time. Architects sneered at it, seeing it more as a work of plumbing than art. How wrong they were. Here was a new renaissance, but rooted in the future and not the past.

CRYSTAL PALACE, LONDON
The innovatory elements in the construction were the use of prefabricated parts and the exploitation of 19th-century England's advanced industrial and transport infrastructure – a presage of things to come.

INDUSTRIAL REVOLUTION
ENGINES OF CHANGE

ISAMBARD KINGDOM BRUNEL

Perhaps the greatest engineer of the British industrial revolution, Isambard Kingdom Brunel was born in 1806, the son of another prominent engineer. Apart from the bridge at Clifton, Brunel's most notable works are the introduction of the broad-gauge railway, which made possible high-speed rail travel; the design of the first steamship to regularly cross the Atlantic (*The Great Western*, 1838); and the *Great Eastern* steamship (1858), which laid the first telegraph cable across the Atlantic. It was the largest vessel for the next 40 years. Brunel died in 1859.

MINERAL ADVANTAGES

By the middle of the 18th century, Britain s natural forests had become depleted and existing shallow coal mines were proving inadequate. The invention of steam pumps at this time meant that coal mines could be drained to a greater depth and deeper coal seams exploited. The new mining techniques and the recent discovery of a method for smelting iron using coke led to a massive increase in the exploitation of both iron and coal. Britain s rich mineral deposits, with coal and iron ore located in the same regions, became the basis of the country s industrial leap forward.

THE INDUSTRIAL REVOLUTION broke out in England in the 1750s. The application of reliable steam power to production machinery, the ability to ship goods worldwide, and the rise and rise of the industrious middle classes were some of the many reasons that Britain was the first nation to industrialize. The results were a mixed bag, to say the least. Industrialism brought misery for those all but forced into mechanized sweatshops and encouraged cities to grow beyond their capacity or ability to provide civilized places to live. Pollution and new forms of accident and disease became rife. At the same time, the Industrial Revolution brought many benefits in its wake, not always apparent to architects, who for a long time were generally either unaware of what it could do for the building design or actively hostile toward that design. The Industrial Revolution promised to mechanize architecture too, and to make the craftsman extinct.

To an extent these fears were well-founded. Nevertheless, even the earliest architectural fruits of the Industrial Revolution had proved to be rather beautiful. Many, beginning with the elegant Iron Bridge that spanned the Severn at Coalbrookdale, Shropshire (1779), were far removed from the aesthetic beat trod by architects. In any case, the first structural monuments of the Industrial Age were largely built by engineers. It took very many years before most architects were prepared to accept the fact that engineers were designing some of the most beautiful yet economic structures the world had ever seen. Meanwhile architects allowed themselves to get caught up in an arcane Battle

CLIFTON SUSPENSION BRIDGE, BRISTOL, 1830–63
Built over a deep gorge, Brunel's virtuoso suspended bridge has a main span of 702ft (214m). In the original designs, the vast pylons were to have had sphinxes and hieroglyphic decoration.

of the Styles that was to rage, more or less, up until World War I, when a newly industrialized and absurdly competitive Europe tore out its own heart with the savage fruits of its factories.

FEATS OF ENGINEERING

Among the great new engineering works that were ultimately to inspire architects were the Clifton Suspension Bridge, Bristol (1830–63) by Isambard Kingdom Brunel (1806–59), its graceful ironwork suspended from imposing Egyptian-style pylons at either end; the iron-framed warehouses, supported on massive Greek Doric cast-iron columns, covering the seven acres of the new Albert Docks, Liverpool (Jesse Hartley, 1845); and the superb Boatstore at the Royal Naval Dockyard, Sheerness (1858–60). This was the first multi-tiered iron-framed building and, like office buildings of a century later, the external timber panels are simply clipped on.

Until the coming of the Industrial Revolution, the walls of buildings carried their own weight. Now the walls were, if the architect or engineer chose, no more and no less than a skin. Of course builders had been doing this in sub-Saharan Africa in the construction of mud-walled mosques for many centuries; but cast-iron and – from 1856 when John Bessemer made it possible – steel are far stronger than timber and bamboo. One look at the Sheerness Boatstore designed by Godfrey Thomas

THE BOATSTORE, ROYAL NAVAL DOCKYARD, SHEERNESS, 1858–60
This utilitarian building measures 210ft (64m) by 135ft (41m) and is lit by a central overhead "nave". It is one of the earliest tiered iron-frame buildings, started in the last decade of Britain's industrial preeminence, but appears to have been built much later.

Greene, Director of Engineering and Architectural Works to the Admiralty, and you can see clearly that because of the nature of its construction, the building could be extended indefinitely. An architecture of indeterminacy had been born; no wonder most architects feared the worst.

In the hands of great engineers, this approach was to lead in time not just to the great railway stations of the nineteenth century, the cathedrals of their age as they are often called, but to such

JEREMY BENTHAM
Born in London, Jeremy Bentham (1748–1832) was a philosopher, economist, and writer on jurisprudence. His attempts to solve social problems scientifically greatly influenced 19th-century thought. His contribution to architecture came in his plan for the Panopticon (1787). The principle of the Panopticon was a central rotunda and – in the case of prisons – a circle of cells facing inward, which could thus be constantly surveyed from the rotunda. The model was to have a profound influence upon the design of hospitals, schools, and prisons. It became a prototype for many later buildings that had surveillance as part of their purpose.

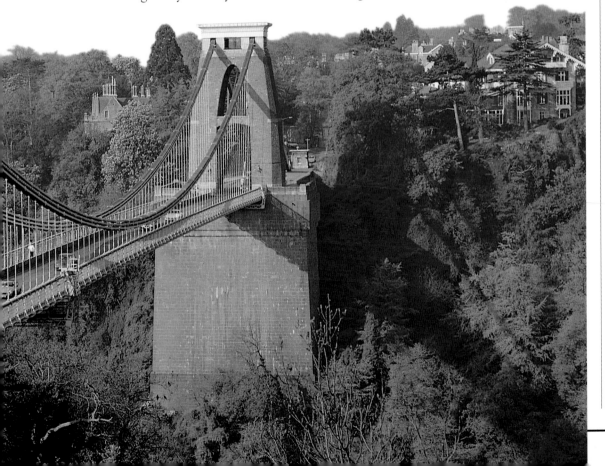

BIBLIOTHÈQUE NATIONALE, PARIS, 1859–67
The light, airy interior of the reading room displays the advantages of the new industrial building materials. The structure also shows how the scale previously reserved for religious buildings was now adopted for secular constructions.

Others found a new voice through adopting the new language of industrial civilization. Two important prototypes of the twentieth-century office building stand out long before the rise and rise of their US counterparts. These were Gardener's Warehouse, Jamaica Street, Glasgow (1855–56) by John Baird I (1798–1859), and Oriel Chamber, Liverpool (1864) by Peter Ellis (1804–84). The former is clad in a handsome cast-iron frame in a Venetian style, while the latter is cast-iron within and without and, although it has a decorative parapet, its bow-windowed style has no real precedent. In such relatively humble designs in cities that built and berthed the new ironclad steamships – which may in some ways have been an inspiration – we see the beginnings of a new architecture increasingly free of stylistic illusions and delusion.

THE USE OF IRON
In Paris, a daring use was made of cast-iron and metal in the grand, almost Byzantine interior of the Bibliothèque Nationale (1859–67) designed by Pierre-François-Henri Labrouste (1801–75). Labrouste had experimented successfully in the 1840s with the cast-iron interior of the Library of St. Geneviève, Paris, but the Bibliothèque Nationale showed real confidence in the handling of the new material. The main reading room is roofed over with nine graceful pendentive domes made of terra-cotta. Each has an eye at its center (as in the unglazed dome of the Pantheon, Rome), filling the room with daylight, but also meaning that readers are unaffected by harsh light late in the afternoon, and especially on bright winter days. Slim cast-iron columns and arches hold up the domes. The overall effect is delicate, almost tentlike. The book stacks are also made of cast-iron and the floors of the stack (store) room are slatted metal, allowing daylight to filter down into its lowest recesses. The central space of the stack room is spanned by latticed metal bridges,

spectacular structures as the Eiffel Tower (1887–89) by the legendary French engineer Gustave Eiffel (1823–1923) and the Galerie des Machines (1889), two awe-inspiring buildings erected for the International Exhibition in Paris, a successor to the Great Exhibition of 1851 in London. The Galerie des Machines was a successful collaboration between engineer (Victor Contamin, 1840–93) and architect Charles Dutert (1845–1906), pointing to the way in which these two professions would work ever more closely in succeeding decades.

THE ARCHITECT'S RESPONSE
How did architects respond to the challenges and opportunities thrown up by the Industrial Revolution? Most, as we have seen, found it hard, or, as we will see later on, simply impossible.

a device that architects would pick up again in France and Britain more than a century later.

The church of St. Eugène, Paris (1854–55) by Louis-Auguste Boileau (1812–96) is straight-forward Gothic on the outside; inside the surprise is to discover that pillars, capitals, vaults, and arches are all made of iron. This would have shocked the fervent architects of the mainstream Gothic Revival who wished to recreate a medieval world, but it was a strong, elegant, and economic solution. Whatever its strengths, however, cast-iron was seen as all right for interiors but not quite the done thing for exteriors. In fact cast-iron frames could justifiably be seen as the skeleton of a building; its skin

TURBINE BUILDING, MENIER FACTORY, NOISIEL-SUR-MARNE, 1871–72
The iron skeleton of Saulnier's extraordinary building is a self-sustaining structure that allows for large windows and a sheer curtain wall of brick, hung outside the iron frame itself.

ought to be something else – stone usually – as it was in these examples, and as it was, too, in the delightful University Museum, Oxford (1854–60) by Benjamin Woodward (1815–61).

The Museum has a display of dinosaur skeletons and these are arranged beneath delicate cast-iron vaults and between a grove of cast-iron columns that echo the dinosaur bones as if designed to do so. Yet the skin of the building is a curious Venetian Gothic design (with the kitchen of the medieval abbey, Glastonbury, thrown in for good measure) encouraged at the time by the great Victorian critic John Ruskin (see pp.154–55) who we will meet later. Ruskin railed against industrialism and the new architecture it spawned.

AN ARCHITECTURAL ASSORTMENT

So architects struggled intellectually with what to do with new materials. Their confusion is often expressed in buildings that are nevertheless delightful. Just look at the Menier Chocolate Factory at Noisiel-sur-Marne (1871–72) by Jules Saulnier (1828–1900). It looks more than a little like a chocolate box, but here the architect pulls off a brilliant mix of decorative design and structural inventiveness. The skeleton of the factory can be seen on the outside – those cross-braces of iron – but these are offset by colorful brick panels that echo their form. In fact this is a perfect machine for making chocolates in; it has the right decorative touch and, in modern terms,

UNIVERSITY MUSEUM, OXFORD, 1854–60
The spandrels of Woodward's iron arches are decorated with foliage and the surrounding arcade has capitals depicting different species of plants, underlining the building's educational purpose.

EARLY FACTORIES

Textile mills were the first real factories. They were brick-built, with heavy wooden floors and beams. Machinery stood on the top floor, where timber trusses gave the wide spans without column support that were needed to house heavy machinery. The first factory to include cast-iron columns was Claver Mill in Derbyshire (1785), but it also had timber beams and load-bearing masonry walls. The first totally iron-framed mill was built in 1796, using flat brick arches supported by iron beams.

GLASS TECHNIQUES

Heavy duties imposed on the sales of glass meant that Britain was backward in glass production at the time Paxton began work on the Crystal Palace. He needed 300,000 panes of glass – and quickly. This was impossible. He turned to France where glass-making was in full swing. The techniques, although excellent in terms of quality, required an immense input of skilled labor. Each pane was hand blown and then fired in the form of a cylinder. As it cooled, the cylinder was cracked open and refired. As it melted, it opened up to form a flat sheet which, as soon as it was cool, could then be rushed, by new steam railway, from the glassworks – which Paxton had set up in Birmingham with French workers – to London, and thus to the site of the Crystal Palace.

it is energy efficient too: it stands on mighty stone piers across a river and the water flowing under the arches between them generates power to drive machinery.

All iron buildings were to remain essentially the preserve of the engineer, and even at the end of the nineteenth century when all-iron, architect-designed structures began to appear, notably in the Métro station entrances of Hector Guimard (1867–1942) in Paris, iron was employed first and foremost for the decorative possibilities it offered.

THE CRYSTAL PALACE

One of the most radical and important buildings of all time, the Crystal Palace (1850–51) was perhaps the Parthenon of the Industrial Revolution. "Was" is the operative word, because this great temple of glass and iron was destroyed by fire in 1936. It had lasted just 85 years, having been moved from its original home in Hyde Park in central London to Sydenham, south London.

The Parthenon has lasted 30 times as long, and, if not still going strong, is there to remind us of the durability of stone and marble as building materials. But the Crystal Palace was only ever meant to be temporary.

It was the masterpiece of Joseph Paxton (1801–65), a gardener, who had experimented with the design and construction of lightweight palm and lily houses in the gardens of Chatsworth House, Derbyshire in the 1840s. The Crystal Palace was designed and built at the last possible moment to house the Great Exhibition of 1851. The exhibition, visited by six million people, was a chance for Britain to show off the fruits of the Industrial Revolution that she had spawned a century earlier. Paxton made maximum use of plate glass – a recent invention – in the design of the Palace, employing 300,000 sheets of the stuff.

The building was designed to be put up as quickly as possible by semiskilled workers. It was the first large-scale, prefabricated building in modern materials the world had seen. It pointed the way forward

CRYSTAL PALACE, 1850–51
Chosen from over 250 designs, Paxton's vast structure measured 1,851 ft (564m long), reflecting the date of its completion. The entire structure – built by 2,000 workers – was in place in three months and was completed without scaffolding. Surely a miracle of the industrial age.

LLOYD'S BUILDING, LONDON, 1978–86

Richard Rogers' central atrium at Lloyd's quotes directly from Paxton's earlier structure. It houses the central "room" of Lloyd's, while the floors around it contain 12 levels of offices; on the outside are service ducts and elevators. At the end of the 20th century Rogers' hi-tech money palace showed how far steel and glass had come.

however, was as much rooted in nature as it was in new materials technology. He studied the structure of the leaves of the giant water lilies at Chatsworth House, Derbyshire, England. These were strong enough for young children to stand on quite safely. What he learned – as a medieval master mason might have done if he had been thinking of the optimum way to vault the nave of a cathedral – was that the lilypad offered the greatest strength possible from the lightest possible structure. Iron and glass could be put to work to do much the same thing in the construction of a building.

THE RAILWAYS

More than this, though, Paxton took full advantage of the coming of the railways to speed the various bits of the building from foundry to construction site. The world's first steam-operated mainline opened between Liverpool and Manchester in 1830, and Birmingham, where many of the components of the Crystal Palace were made, was linked to Euston Station, London in 1837. In every sense, then, the Crystal Palace was a new type of building. It employed not only the new materials and forms of industrial architecture, but exploited the new industrial society itself. It was truly the fruit of Britain's Industrial Revolution.

> *"Above the visitors rose a glittering arch far more lofty and spacious than the vaults of even our noblest cathedrals"*
> THE TIMES, LONDON

to a new way of building, free from the style and materials that had held architecture in their grasp from Mesopotamia to nineteenth century-England. In fact, it foreshadowed the great glazed buildings of the late twentieth century – office atriums and shopping malls. These were a long time coming because very many architects in 1851 would have seen the Crystal Palace as a threat, or if they had no sense of the future, would have dismissed it as a large greenhouse and not proper architecture. Ultimately, not only did the Palace give a lead to the steel-and-glass architecture of the twentieth century, but it remained in the back of the minds of forward-looking architects. Look at the great glazed atrium of the Lloyd's Building (1978–86) in the City of London, designed by the Richard Rogers Partnership: it owes more than a little to Paxton's great greenhouse of 125 years earlier. Paxton's basis for the structure of the Palace,

THE CRYSTAL PALACE UNDER CONSTRUCTION
The building was put together from millions of identical prefabricated units with a network of pipes to stabilize the structure. This network had nodes at regular intervals into which columns could be inserted and erected literally in minutes.

RAILWAYS
STEAM-AGE DESIGN

LINE ARCHITECTURE
Engineers either gave bridges, tunnels, and viaducts the look of Roman aqueducts or dressed them in medieval garb complete with battlements and arrow slits. This road bridge and tunnel got up as a medieval castle stands at Clayton on the London-Brighton railway line. Only gradually did railway companies relax and allow impressive engineering works to speak for themselves.

THE FIRST RAILWAY BUILDINGS reflected the split in the nineteenth century mind as to what was properly the realm of engineering and what was the realm of architecture. The difficulty faced by the pioneer railway companies was how to entice custom and how to civilize an unfamiliar world of steam, smoke, and pounding piston strokes. It seems rather charming now, yet early locomotive builders decorated their iron-horses with Classical ornamentation: a tall chimney might become a fluted Doric column, a dome on top of a boiler could be tricked up as a sort of steamy Temple of Vesta at Tivoli. In fact, locomotive builders got into their stride as quickly as the engines themselves; they soon found that the aesthetic of the locomotive that followed naturally from its essential workings was good looking without help from the Classical Muses. Over time, the locomotives became a much-loved (and today much-missed) part of the landscape.

As for stations and intrusive engineering structures such as bridges and tunnels, what should they look like? Quite simply, early railway architects threw the book at their subject: stations and other essential structures

emerged in every style going. Only rarely did boards of directors agree to let their buildings speak for themselves in the equivalent of plain English. Stations appeared in the guise of Greek temples, Roman baths, medieval cloth halls and cathedrals, country cottages, and grand civic palaces, but virtually never as straightforward expressions of railway design. Still, passengers may well have needed to be wooed by such architectural conceits and deceits; in any case, the results were often glorious.

BRITISH STATIONS
Railways began in England. Richard Trevithick, the Cornish engineer, demonstrated one of his early locomotives the "Catch-me-who-can" on a circular track years before the London & Birmingham Railway arrived in a puff of Grecian glory at the same site on London's Euston Road in 1837. Their chosen style, as we have seen, was Greek Doric (and later Greco-Roman; today Euston Station, rebuilt in 1967 is neither Greek nor Roman, just very dull). When the Great Northern Railway arrived a few hundred yards to the east at King's Cross in 1852, it chose a handsome, undecorated arcaded style, realized in yellow stock brick, that recalled the functional grandeur of Roman bridges and aqueducts. It was the work of Lewis Cubitt (1799–1883) and was always preferred by early functionalist Modern Movement architects in Britain to the fairy-tale Gothic hotel of St. Pancras that announced the arrival of the Midland Railway between King's Cross and Euston in the mid-1860s.

In fact, St. Pancras Station (1864–68) itself was a triumph of the civil engineer's art; it was just that William Barlow (1812–1902) had to hide his much-admired train shed behind Sir

ST. PANCRAS TRAIN SHED, LONDON, 1864–68
In the foreground we see Barlow's train shed, its slightly pointed arch echoing the Gothic detailing of the building's exterior. At its base the arched vault is secured by 3-in (8-cm) rods. In the distance to the left of the image is Scott's Grand Midland Hotel.

VICTORIA STATION, BOMBAY, INDIA, 1887
Frederick Stevens' hybrid confection shows his predilection for mixing European Gothic with indigenous forms of architecture — here, with elements of Indo-Islamic styles.

& White, and Grand Central (1903–13) by Reed and Stem, Warren, & Whitmore. Both drew their inspiration from the great basilicas and imperial baths of ancient Rome, yet both were magnificent examples of sophisticated construction, engineering, and urban planning.

THE RASH OF SPEED

A very important aspect of the coming of the railways was the way in which they allowed architects and builders to transport ideas, drawings, and materials at unprecedented speed through countries and across continents. This had its good side and its drawbacks; it meant that good architects could be employed to raise standards in previously neglected towns, but there was also a danger of buildings getting to look too much like one another. The rash of redbrick houses that smothered Victorian England was helped along by the railways.

BATHS OF CARACALLA, ROME, AD 212–216
This enormous complex could house over 1,500 bathers and included exercise areas, libraries, art galleries, and gardens. Built by Emperor Caracalla, the baths functioned for over 300 years.

George Gilbert Scott's Grand Midland Hotel (1865–71). Barlow's iron and glass train shed was magnificent; at 237 feet (74 meters) wide and 96 feet (30 meters) high, it boasted the world's greatest single span. This great roof was held in place by iron rods that passed underneath the platforms. For many decades, progressively-minded architects would tut-tut at what they saw as the incongruity of Barlow's functional master-piece and Scott's outlandish Gothic fantasy; today we see the two working happily hand-in-gauntlet.

LATER FANTASIES

Such fantasies were taken ever further during the course of the nineteenth century and well into the twentieth. Victoria Station, Bombay (opened 1887), styled in a fruitcake-rich blend of Indo-Saracenic and Gothic Revival styles by Frederick Stevens (1848–1900), rarely fails to draw a smile from seen-it-all travelers. But the grandest examples of railways successfully meeting revived historic styles were to come only shortly before the cataclysmic World War I. They were both in the United States, both in fact in Manhattan. These were Pennsylvania Station (1902–11; demolished for no good reason in 1963) by McKim, Meade,

CONCOURSE, PENNSYLVANIA STATION, NEW YORK CITY, 1902–11
While clearly influenced by the vast public buildings of ancient Rome, the simple yet monumental central chamber had a clear, functional aspect, allowing the maximum freedom of movement between different parts of the station. It also served as an impressive entrance to the city itself.

INDUSTRIAL CITIES
HOUSES FOR WORKERS

WORKERS OF THE WORLD, UNITE!
Prussian-born socialist philosopher Friedrich Engels (1820–95) is recognized as one of the two founders of modern Communism. From 1842, he spent much of his life in Manchester, England, where he wrote The Condition of the Working Class in England *(1845). He began a long collaboration with Karl Marx (1818–83) in 1844. They were jointly responsible for the* Communist Manifesto, *published in 1848.*

THE STORY OF architecture is principally the story of great buildings, those that have pushed the art of construction and represented the image we have of ourselves as societies, our beliefs, codes, and values. The ordinary, everyday buildings that most humans have lived in through history are either forgotten or are thought of as the concern of archaeology: mud huts, clay and wattle cabins, straw huts, timber shacks. But, when we reach the 19th century, it becomes impossible to ignore ordinary housing.

The Industrial Revolution not only drew working people from the country to towns and cities in their thousands, but fired a boom in the construction industry now that houses could be mass produced. The factory way of doing things was applied to the building of homes for industrial workers. Aided and abetted by the new railways, mass housing — row upon row of small red-brick terraced cottages — rose by railway stations, beside viaducts, along the banks of canals, and in the shadow of smoking factories. The urban landscape of at first Britain, and then Europe, the United States, and bit by bit much of the rest of the world, was changed forever.

SLUM CLEARANCE
The speed at which these instant slums were built was as astonishing as the rate at which railways traced their tracks across, again, first Britain and then Europe and the United States. The industrial city was born. The problems it threw up were, of course, impossible for architects to solve alone. Because mass housing was built without much thought to sanitation — sewage, running water, light, and fresh air — industrial cities were prey to terrifying bouts of cholera and other foul diseases.

Now a new type of designer was needed, the urban planner, someone who could keep a larger picture in mind of how a city might work and might be a healthy and decent place to live. The role of the planner was to develop slowly over the next century. In the meantime, it was left to philanthropists, critics, and novelists with a social conscience, like Dickens, to raise hue and cry and demand practical action to raise the standard of living for those condemned to live in industrial squalor. At first, it was city engineers who tackled some of the problems of slum clearance and the construction of adequate sewers and water supplies.

It was not that all industrialists were oblivious to the wretched conditions their workers lived in; true, labor was dirt cheap in the nineteenth century, but skilled labor became increasingly valuable as the machines that the factories made — the locomotives, for example, that drove the

TODMORDEN, WEST YORKSHIRE, ENGLAND
The expansion of Todmorden was due to the cotton industry. The Rochdale Canal (1804) and the Manchester–Leeds Railway (1841) transported the coal that fired the steam-powered looms.

LOWER ROAD, PORT SUNLIGHT VILLAGE, CHESHIRE, BEGUN 1888
Port Sunlight Village was created by William Hesketh Lever to meet the cultural, recreational, and domestic needs of the workers at his soap factory.

HONOR DAUMIER
The caricaturist, painter, and sculptor Honoré Daumier (1808–79) is renowned for his cartoons and drawings satirizing 19th-century French society. For 40 years he worked in Paris as a cartoonist, executing some 4,000 lithographs and an equal number of drawings. He made fun of the middle classes and depicted an unsentimentalized view of poverty. His work played an important part in drawing attention to the negative effects of industrialization.

Industrial Revolution ever onward – became more complex and demanded not just factory hands, but an educated workforce. In fact it was industrialists themselves, many of them spurred on by religious conviction, who began to employ architects to build model villages for their workers.

In Britain, the textile manufacturer Titus Salt commissioned Lockwood and Mawson to design handsome Italianate villas for his workforce in his model village Saltaire, Yorkshire (from 1851). That year, Prince Albert had commissioned model workers' housing in London as part of what we now call the outreach program of the Great Exhibition. Sir Giles Gilbert Scott was asked to design factory cottages for mill workers at Ackroyd, Halifax, Yorkshire in 1859. Other industrialists followed suit; there were the Quaker chocolate makers, Rowntree and Cadbury, who built ideal villages at New Earswick, York (1902), and Bournville (1895), the soap manufacturers Lever at Port Sunlight, Cheshire (1888), and finally local authorities themselves.

PLANNING THE INNER CITY

In the 1890s, the young radical architects of the newly created London County Council, steeped in the writings of John Ruskin and William Morris, designed some of the finest inner-city housing developments of their time: the first was the Boundary Estate, Shoreditch, east London, realized in an elegant Arts and Crafts style. Britain was not alone, but it was here, the furnace of the Industrial Revolution, that the problems first arose and were first addressed. By the end of the nineteenth century, the issue of not just how

workers should live but what a healthy modern town ought to be like was high on the architectural agenda. The most radical solution at the time was the creation of garden cities pioneered by the social reformer Ebenezer Howard who imagined England potted with self-sufficient towns of up to 35,000 people, the creation of which would stem the growth of great wens like London, Birmingham, and Manchester.

Letchworth, Hertfordshire, was the first of these ideal towns (begun 1903), but because it was set up on rather eccentric lines, it was initially a paradise for fashionable vegetarians, teetotallers, nature-cure cranks, and men who wore sandals and smocks and read Nordic sagas by William Morris. Industrial workers from the slums of London came up on bus tours and on excursion fares on the Great Northern Railway to laugh at Letchworth people. Amusing perhaps, but mass housing and the problem of how to contain the growth of industrial cities was to become a major theme preoccupying many of the best architectural minds in the 20th century and beyond.

LETCHWORTH, HERTFORDSHIRE, ENGLAND, BEGUN 1903
In the garden city of Letchworth the public buildings, green, and train station lie on a central plateau surrounded by residential areas ranging from suburban villas to working-class housing.

AUGUSTUS PUGIN

THE HUMAN FIREWORK

"I AM SUCH A LOCOMOTIVE, being always flying about." Augustus Welby Northmore Pugin (1812–52) was the mainspring of the archaeologically correct Gothic Revival that from the late 1830s emerged as a potent force in European and, remarkably quickly, global architecture. A force of nature, Pugin lived life quickly and died young and insane. The son of Auguste Pugin who fled the French Revolution and came to London, where he became a principal assistant of John Nash, Pugin wished passionately to recreate a medieval world and above all a Catholic world. (The Catholic faith, driven

A. W. N. PUGIN
Pugin's personal life was as eventful as his professional life was ambitious. He was married three times in the space of 20 years.

underground in England from the reign of Henry VIII, was only officially sanctioned again in 1829.) Pugin had no problem with industry, using brand new railways to their utmost to travel the length and breadth of Britain to build churches, rectories, houses, and monasteries wherever a revived Catholic community wanted one.

As a result of earlier suppression, the Catholic community had much catching up to do and Pugin was its architect champion. He built many Gothic churches, often too quickly and with too small a budget to do justice to his ambitious, romantic designs. His finest churches, which were greatly influential on the development of the Gothic Revival, were St. Giles, Cheadle (1841–46) and St. Augustine's, Ramsgate (1845–51). St. Giles is a proud Decorated Gothic stone church with a tall spire; its interior is a Gothic Aladdin's cave, a sequence of magical spaces, every last inch covered in gorgeous polychrome decoration. As in all his projects, Pugin designed every last detail, including the interiors (and exterior details) of the new Palace of Westminster (with Charles Barry, from 1836).

A GOTHIC FIGUREHEAD

A prodigious designer of furniture, fabrics, vestments, church plate, ceramics, and stained glass, Pugin was also a pugnacious author whose books – notably *True Principles of Christian or Pointed Architecture* (1841) – were to have a major effect not just on the architecture of the Gothic Revival but also on that of the Arts and Crafts movement at the end of the nineteenth century and on the background thinking of the Modern Movement in the twentieth. Pugin believed a building should have no features that were not necessary for convenience, construction, or propriety, and that ornament should be limited to the building's essential structure. He was against all forms of sham and mocked

CENTRAL LOBBY, PALACE OF WESTMINSTER, LONDON
Pugin was responsible not only for the interior modeling and exterior detailing of the façades of the Palace of Westminster, but also for such styling as the wallpaper and inkstands. His designs are still preserved to this day.

"Only a restoration of the ancient feeling and sentiments; 'tis they alone can restore Gothic architecture"

AUGUSTUS WELBY NORTHMORE PUGIN

PUGIN S KEY WORKS
Palace of Westminster, London (with Barry) *1836–68*
St. Wilfrid, Hulme, Manchester, England *1839–42*
St. Giles, Cheadle, Staffordshire *1841–46*
Nottingham Cathedral, England *1842–43*
The Grange, Ramsgate, Kent *1843–44*
St. Augustine's, Ramsgate, Kent *1845–51*

THE GRANGE, 1843–44, AND ST. AUGUSTINE'S, 1845–51, RAMSGATE, KENT
Pugin's sketch shows his house, the Grange, to the left and St. Augustine's on the right. His asymmetrical designs were to have a major influence on Victorian architecture.

what he saw as the gimcrack, cardboard cut-out architecture, got up in fairy-tale historic styles – mock Chinese, Egyptian, Greek, Roman, Hindu, and Gothick – he had witnessed as a youth. Gothick with a k, by the way, was the predecessor of the full-blooded Gothic Revival Pugin spurred on. The former was the by-product of a literary movement (Horace Walpole's *The Castle of Otranto*, 1765, and William Beckford's *Vathek*, 1787, were its gospels). The latter was an architectural adventure driven by religious feeling and as a reaction to the by then often tired Neo-Classicism. The Revival had reached its peak by the time Pugin was asked to help Barry – a classicist – with the Gothic detailing of his successful competition entry for the Palace of Westminster.

Beginning his career at fifteen, designing Gothic furniture for George IV at Windsor Castle, Pugin went on to become a theater-set designer in Covent Garden, before converting to the Catholic faith in 1831, eloping with his first wife Anne, and building his first home, St. Marie's Grange, Alderbury (1835–36; much modified since), near Salisbury with its great medieval cathedral. He later moved to Ramsgate where he built The Grange (1843–44), a house facing the sea with an asymmetrical plan arranged around his family needs rather than dictated by architectural style or theory. The Grange played a key role in the development of later nineteenth-century domestic architecture. Here, Pugin created an ideal Catholic way of life. A passionate sailor, he would even make

THE ROYAL THRONE, HOUSE OF LORDS, COMPLETED 1847
Pugin had already established his credentials for this later commission by designing furniture for Windsor Castle in his teens.

his architectural drawings while bobbing around at sea, never stopping to revise them. Many of his trips by boat were to France, where he collected medieval antiques. A quick-witted, passionate, funny, but opinionated man, he led a colorful life very much on his own terms, served diligently by a team of craftsworkers and builders to whom, like a medieval mason, he could speak or write – in shorthand fashion – and who understood as if intuitively what this human firework was driving at. Treated with mercury for an ailment of the eyes, Pugin went insane, was committed to Bedlam (Bethlehem Hospital for the Insane, housed then in what is today the Imperial War Museum, London) but was taken home by his third wife where he drew a handsome weathervane for the steeple of a church and then died. He was forty.

GOTHIC REVIVAL

THE HOUSE STYLE OF VICTORIAN BRITAIN

> *"In architecture there are two necessary ways of being true. It must be true according to the program and true according to the methods of construction"*
> VIOLLET-LE-DUC

THE GOTHIC REVIVAL reached virtually every part of the world. In some ways it became the house style of High Victorian Britain, driven along on a tide of vigorous and revived Christianity. It accompanied missionaries wherever they went. This is why you will find the Pugin-like St. Patrick's Cathedral in Melbourne, New South Wales (1858) and lesser revived Gothic designs in Shanghai, Bombay, and even in Nagasaki, Japan, and Seoul, Korea.

The Gothic Revival, however, held more than just a religious appeal for architects following in the footsteps of Pugin. It was a liberating force, freeing them from what young designers at the time saw as the constricting forms of Classicism. This, of course, was only a point of view, although a widely shared one, for architects like "Greek" Thomson in Glasgow and Cuthbert Brodrick (1822–1905) with the design of the inventive Town Hall, Leeds (1853–59) were proving that the Classical tradition was far from being exhausted. Yet, as Newton had proved in his 17th-century Third Law of Motion, to every action there is an equal and opposite reaction.

The Gothic Revival, as begun in England, was also perhaps a vote of self-confidence by young home-spun talent in English history and artistic values, as opposed to French or Italian. Britain was now at the height of its powers and, until the United States took over toward the end of the century, the most powerful country in the world, governing the largest empire. English history, and soon enough all things Welsh, Scottish, and Irish, too, became valued as perhaps never before. To a young architect in the 1840s and 50s then, Salisbury Cathedral was worth more than all the churches and villas of Andrea Palladio.

NEW BUILDING TYPES

The revived Gothic style was not just for churches. The nineteenth century spawned many new building types – town halls, opera houses, courts of justice, railway stations, grand hotels – and Gothic, being a flexible form of design as Pugin demonstrated, was pressed-ganged successfully into designs of all sorts. The Royal Courts of Justice, London (1874–82) by George Edmund Street (1824–81; work on the law courts precipitated his early death) is a masterly play of largely fourteenth-century Gothic forms drawn from across Europe. These are gathered around a stirring Gothic

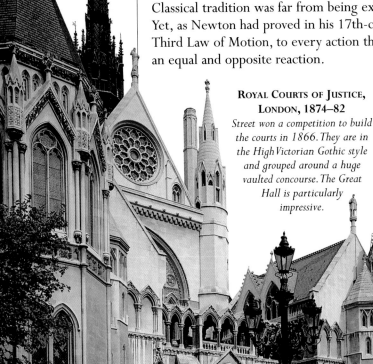

ROYAL COURTS OF JUSTICE, LONDON, 1874–82
Street won a competition to build the courts in 1866. They are in the High Victorian Gothic style and grouped around a huge vaulted concourse. The Great Hall is particularly impressive.

concourse. Equally impressive is the grandiloquent Town Hall, Manchester (1868–77) by Alfred Waterhouse, a thing of towers, turrets, and spires arranged ingeniously around an awkward triangular site. Inside, every detail down to the cisterns in the impressive lavatories has been thought through with care and precision. The council offices lead off corridors that run around the perimeter of the building, offering complex and rewarding views across serpentine vistas of pointed arches, twisting stairs, and richly marbled surfaces.

Pressed into service for buildings of every type, Victorian Gothic was mostly used, as one would expect, for churches and although many of these are of pedestrian design, there are many exceptions. In England one of the most inventive Goths was the formidable William Butterfield (1814–1900), on one level a devotee of Pugin, but also the champion of "structural polychromy" whereby churches were built in rich mixes and striations of colored stone and bricks and their interiors saturated with different colored marbles and mosaics. Butterfield and his ilk were influenced by the North Italian churches; these were much written about at the time by Street amongst others. Butterfield's high-minded polychrome masterpieces are the Anglo-Catholic church of All Saints, Margaret Street, London (1849–59) squeezed into a tiny yard but making its presence known with a very tall tower, and Keble College, Oxford (1867–83), a *tour-de-force* by any standards.

Non-English Gothic

Outside England, the Gothic Revival was widespread and yet rather anaemic. The French theorist Eugène-Emmanuel Viollet-le-Duc (1814–79) had a very impressive name and several key treatises on the development of European Gothic to offer, yet his own buildings are either dull – St. Denys-de-l'Estrée, Paris (1864–67) – or quite mad – the spiky pilgrimage church at Lourdes. In Germany and Austria much the same was true. Look at the hard-edged and ultimately soulless profile of the Votivkirche, Vienna (1856–79) by Heinrich von Furstel (1828–83): it looks like the sort of church

a long-term prisoner in an Austrian jail might have made out of matchsticks.

The Gothic Revival stretched into the twentieth century (just); perhaps its final and one of its most dramatic late flowerings was the Anglican cathedral, Liverpool (1903–1978) by Sir Giles Gilbert Scott (1881–1960), a mountain peak of red sandstone notable for its awesome interior which owes much to Spanish precedent. Even then, it has nothing of the warmth of medieval work and, although inventive and impressive, is best compared to the power stations the architect built at Battersea and Bankside in London later in the mid-twentieth century. In any case, by the time of its completion, Liverpool Cathedral, intended as a powerhouse of muscular Christianity, braved a world in which church attendances had declined remorselessly and Christianity itself was increasingly divided up into sects, and no longer played such a central role in the life of the community.

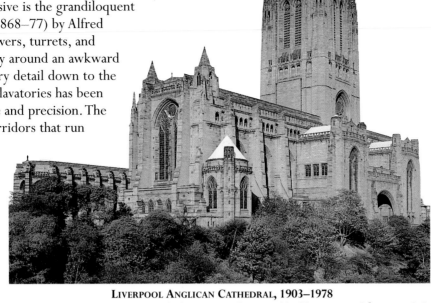
LIVERPOOL ANGLICAN CATHEDRAL, 1903–1978
Scott's Anglican cathedral is among the last major Gothic Revival buildings. Original features include the doubling of the transepts, the space between them given to an immensely tall lantern tower.

EUGÈNE-EMMANUEL VIOLLET-LE-DUC
The French architect and writer, Viollet-le-Duc (1814–79) was especially skilled in restoring medieval architecture. He designed and supervised the restorations of the walled city of Carcassonne and the cathedrals of Laon (above), Amiens, and Notre Dame. To Viollet-le Duc, the Gothic style was one of rational construction based on the system of rib vault, flying buttress, and buttress.

VOTIVKIRCHE, VIENNA, 1856–79
The Votivkirche by Heinrich von Verstel was built in thanks to God when an attempt on the life of Emperor Franz Josef failed. The church has tall, slender towers with crocketed (ornately carved) steeples.

MONUMENTAL DECADENCE

FLIGHTS OF FANTASY

LUDWIG II OF BAVARIA

Born in 1845, the son of Maximilian II and Marie of Prussia, Ludwig united with Prussia against France and in 1870, on the advice of Bismarck, called on the German princes to form a German empire. A patron of theater, opera, and Wagner (see opposite), he was responsible for a series of outlandish castles, among them Linderdorf, Herrn-Insel (based on Versailles), and Neuschwanstein. Increasingly mad and reclusive, Ludwig drowned himself in 1886.

NEWFOUND WEALTH and new ways of building seem to have been at least two of the many complex factors that encouraged a spate of wild and eccentric building in the second half of the nineteenth century. What had been agreeable follies secondary to architecture proper a century earlier now became the architecture itself. One of the greatest of these follies blown into larger than life reality is Neuschwanstein (1869–81), a fantastic mountain palace in the guise of the most romantic castle ever built. This has been the source of countless illustrations of fairy-tale castles ever since and was used as a source of inspiration in Walt Disney's feature cartoon *Sleeping Beauty* and in Disneyland itself. Neuschwanstein ("the New Swan Castle") was commissioned by the young, rich, and unbalanced Ludwig II

of Bavaria and designed by Eduard Riedel (1813–85) and Georg von Dollmann (1830–95). Ludwig, a popular but profligate ruler who later died in suspicious circumstances, liked to dress up and pretend he was Lohengrin, the swan prince of legend and star of Richard Wagner's opera of the same name; Ludwig was Wagner's chief patron. The castle is a wonderful sight in the heavy snows that fall here and, although inordinately costly when built, it has now become Germany's top tourist attraction.

On a much smaller scale, but just as nutty and equally delightful, is Castell Coch (1875–91), near Cardiff, Wales, rebuilt for the Marquess of Bute by William Burges (1827–81). Burges was one of the most inventive nineteenth-century Goths and designed much playful and meticulously crafted furniture; his interiors are loved by children of all ages and Castell Coch is exactly what in a child's mind's eye a castle ought to be like. It looks most of all like the kind of castle to be found in the pages of an illuminated medieval psalter or breviary (illustrated books of prayers). Sadly, instead of knights in armor and

NEUSCHWANSTEIN, BAVARIA, 1869–81

Inspired by Wartburg Castle in Thuringia, the magnificent 11th-century setting of Wagner's Tannhäuser, *Neuschwanstein was the first of Ludwig's fairy-tale castles, but was not completed until after his death.*

SLEEPING BEAUTY CASTLE, DISNEYLAND, CALIFORNIA, 1955

There is a strong resemblance between Ludwig's Neuschwanstein – the ultimate fairy-tale castle – and the Sleeping Beauty Castle in Walt Disney's family theme park, Disneyland, Anaheim, California. Sleeping Beauty Castle is located in an area called Fantasyland.

INTERIOR, CASTELL COCH, NEAR CARDIFF, 1875–91
Burges' lavish interior shows the 19th-century love of medieval craftsmanship and embellishment. In contrast, the exterior with its solid towers, conical roofs, and smooth brickwork is quite plain.

damsels in distress, today you will only meet fellow tourists beyond its working portcullis and stocky stone walls. The decoration, however, raises your eyes above the mundane and whirring video cameras to vaults enlivened with monkeys, peacocks, and birds of paradise. Nowhere more than at Neuschwanstein do you get a feel of how wealthy Victorians who lived on the back of the poor wanted to escape the sulfurous reality of industrial society. Among those who tried to improve

the lot of those at the bottom of the pit of industrial society was Prince Albert, a close relative of Ludwig II's and the industrious husband of Queen Victoria. When he died of typhoid at the age of 42, the Queen commissioned Sir George Gilbert Scott to design a wonderfully over-the-top monument to his memory. The Albert Memorial (1863–72), London, is a high Gothic polychrome canopy crowned with a richly encrusted spire and rising from a base at the top of long flights of stairs decorated with relief carvings of the Prince's greatest contemporaries; Scott himself and Pugin, too, are there if you look.

OUTRAGEOUS MONUMENTS
Monument mania swept Europe at this time as newly unified nation-states (Italy and Germany, 1871) emerged from a mass of rival and warring dukedoms and principalities. Many of these monuments were quite ludicrous, but perhaps none more so than the wonderfully pompous Victor Emmanuel II monument, Rome (1885–1911) by Giuseppe Sacconi (1854–1901), built to commemorate Italian unification and in homage of Italy's first king; you can see the king riding a bronze horse in front of this frothing tide of white marble. Romans call it "the typewriter"; it is extremely funny. In part it was this monumental decadence that encouraged the rise of the earnest and moralistic Arts and Crafts movement that saw a return to the modest and the homespun toward the end of this overactive century.

VICTOR EMMANUEL MONUMENT, ROME, 1885–1911
Variously called "the typewriter" and "the wedding cake," this oversized monument to Italy's first king houses a museum to the Risorgimento, the events that led up to the unification of the country in 1871.

RICHARD WAGNER
The leading German composer of the 19th century, Wagner's overwhelming influence on the subsequent history of opera was due to his dual role as composer and musical dramatist. In his greatest work, Der Ring des Nibelungen (1876), he developed a completely new style of musical performance. The romantic force of Wagner's work and its intense emotional and psychological expression is reflected in the building projects of the composer's patron, Ludwig II (see opposite), who decorated his castles with scenes from Wagner's works. The influence of Richard Wagner on Ludwig cannot be over-emphasised. If it were not for Ludwig, most of Wagner's later operas may never have been written.

FREE STYLE

ANYTHING GOES

JEAN-LOUIS-CHARLES GARNIER

Born in Paris in 1825, Garnier studied at the Ecole Des Beaux-Arts and traveled in Italy. In 1860 he won the competition to design the Paris Opéra, a project that, with the interruption of war in 1870, took 15 years to complete. Garnier was a leading figure in the Beaux-Arts movement and created several influential designs on the French Riviera. For the 1889 Paris Exposition, he created the Exposition des Habitations Humaines, later the subject of a book. Garnier died in Paris in 1898.

IDEAS, MATERIALS, AND PEOPLE traveled far and fast in the second half of the 19th century. It must have seemed as if anything was possible, and to many architects it was. With Classicism in decline and the Gothic Revival offering great diversity, an increasing number of architects chose to have their cake and eat it: they stirred the whole lot together, domes and pointed arches, Doric columns and Egyptian pylons, Indian stupas and Mesopotamian ziggurats. At best this led to some intriguing fusions of styles and traditions;

at worst, it was rather like a child stirring strawberry jam into a bowl of rice pudding: the result is a sticky, and to refined tastes, unpalatable mess. Why, though, take a position in the mid-century Battle of the Styles, when you could play both sides off one against the other by combining the two in one building?

FUSION

The Palais de Justice, Brussels (1866–83) slouches to mind when one thinks of this fusion, or just confused, approach to architecture. A colossal piling-up of stone, this is the nineteenth-century equivalent of a Mesopotamian ziggurat and seems to eyes at the beginning of the twenty-first century to be equally unreasonable and unfathomable. It was the work of Joseph Poelaert (1817–79), who here squeezed monumental Classical elements together as if designing with a vice rather than a T-square. The oddest thing about this building and others like it – the Rijksmuseum, Amsterdam (1877–85), the Reichstag, Berlin (1884–94) – is that, although huge, they seem somehow unreal.

The Opéra, Paris (1861–74) by Jean-Louis-Charles Garnier (1825–98) is equally pretentious, but rather lovable. It has something of the look and feel of a wedding cake too far; in fact, behind its highly mannered entrance façade is an interior richer than the richest fruitcake. This is Baroque-in-excelsis and, although so lavish that a pair of sunglasses comes in handy when casting an eye over acres of gilding lit by voluminous chandeliers, it is perfectly in keeping with the spirit of the operas it was designed to show. The sense of drama is maintained by the fact that it takes nearly forever to reach the auditorium, which is a surprisingly small part of this saccharine-sweet confection.

Much less immediately colorful yet equally vulgar and bizarre is the Church of the Sacré Coeur, Paris (1875–1919), a strangely lifeless concatenation of white arcades, pediments, campanile, and domes – Byzantium here, 12th-century French there – looming over the city center from the artistic heights of Montmartre. The design is by Paul Abadie (1812–84) and best seen from a distance.

ESCALIER D'HONNEUR, THE OPÉRA, PARIS, 1861–74
Garnier intended his resplendent staircase as a setting for the public to show off: "the view of broad staircases crowded with people was a spectacle of pomp and elegance too," he wrote.

The Byzantine tradition was used much more convincingly by John Francis Bentley (1839–1902) at Westminster Cathedral (1895–1903). Here, soft red brickwork on the outside, a single elegant campanile, and a numinous interior – a great brooding nave vaulted over with saucer domes that vanish into a high and holy gloom – do much to redeem an aesthetic, the Byzantine, that seemed rather out of place in the cities of London and Paris.

BARONIAL

Two successful examples of Free Style design are two buildings, one in London, one in Banff, that both have at least one foot in the baronial architecture of medieval Scotland. New Scotland Yard, Westminster (1887–90) by Richard Norman Shaw (1831–1912), is a polished performance, a police headquarters that rises besides the Thames from a stern granite base only to break into courses of warm red brickwork broken by a catalog of windows ranging from Elizabethan to Baroque. Four towers sprouting above the granite base patrol the building, each capped with a lead roof modeled on those, appropriately for a police station,

BANFF SPRINGS HOTEL, BANFF, ALBERTA, 1886–88
Situated in the Canadian Rocky Mountains, and originally built as a recreational outpost on the new railroad, the hotel dominates the town. Later additions were made in 1903–14 and 1926–28.

that give the Norman towers of the keep of the Tower of London their curiously jaunty character. Shaw's roofscape is a happy play of split Baroque pediments, obelisks, tiers of dormer windows, and high chimneys. It all goes together delightfully.

As does the theatrical mountainscape of the Banff Springs Hotel, Banff, Alberta (1886–88) by the Canadian firm Bruce Price. Not only did parts of Canada remind Scottish settlers of the Highlands back home, but the Scots came here in force in the nineteenth century. Not surprisingly, then, this grand resort hotel has something of the air of a Scottish castle; yet it is also an original composition, employing massive elements to make the building's mark against a daunting backdrop of pine-clad mountains. There is a freshness here that suggests a freedom from the artistic constraints and pretensions of contemporary Europe. This was the heyday of resort hotels aimed at busy city professionals wanting to get back to nature, albeit in style and comfort. These ambitious Canadian hotels came with the driving through of the railroads from Quebec to Vancouver and further examples can be seen looming above the tracks.

RICHARD NORMAN SHAW
Born in Edinburgh in 1831, Shaw was one of the principal exponents of the English Domestic Revival. His many buildings use a variety of styles, ranging from Gothic Revival to his own adaptation of the Queen Anne Style, versions of 16th-century manor houses and English Palladian architecture. His examples of the latter became the standard style for British government buildings in the 1920s and 1930s. Shaw's domestic designs were to have an influence on the American Shingle style. He died in London in 1912.

WESTMINSTER CATHEDRAL, LONDON, 1895–1903
Bentley broke with his typical Gothic style when he based his design for Westminster Cathedral on Byzantine examples. The cavernous interior is gradually being covered with marble and mosaic, in accordance with Bentley's original intention.

MORALITY & ARCHITECTURE

OPPONENTS OF INDUSTRIALISM

WILLIAM MORRIS

Designer, craftsman, writer, and socialist, William Morris (1834–96) was born into a wealthy family in Walthamstow, London, and educated at Marlborough School and Exeter College, Oxford. Morris became associated with the Pre-Raphaelite Brotherhood, particularly the painter Edward Burne-Jones and the poet Dante Gabriel Rossetti. In 1861 he founded the firm of Morris, Marshall, Faulkner and Company, designing and making wallpaper, textiles, stained glass, and furniture. In 1890 Morris set up a publishing house, the Kelmscott Press, for which he designed typefaces and ornamental borders.

> "*Have nothing in your houses that you do not know to be useful, or believe to be beautiful*"
> WILLIAM MORRIS

PERHAPS SOMETHING had to give in nineteenth-century architecture; for the most part, although substantial and well serviced with new developments in heating, lighting, and drains, it was becoming decadent. In previous ages, styles of architecture had grown more or less naturally out of expediency: from the discovery of new technologies, the use of available materials, or from a desire to stand still (as it seems to us to have been in, say, ancient Mexico or Egypt) or move forward. But, never back. The architects of the Renaissance explored the past but reworked it for new ends.

From the mid-19th century, not only did architects and their clients look back to a past, whether this was the Greece of Pericles or the England or King Arthur and his Round Table, but they tried to recreate it. More than this, they had the means, technological and financial, to do with the Pandora's box of architectural history whatever they wanted to. Their imaginations, as we have seen, could and did run riot, and the result was a spate of meretricious if entertaining nonsense. It is fashionable today to say that all styles of architecture of whatever period are equally valid and should not be judged in hindsight; but, this is cowardly and overly academic. We judge as much by eye and gut feeling as we do by the intellect. This is what John Ruskin (1819–1900) and William Morris (1834–1896) did and why these eminent Victorians were also among the fiercest critics of their age. And with these two romantic if flawed figures the critic came of age; it was not enough just to do: society needed to think about what it did and why.

GOTHIC REVIVAL

Both Ruskin and Morris were born into well-to-do families. Both were educated at Oxford and both detested industrialism and all its ways. The steam locomotive, Pugin's friend, was foe to these two high-minded artists and writers. Ruskin, in fact, owed much to Pugin, but because Pugin was (a) a Catholic, (b) first off with ideas that Ruskin would have liked to have been his own, and (c) insane (see pp. 146–47), he belittled this great man. Pugin had suggested, by implication, that there was a direct link between architecture and morality. Greek and Roman architecture he found abhorrent because it was pagan and England was a Christian country. Moreover, most contemporary architecture was immoral because dishonest, and dishonest because it squeezed

INTERIOR DESIGNED BY MORRIS AND HIS FOLLOWERS
Many original William Morris fabrics and wall coverings are used in Wightwick Manor, Wolverhampton, England. The walls of this room are lined with Morris' Honeysuckle printed linen; the furniture is by his followers.

its functions into buildings that were meant to be temples and not houses, banks, town halls, or railway stations. And corrupt, because they were all too often encrusted with gratuitous and meaningless decoration.

Ruskin agreed. At first, because of his love for Venice and its legendary painters – Tintoretto above all – he encouraged young contemporary architects to design a pseudo-Venetian style that he came to loathe. What he was looking for was the sort of honesty of construction he saw in the work of medieval masons. The beautiful chapter "On The Nature of Gothic" he wrote in the second volume of *The Stones of Venice* (1851–53) helped set the tone of the zealous Gothic Revival developing as he thundered away in the prose style of an archangel. Ruskin supported, in print and with money, the Pre-Raphaelite school of painters and craftsmen, William Morris among them.

Morris championed the cause of the craftsman and encouraged a return to the skills of weaving, hand-printing, fresco painting, and the writing of interminable sagas based on Norse and other legends. Morris had Philip Webb (1831–1915) design him an honest-to-goodness home, the Red House, Bexleyheath, Kent (1859–60), the precursor to the Arts and Crafts houses of the next generation. Both men became increasingly radical with age, so much so that in the 1880s

Morris took part in great popular demonstrations demanding social and political reform and finally became a Marxist. Ruskin railed ever more eloquently against the evils of industrialism and wrote one of the greatest socialist pamphlets (he would not have called himself a socialist), *Unto This Last* (1859), in which he likened the political economy of capitalist society to that of a skeleton bereft of skin, muscle, and, above all, a soul.

THE VICTORIAN LEGACY

The legacy of Morris and Ruskin was great. They were to affect the thinking and work not just of Arts and Crafts architects, designers, and craft workers, but of the architects who came to build local authority homes across Europe for industrial workers, and of some of the greatest and most radical architects of the 20th century, Le Corbusier the greatest of them all. Architecture had lost its innocence in the nineteenth century; it had become self-conscious to a degree that it had never been even when the Mannerists were at their height in 16th-century Italy. Because anything could go, it was time to stop and think. What really mattered? How should architecture best serve society and, if there was a better society to be had, what could the architect do to help jostle it along? These were questions that, sometimes intelligently and sometimes disastrously architects were to try and answer during the 20th century. Ruskin and Morris posed them; no one yet has the answers.

JOHN RUSKIN
The English writer and critic John Ruskin (1819–1900) was born in London, and tutored privately. In 1836 he went to Christ Church, Oxford, where he won the Newdigate prize for poetry. Shortly after graduating he met J. M. W. Turner and supported his painting in his book *Modern Painters* (1843–60). Along with *The Seven Lamps of Architecture* (1848) and *The Stones of Venice* (1851–53), where he championed the Gothic style, this book established him as the major art and social critic of his day. In 1869 he became the first Slade Professor Fine Art at Oxford. His letters, lectures, and essays to working men were published in collections, including, *Time and Tide* (1867).

THE RED HOUSE, BEXLEYHEATH, KENT, 1859–60
Philip Webb designed the Red House for his close friend William Morris. The house is asymetrically arranged, its style drawn from the vernacular. It took its name from the red tiles and bricks used in its construction.

The
MACHINE
AGE

THE MACHINE AGE THREW ARCHITECTS INTO
A CREATIVE MAELSTROM. NEW METHODS
OF CONSTRUCTION, NEW MATERIALS, AND NEW
PURPOSES TOOK THEM BY SURPRISE. A LARGE
NUMBER IN EUROPE AND THE US REACTED BY
RETREATING TWO STEPS BACKWARD, ONE STEP
FORWARD INTO A MAKE-BELIEVE WORLD IN WHICH
THEY TRIED TO ESCAPE FROM OR SIMPLY IGNORE THE
ONWARD MARCH OF INDUSTRY. THE ARTS & CRAFTS
MOVEMENT REPRESENTED ONE SUCH VENTURE INTO
RETRO DESIGN, ITS ARCHITECTS CELEBRATING THE
WORK OF THE KIND OF SKILLED AND GNARLED
CRAFTSMEN WHOM THEY LIKED TO THINK OF AS
SUCCESSORS TO THE GREAT CATHEDRAL BUILDERS
OF THE MIDDLE AGES. THE FLORID AND OFTEN
DECADENT ART NOUVEAU STYLE WAS ANOTHER SUCH
RETREAT, WHILE THE BRILLIANT, VEGETABLE-LIKE
DESIGNS OF ANTONI GAUDÍ OFFERED AN
ALTERNATIVE VISION OF WHAT ARCHITECTURE
COULD BE AT THE BEGINNING OF THE CENTURY THAT
WITNESSED HUMANKIND LAUNCHING ITSELF INTO
SPACE. YET IT WAS THE MIGHTY SKYSCRAPERS OF
NEW YORK AND CHICAGO THAT POINTED THE WAY
TO AN ARCHITECTURE OF MACHINE-AGE SUPREMACY.

EQUITABLE BUILDING UNDER CONSTRUCTION, NEW YORK CITY
*The Equitable Building was so vast that it deprived surrounding buildin
of light. In 1905, the year after it was built, a zoning law was passed
in New York City requiring skyscrapers to be set back from the street.*

MACHINES FOR WORKING IN

THE BUILDING STRIPPED BARE

MASS PRODUCTION

The outstanding contribution of the automotive industry to technological advance was the introduction of full-scale mass production. Henry Ford (1863–1947) revolutionized factory production with his assembly-line methods. In 1903 he and his partners formed the Ford Motor Company. His business philosophy was to reduce the unit cost and increase the volume of sales. The Model T appeared in 1908. By 1913, mass production enabled him to reduce the price to produce "a motor car for the great multitude."

OCEAN LINERS

The early years of the 20th century saw the golden age of the great transatlantic ocean liners. It was a time of great achievement for the engineers and craftsman who worked on these ships. Built at the Harland and Wolff shipyards in Belfast, White Star's *RMS Olympic* (above) was launched in October 1910 and was capable of a speed of 21 knots (24 mph).

THERE WAS AN END, even if in the great sweep of history it was really no more than a cease-fire, in the long-running Battle of the Styles. It came more or less at the end of nineteenth and the beginning of the twentieth centuries. What brought it about? Steel frames, reinforced concrete (perfected by François Hennebique in 1892), the electric lift or elevator, curtain walling, rising land prices in cities – and thus the need for ever taller buildings if developers were to make a profit. In addition, the final recognition that the buildings which emerged from these new developments looked just fine stripped of historic garb and standing proud in all their naked machine-age glory.

RAPID CHANGE

The world really did change very quickly in the three or four decades leading up to World War I (1914–18). Railways became fast, safe, and reliable; propeller-driven steamships could cross the Atlantic rapidly; the Wright brothers introduced the world to powered flight in 1903; machine guns and other new weapons changed the ugly face of war, and, above all, the mercantile and professional classes assumed power in Britain, France, and the United States and were the effective force behind crumbling thrones – elsewhere many of these were to vanish in the

carnage of World War I. Instead of churches, cathedrals, and palaces, the buildings that mattered most were now office buildings, the department store, and above all the factory. Mass production was born with Henry Ford's Model T in 1908. The first cars or automobiles had appeared in Germany in 1886 and, until Ford took up the principles of scientific management set down by the American business efficiency expert Frederick Taylor (the first of an interminable breed), it had been a handcrafted plaything for the rich. Ford's ever-increasing efficiency enabled him to more than halve the cost of the first $850 Model Ts: the era of mass private transportation had arrived.

The United States drove these new developments with a dynamism that shocked Europe. By the 1880s, it seemed that nothing could hold the US back, and by the outbreak of World War I, the land of individual rights, freedom of speech, and free enterprise was clearly the world economic leader. It was here, then, in the US, that architecture began its great break from the past. Not that it was easy. During the 1880s and 1890s architects themselves still trained in old traditions struggled to find forms for buildings that were bursting beyond the old order of columns, cornices, and pediments. We

THE BOSTON PUBLIC LIBRARY, 1887–93

The Boston Public library by McKim, Mead, &White was described as "a palace for the people." The building is of traditional construction with load-bearing walls. The main reading room has a barrel-vaulted ceiling and a richly carved limestone balcony.

see influential architects like Henry Hobson Richardson (1838–86) and McKim, Meade, & White in the design of the Marshall Field Wholesale Warehouse, Chicago (1885–87; demolished) and the Boston Public Library (1887–93) inventing a grand, muscular Neo-Romanesque style to match the scale of the buildings. Impressive but bulky, they quickly became outdated. And then, finally, we see the steel frame and the essential architecture of the twentieth century breaking through.

THE SKYSCRAPER

In 1894–95, Charles B. Atwood (1849–95), working for Daniel Burnham (1845–1912) built the 15-story Reliance Building, Chicago, perhaps the purest expression of the first generation of skyscrapers. Chicago was the spiritual home of the new architecture ever since a great fire had swept through the Windy City in 1873 and given its architects an unprecedented opportunity to build anew with new materials, techniques, and inventions. Yet it was the City of New York that made the new style world famous at the start of the new machine-age century.

RELIANCE BUILDING, CHICAGO, 1894–95
The elegant, skeletal design of the Reliance Building is based on the proportions of its fifteen-story steel frame. The building has bay windows and the spandrels are clad in a light terra-cotta.

> *"[The skyscraper] must be every inch a proud and soaring thing, rising in sheer exultation..."*
> LOUIS SULLIVAN

STEEL-FRAMED BUILDINGS

In cities such as New York and Chicago, steeply rising land values provided the incentive to build higher buildings. In response to this need a load-bearing metal framework (structurally independent of the external walling) was developed that allowed construction to a great height. The steel skeleton supported its own weight, as well as the walls and floors. The external cladding was carried by metal shelves riveted to the metal core. This change from masonry to steel reduced the weight of the building. Lightweight construction allowed bigger windows and generated large, clear internal spaces.

REACH FOR THE SKY
MANHATTAN'S SKYSCRAPERS

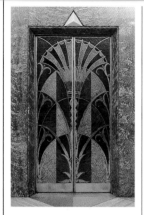

ART DECO
The dominant style in the decorative arts and architecture of the late 1920s and early 30s, Art Deco derives its name from the *Exposition Internationale des Arts Décoratifs et Industriels Modernes*, held in Paris in 1925. It is characterized by the use of luxury materials, stylized motifs, and streamlining. In architecture, Art Deco found its greatest expression in skyscrapers and movie theaters. The most notable example is the Chrysler Building, which was decorated both inside and out with Art Deco motifs. The ornamentation on the elevator doors (above) recalls the building's sunburst lantern.

FOR A QUARTER of a century the Woolworth Building was the world's tallest. It dominated the upward-rising skyline of New York and, aside from the Statue of Liberty, was the first sight visitors and immigrants to the United States saw if they came by way of the Atlantic and the eastern seaboard. And what a sight it was! A 792-foot (241-meter) tower crowned with a steep medieval roof and lantern. From the streets where it rose gracefully in a display of good civic manners, up through four successive stages, each one narrower than the last, the Woolworth Building spoke of a supremely confident, commercially driven United States.

MEDIEVAL INSPIRATION
It was designed by Cass Gilbert (1850–1934) and built between 1910 and 1913. Gilbert used all the new technology and materials available to him, yet clad his tower in a fine sheath of terra-cotta molded with Gothic details. This works well on two levels. Terra-cotta washes in rain, which means the world's first real skyscraper stays clean, and the Gothic details are there to suggest that our notion of a tower is forever set in a medieval world of knights and courtly love.

SAN GIMIGNANO, ITALY
The skyscrapers that sprang up in New York City in the early decades of the 20th century recall the 13 towers that dominate San Gimignano's picturesque skyline. Here, the towers were built by two rival noble families – the Ardinghelli (Guelf) and the Salvucci (Ghibelline) – in the 12th and 13th centuries.

Significantly, however, the Woolworth Building was a fanfare not for the wealthy, no matter how wealthy the Woolworth dynasty itself had become by 1910, but for the common man. Woolworth in the public eye meant big, cheap, and cheerful stores where everything could be bought for much less than a fistful of dollars; a few nickels and dimes would do. The lofty new architecture of the twentieth century was thus rooted in the commonplace.

Over the next few decades the design of these new versions of the merchant princes' towers that had tried to outreach one another in medieval Italian towns matured as they reached for the sky. Opened in 1930, the Chrysler Building (by William Van Alen, 1883–1954) outreached the Woolworth Building. Within a year, however, it too had been convincingly overtaken by the Empire State Building (1929–31) designed by the firm of Shreve, Lamb and Harmon. The two buildings have long been considered the

WOOLWORTH BUILDING, NEW YORK, 1910–13
Although Gilbert claimed that his design was based on secular models, his choice of the Gothic style for the Woolworth Building earned it the nickname "Cathedral of Commerce."

zenith of the skyscraper design. They are not simply very tall, but have a grace that belies their breathtaking scale, and although they are undeniably show-off buildings, they share the same good manners displayed by the earlier Woolworth Building. Both rise from bases that make them a part of the streetscape; the towers are set back (or "zoned") and rise, again like the Woolworth Building, in diminishing stages and are topped by spires that truly vanish into the clouds on winter and stormy days. Both are decorated, but not overly so, with smart Art Deco details and make use of new weatherproof materials like stainless steel, as well as chromium plating. Both look as good as new nearly three-quarters of a century on from their construction. They are also very strong, as the Empire State Building proved one stormy day in 1945 when an Army Air Corps bomber crashed into the 79th floor.

TALL STORIES

Both are hugely popular tourist attractions as well as thriving commercial complexes, and have achieved a mythical status over the years fueled by films like *King Kong* (see right) and *Bladerunner*. The close relationship between the two buildings was amusingly illustrated in a painting by the Dutch architect Rem Koolhaas (see p.224) for his book *Delirious New York* (1978): the Chrysler and the

EMPIRE STATE BUILDING, NEW YORK, 1929–31
The ziggurat profiles of the New York skyscrapers were partly determined by the 1916 zoning laws. These required the buildings to be progressively stepped back, admitting light and air to the lower levels and to the streets below.

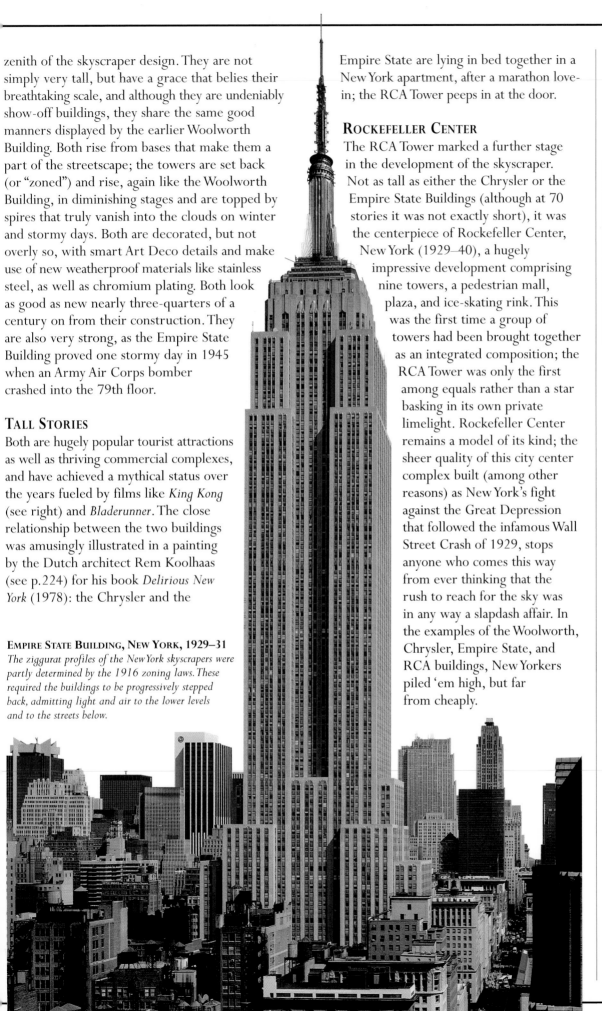

Empire State are lying in bed together in a New York apartment, after a marathon love-in; the RCA Tower peeps in at the door.

ROCKEFELLER CENTER

The RCA Tower marked a further stage in the development of the skyscraper. Not as tall as either the Chrysler or the Empire State Buildings (although at 70 stories it was not exactly short), it was the centerpiece of Rockefeller Center, New York (1929–40), a hugely impressive development comprising nine towers, a pedestrian mall, plaza, and ice-skating rink. This was the first time a group of towers had been brought together as an integrated composition; the RCA Tower was only the first among equals rather than a star basking in its own private limelight. Rockefeller Center remains a model of its kind; the sheer quality of this city center complex built (among other reasons) as New York's fight against the Great Depression that followed the infamous Wall Street Crash of 1929, stops anyone who comes this way from ever thinking that the rush to reach for the sky was in any way a slapdash affair. In the examples of the Woolworth, Chrysler, Empire State, and RCA buildings, New Yorkers piled 'em high, but far from cheaply.

ICONIC IMAGERY
Since its opening by President Hoover in May 1931, the Empire State Building has captured the public imagination. Its status as an icon of popular culture was ensured as early as 1933 by the classic film *King Kong*. The still above shows the giant ape on top of the skyscraper. The helpless Fay Wray clings to the base of the mast tower, while Kong fights vainly against attack by fighter planes.

"...the Cathedral of Commerce"
REV. S. PARKES CADMAN, AT THE OPENING OF THE WOOLWORTH BUILDING

FRANK LLOYD WRIGHT

MONSTER AND GENIUS

HIS WIFE AND CHILDREN were murdered. His house burned down twice, but the hotel he built in Tokyo survived the devastating earthquake of 1926. He ran away to France with a mistress. His career spanned 70 years. His autobiography was a bestseller. His life was turned into legend in Ayn Rand's *The Fountainhead*. He designed some of the most radical, and memorable buildings of all time. He was Frank Lloyd Wright (1867–1959), monster and genius, best known for his suburban homes in the Chicago suburb of Oak Park, Illinois early in his career, the ingenious and much published Fallingwater (1936–39), Bear Run, Pennsylvania, and the controversial Solomon R. Guggenheim Museum (1943–59), New York City.

Wright trained briefly as an engineer and worked with Louis Sullivan before setting up on his own in Chicago in the 1890s. He had built a home for himself in Oak Park in 1889, and this became the prototype of many such houses for Chicago's newly wealthy. Wright claimed to have invented the open-plan interior, and perhaps he did. Certainly, this was to be one of the threads running throughout the many buildings – houses, ambitious and modest, churches, offices, and museums – he designed

FRANK LLOYD WRIGHT
Although he lived to be 90, it was not until the final 20 years of his life that Wright consistently received major commissions.

over his long career. Such houses put an end to the idea of the home as a sequence of separate boxes; they made space flow.

Although modern in this sense and in their use of the latest developments in heating, lighting, and domestic gadgetry, Wright's houses were built of local natural materials. Although unafraid of new technology – he loved fast cars and in the 1930s drove a Cord, one of the most advanced automobiles of its day – he liked to get close to nature and was a brilliant manipulator of daylight as well as interior space. The most adventurous of his early houses is Robie House, Chicago (1909–10). Here, family rooms flow as they might in a Pullman train or ocean liner, gathered under sweeping horizontal roofs and provided with seamless rows of windows. Even so, the house is adorned with Wright's quirky take on Arts and Crafts décor and detailing, which makes it seem fussier than the clarity of its overall form and plan suggest.

NATURE AND ARCHITECTURE

His most famous house, Fallingwater (1936–39), brings Modern architecture and nature together in a poetic and convincing manner. The house comprises several concrete trays jutting out over a masonry core sited over a waterfall. The way the rooms are arranged on, around, and through these trays is quite magical and very clever. Interior and exterior merge as they do in the best traditional Japanese houses, which Wright would have known firsthand; the overall effect is one of Modern man living in harmony rather than triumphing over nature. Fallingwater was an expensive house, yet in the same decade, Wright experimented

FALLINGWATER, BEAR RUN, PENNSYLVANIA, 1936–39
This residence is perhaps Wright's greatest integration of architecture and nature. The architect commended its occupants to "not simply look at the waterfalls, but to live with them."

SOLOMON R. GUGGENHEIM MUSEUM, NEW YORK, 1943–59
Wright's intention was to create a structure where forms flowed into one another in a "quiet, unbroken wave," thus ceasing to rely on the post-and-beam constructions of earlier periods.

with and built a number of what he called Usonian houses; these were made up from easy-to-assemble, prefabricated wood sandwich panels designed to be erected on a simple concrete base. Wright may have been supremely arrogant and cocksure, but he was never aloof from the needs of those struggling to make ends meet.

At the same time as he built Fallingwater, he designed one of the most unusual and special corporate headquarters yet seen. This was the Johnson Wax Administration Building, Racine, Wisconsin (1936–39; tower added later). The core of the building is an open-plan office in which clerks and typists worked at Wright-designed desks (like Pugin, he liked to design every last detail of his buildings himself); the glazed roof is held up by a forest of slim, yet immensely strong, concrete columns that mushroom out at the top. If Martians built, this is how you imagine they would design columns. Not surprisingly, Wright's buildings from this time became the source for many science fiction illustrations, notably in the colorful pages of the English boy's comic *The Eagle* (founded, 1951), where Dan Dare, Pilot of the Future, took off from a Space Fleet headquarters that looked as if Wright had designed it. One disturbing feature of the streamlined, space-age Johnson Wax Building, no matter how brilliant it was in other ways, was the fact that those clerks and typists had no view out; all the better, one supposes, to stop them from daydreaming in scientifically costed office hours.

WRIGHT'S LEGACY

At the same time, Wright built himself a summer house, Taliesin West, in the desert beyond Phoenix, Arizona. This long, low home was designed as a kind of crystalline structure emerging as naturally as possible from the dry and boundless landscape of which it was so much a part.

It also served as Wright's atelier where he taught generations of young architects to follow in his footsteps, and it may be seen as the architect's enduring legacy.

His later works include the weird and wonderful H.C. Pirie Tower, Bartlesville, Oklahoma (completed 1956) – a tall concrete office with its cantilevered structure based on that of a tree – and the highly idiosyncratic Guggenheim Museum, New York, commissioned in 1943 and completed, after much wrangling with the city authorities, six months after Wright's death in 1959. Here, Wright broke away entirely from the conventional museum format: instead of a sequence of individual galleries, he came up with one continuous flow of spaces, gained by a spiral ramp ascending the inward tapering walls of a giant, inward-looking and top-lit concrete shell. This was, in one sense, the Pantheon reinvented for the mid-twentieth century. It is a masterpiece of sorts, even though it willfully subverts the streetscape it blooms in and requires visitors to look at paintings while standing at an angle on the ramp.

The last project to bear Wright's name, the Marin County Civic Center, California (completed 1964) shows a descent into kitsch. Like an alien spaceship crash-landed into a hillside, it is big and gimmicky, and more razzmatazz than substance. Despite Taliesin West, Wright's adventure in architecture failed to outlive the Grand Old Man.

"*Every great architect…must be a great original interpreter of his time, his day, his age*"

FRANK LLOYD WRIGHT

ARTS & CRAFTS
SPECTACULAR VERNACULAR

I AM WRITING THIS BOOK in England, one eye on a computer screen, the other on the sensational views of an Iron Age fort in front of me, the largely unspoiled farmlands of Herefordshire and the not-so-distant hills of the Welsh borders to my right. This romantic view is framed by a band of low windows, shaded from the sun by deep eaves projecting from a steep-tiled roof topped with tall chimneys, and supported by deep, sloping buttresses emerging from white, roughcast walls. The house is Perrycroft, Colwall, Herefordshire (1893–95), a handsome, lovingly built Arts and Crafts house designed by Charles Francis Annesley Voysey (1857–1941).

Although Voysey's style is very much his own, it belongs to a spirit of the times and a way of making buildings that is nevertheless unified by strong and passionately held beliefs. I can feel these at Perrycroft. The house is a touch quaint, yet clearly a strong reaction to the fustiness and fussiness of much late Victorian design. It boasts a free-flowing plan (Voysey was as quick off the mark here as Frank Lloyd Wright), gloriously light interiors and a sense of harmony and well-being expressed in the sheer solidity of its structure and in superb hand-crafted details – window latches, door handles, fireplaces. It is what Arts and Crafts architects would have called an "honest" house. It is entirely free from gratuitous decoration, is wonderfully easy to live in, and a delight to come home to. Although

idiosyncratic, in the sense that it is clearly the work of a particular and special mind, it feels as if it belongs to the spectacular landscape it adorns. It was Voysey's first major commission; he did his client proud. Voysey was a tiny, birdlike man, high-minded and religious, who designed his own clothes – blue suits without cuffs or lapels so as to gather no dust. He wrote a fascinating essay, *Individuality* (1915), and, aside from being a fascinating individual, was a great fan of Pugin (he disapproved of Morris' strident socialism) and the designer of furniture, fabrics, and wallpaper.

TRADITIONAL BUILDING CRAFTS
Encouraged by Ruskin and Morris, the architects of the English Arts and Crafts movement abhorred the machine age and detested the use of steel frames and reinforced concrete that had just come into their pseudo-medieval view. They wanted English homes (churches, village halls, and pubs too) built by honest English craftsworkers, descendants of the cathedral builders. Everything must be made by hand. Only local materials should be used. Forms of construction must be honestly expressed. This was a new style for a new client – well-to-do middle class patrons steeped in the poetry of Tennyson and keen on the paintings of the Pre-Raphaelites. For them, Arts and Crafts houses offered an escape from the harsh reality of industrial England.

THE PRE-RAPHAELITE BROTHERHOOD
Established in 1848, the Pre-Raphaelites were a group of artists who reacted against the Neo-classical conventions of the day. They called themselves the Pre-Raphaelite Brotherhood to indicate that they were inspired by medieval and Renaissance art up to the time of the Italian painter Raphael. The nucleus of the group was formed by three fellow students at the Royal Academy – John Everett Millais, William Holman Hunt, and Dante Gabriel Rossetti. The group were also influenced by the poetry of John Keats and Lord Tennyson. Rossetti was a distinguished poet as well as a painter. The painting above is his *The Damsel of Sanct Grael* (1857).

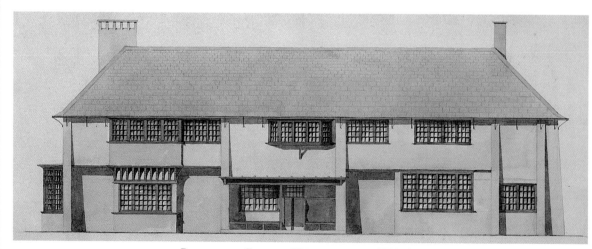

PERRYCROFT, COLWALL, HEREFORDSHIRE, 1893–95

Voysey's Perrycroft is situated in the Malvern Hills. The house is based on an L-shaped plan and has a long horizontal roof line and a wide front door. The dining room, smoking room, and drawing room are arranged along the south side of the main wing.

DEANERY GARDEN, SONNING, BERKSHIRE, 1899–1902
Lutyens' Deanery Garden was built for the founder of Country Life *magazine, Edward Hudson. The long roof is broken by the hipped bay of the hall window and the prominent chimney stack.*

There was no fixed style. Voysey's white houses were very different, for example, from those of E. S. Prior (1852–1932) which are built of materials excavated from their sites and take Arts and Crafts logic to an extreme. The Barn, Exmouth, Devon (1896–97) and Home Place, Holt, Norfolk (1904–06) are prime examples of his eccentric and determined style. These ideas were expressed more subtly and smoothly in the supremely competent English country houses of Edwin Lutyens (1869–1944). These ranged greatly in style and character, although all his early houses made use of local materials and played intelligently with vernacular building design. So Marsh Court, Stockbridge, Hampshire (1901–04), the lovely white chalk house he built for Herbert Johnson, a stockbroker retired at 50 with half a million pounds to his name, was very different from Deanery Garden, Sonning, Berkshire (1899–1902), the imposing red-brick house built for Edward Hudson, the founder of *Country Life* magazine and the man who introduced Lutyens to Johnson.

EQUIVALENT MOVEMENTS

Beyond the refined world of the English country house, the Arts and Crafts movement was to affect the design of the common or stock suburban home in the 20th century, that of early local authority housing developments and homes both grand and humble across what was the British empire and in parts of Central Europe, notably Vienna (the Viennese Secession, see p.166, had close links with Arts and Crafts practitioners). In the United States, McKim, Mead, & White perfected their Shingle Style in the 1880s with such splendid clapboard (shingle) designs as the William Low House, Bristol, Rhode Island (1887–88), and Charles S. (1868–1957) and Henry M. (1870–1954) Greene worked in an American Arts and Crafts idiom in Northern California.

In Scandinavia, contemporaries of Voysey, Prior, and Lutyens reworked old traditions in a bid to reassert their national characters through architecture. Spain – Catalonia to be more precise – had Gaudí (see p.168–69). And Scotland had the singular talent of Charles Rennie Mackintosh (1868–1928), whose impressive Glasgow School of Art (1897–1909) showed how history could be interpreted in radically new ways. If the architects of the Arts and Crafts movement had scraped away the excesses of Victorian design, they were not, as has been suggested many times, precursors of the Modern Movement. At heart, they were still Victorians and their dreams delved into a distant and fictional past when England was "merrie" and the Industrial Revolution, with its steam, steel, and reinforced concrete, was unimaginable.

CHARLES RENNIE MACKINTOSH
The work of Scottish architect, designer, and artist Charles Rennie Mackintosh (1868–1928) greatly influenced modern European architecture and design. As an architect, Mackintosh's masterpiece is the Glasgow School of Art (see below). He was also famous for his interior decoration and furniture design, often in association with his wife Margaret Macdonald (1865–1933).

GLASGOW SCHOOL OF ART, 1897–1909
The main studios are arranged along the north façade (above). Additional teaching spaces and offices are on the east wing, with a lecture theatre, library, and studio spaces on the west façade.

ART NOUVEAU & SECESSION

CURLS AND SWIRLS

SAMUEL BING opened his shop, Art Nouveau, in Paris in 1895, giving its name to a short-lived but highly expressive style that was perhaps better suited to interior décor and illustrations than it was to architecture. Yet, Art Nouveau was an attempt, very different in spirit from that of the English Arts and Crafts or the Shingle Style of the US East Coast, to find a new look for a new era. It always looked decadent and it is hard to look at say one of the surviving Art Nouveau entrances to the Paris Métro (by Hector Guimard, 1867–1942) and not think of the nightmarish erotic drawings of Aubrey Beardsley or the stories of Oscar Wilde. Used as a form of decoration in fin-de-siècle theaters, shops, restaurants, and cafes, Art Nouveau was translated into the modern, solid, and serious realm of architecture with relatively little success. However, the Hotel Gellert, Budapest (1912–18) stands out as a grandiose exception, while on a more subtle scale there are the Brussels houses of Victor Horta (1861–1947). The Hotel Tassel (1892–93) is a fascinating home, a thing of richly mosaiced floors and painted walls centered on a highly decorated stairwell which makes a refined play on the vegetable and flower forms that characterize Art Nouveau. It looks far too precious to live in, but this, my dears, was a precious moment in the development of modern aesthetics, the age of *The Yellow Book*, of the sipping of absinthe, the smoking of cheroots, of silk dressing gowns, and the coming of the Ballet Russe.

NEW FORMS

The flowery forms of Art Nouveau decoration can be seen to delightful and memorable effect on the façade of the Majolica House, Vienna (1898–99), a six-story apartment building designed by Otto Wagner (1841–1918). Wagner was a substantial architect who was professor at the time of the Academy of Fine Arts in Vienna and who taught all the young bloods who formed the Secession, a further attempt to find

EMILE GALLÉ

Born in Nancy, the French designer and glassmaker Emile Gallé (1846–1904) was a leading initiator of the Art Nouveau style. He studied philosophy, botany, and drawing, later learning glassmaking. By 1874 he was running a glass workshop, which grew to employ 300 workers, as well as managing what had been his father's pottery company. He developed the use of deeply colored glasses in heavy masses, often layered in several thicknesses and carved or etched to form plant motifs.

HECTOR GUIMARD

The architect and designer Hector Guimard (1867–1942) was born in Lyons, France. Influenced by the ideas of Viollet-le-Duc and the architecture of Victor Horta, he filled his designs with fluid, curvilinear lines that became synonymous with the Art Nouveau. Several entrance structures for the Paris Métro (1898–1901) made from cast iron in plantlike forms are his best known works.

HOTEL TASSEL, BRUSSELS, 1892–93
The staircase of Horta's Hotel Tassel has sinuous iron supports and tendril-like floral iron ornamentation. Horta also uses vegetal shapes in the design of banisters, wallpaper, and mosaics.

a new architecture for what was seen as a new age. Among these young bloods starting out in the Vienna of Sigmund Freud and Egon Schiele were Josef Maria Olbrich (1867–1908) and Josef Hoffman (1870–1956). Olbrich designed the Secession Building (1897–98), Vienna, a clean-cut, white art gallery, almost but not quite Modern in its sensibility, adorned with a sphere, or globe, wrapped around with gilded laurel wreaths.

Hoffman's most ambitious work was the Palais Stoclet, Brussels (1905–11), a luscious house made up of white cubes and rectangles ascending towards a central tower decorated with statues; the feel is cinematic, almost Art Deco. The interiors are light and bright, yet richly decorated in parts with the gilded artworks of the painter Gustav Klimt. One of Hoffman's enduring creations was the Wiener Werkstatte, a workshop that produced furniture (still in production) and decorative objects for Secession buildings.

Another of Wagner's gifted pupils was Adolf Loos (1870–1933), famous for his book *Ornament and Crime* (1908). Here Loos equates unnecessary

decoration with the workings of not just the decadent, but the criminal mind. He went to inspect prisoners in Vienna's jails and found (well he would, wouldn't he?) that their skins were mostly ornamented with tattoos; therefore, although the logic here is rather thin, ornament is a crime. Well, Wagner thought so anyway. Like Voysey he preferred cuffless suits, admired the cult of the English gentleman, and was uncommonly well traveled. He spent three years in the United States as a manual worker, getting up to speed on the new architecture emerging in New York and Chicago.

The results of his investigations were a stream of pamphlets and ultra-refined houses. The houses are remarkable both for their wilfully plain exteriors and their opulent interiors. But, opulent only in the sense that they made extensive and costly use of rich materials – marbles, brass, bronze, stone. Loos believed that all the richness of a house could be realized in flat surfaces. The houses are legendary; perhaps the best are the Scheu House, Vienna (1912), and the Muller House, Prague (1931).

GUSTAV KLIMT

The Austrian painter Gustav Klimt (1862–1918) founded the Vienna Secession in 1897, a group of architects and artists with a highly decorative style similar to that of Art Nouveau. Klimt is famous for his portraits, characterized by flat, decorative patterns of color and gold leaf. Among his decorative commissions were the murals he designed for the dining room of the Palais Stoclet, designed by his friend Josef Hoffmann.

PALAIS STOCLET, BRUSSELS, 1905–11
The composition of Hoffman's Palais Stoclet is balanced, but asymmetrical, the main points of emphasis being the stair-tower and bow windows. The lavish cladding is white marble framed by geometrical bronze moldings.

ANTONI GAUDÍ
SAINT ANTONI OF BARCELONA

FROM 1998, ATTEMPTS were made by Catholic clergy in Barcelona to canonize Antoni Gaudí (1852–1926), possibly the most pious and certainly one of the most original architectural talents of all time. St. Antoni, as he may yet be (he needs two miracles to his name before the Pope can declare him a saint, yet surely all his mature buildings are themselves miraculous), gave up all other work late in life so that he could devote himself exclusively to his still far from finished masterpiece, the Expiatory Church of the Holy Family, Barcelona (the "Sagrada Familia"; 1882 onward). There is no other building like this tall bed of stone

ANTONI GAUDÍ
The son of a metalworker, Gaudí never married and in the later years of his life lived with his niece.

vegetation anywhere in the world. Gaudí lived austerely in the crypt of his building. One day he stepped back to look up at the strange tower that soared above the church's Nativity porch (three more were later added) and was run over by a tram. Hurried to the hospital, the old man was taken for a tramp. A few days later, however, Barcelona came to a halt and his vast funeral procession snaked slowly through the city. Then as now, Gaudí has been the city's patron saint whether or not the Pope agrees.

Gaudí's talent emerged with the rise of Modernismo, an artistic movement in Catalonia that was part and parcel of the region's attempt to reestablish a local identity that Castillian Madrid had done its best to stamp on for several hundred years. It led in one direction to the whimsy of Art Nouveau, but in another to the extraordinary and unprecedented designs of Gaudí. His first major work, the Palau Güell (1885–89; all his key works are in or very near Barcelona) was odd from its twin parabolic gateways in – they are more like the entrance to a cave than to a grand city-center house. Inside, the main room is a fantastic cavern, complete with organ, minstrel's gallery, and a blue tiled dome.

THE DIVINE PARABOLA

The Park Güell (1900–14) was an attempt to build a garden suburb high above, but near, the city center. In the event only two houses were built (Gaudí lived in one before he moved to the crypt of the Sagrada Familia), but we are left with a glorious, snaking park, the best part of which is what was intended to be an open-fronted market hall, its roof held up by a conga dance of Greek Doric columns. The roof is capped with a colorful parapet decorated with deliberately broken glazed ceramic tiles. People sit and chat on benches built into the parapet walls. This is a magical place.

THE SAGRADA FAMILIA, 1882 ONWARD
After Gaudí's death in 1926, work on the church was continued by his associates. Some of the original design models and plans were destroyed during the Spanish Civil War, but the project was resumed in 1954.

The two urban apartment houses Gaudí designed, Casa Batlló (1904–6) and Casa Milà (1905–10), are again like nothing else. The former is known as the House of Bones, its façades are like the skin of some scaly, horny lizard; balconies appear to be made of the bones of mythical creatures and even appear to have teeth. Odd. Odd, too, the elephantlike skin of Casa Milà (known as *La Pedrera*, the Stone Quarry). Behind those undulating walls are flats arranged around a circular central courtyard; you will look in vain to find a straight line inside or outside one of these highly prized if unusual homes. Weird sculptural chimneys ornament the roof of the building.

MOSAIC IN CASA MILA
The surfaces of Gaudí's buildings were decorated with patterned brickwork, ceramics, and florid metalwork.

Strangest of all Gaudí's buildings is the church of Santa Coloma de Cervello (1898–incomplete), centerpiece of the Güell industrial colony (a Catalan version of Bournville or Port Sunlight – see p.145). The roof of the crypt is supported by stone columns that lean over at what appear to be crazy angles; the pews, also designed by the architect, follow suit. This is as strange a space as was ever shaped by an architect; it is also quite wonderful. Gaudí's work was unique. It is extreme, yet his structures are logical and his apparently weird geometry is rooted in nature. He was trying somehow to nurture an architecture that connected humans both to God and to nature. He is a saint in all but name.

"*The straight line belongs to man, the curve to God*"

ANTONI GAUDÍ

CASA MILÀ, BARCELONA, 1905–10
The undulating forms of this apartment building, with its cast-iron balconies, resemble the curved motifs of Art Nouveau.

BRAVE NEW WORLD

THE END OF WORLD WAR I MARKED HUGE CHANGES IN THE WAY ARCHITECTURE WAS EXPERIENCED. IN THE SOVIET UNION, FASCIST ITALY, AND NAZI GERMANY, NEWLY CONSTITUTED TOTALITARIAN POLITICAL REGIMES USED ARCHITECTURE AS A FORM OF THREE-DIMENSIONAL PROPAGANDA, A CULTURAL SLEDGEHAMMER. SOCIALIST GOVERNMENTS TOO EMPLOYED ARCHITECTURE AT BOTH A NATIONAL AND LOCAL LEVEL — MODERN AS OPPOSED TO NEO-CLASSICAL (ITALY AND GERMANY) AND SOCIAL REALIST (THE USSR UNDER JOSEPH STALIN). AS EUROPEAN SOCIETY POLARIZED INTO HARD-LINE LEFT AND RIGHT, ARCHITECTURE FOLLOWED. WITH MUCH OF THE REST OF THE WORLD UNDER THE YOKE OF EUROPEAN EMPIRES, THESE STYLES OF ARCHITECTURE WERE SHIPPED ABROAD. AFTER WORLD WAR II, THE US TOOK UP THE MANTLE OF ARCHITECTURAL PIONEER AND THE NEW, MIESIAN STYLE THAT FOLLOWED SET THE TONE FOR AN ARCHITECTURE REPRESENTING A FORM OF DEMOCRACY UNDERPINNED BY CORPORATE CAPITALISM. ALL OTHER STYLISTIC MOVEMENTS, NO MATTER HOW COLORFUL, WERE TO PLAY SECOND FIDDLE TO THIS DOMINANT CULTURE, WORLDWIDE.

OPERA HOUSE, SYDNEY
Jørn Utzon's stunning design, built between 1957–73, is a mixture of abstraction and naturalism: the sails that rise into the sky resemble the boat sails of the harbor, but also express the building's aspirational quality.

REVOLUTIONARY RUSSIA
COMMUNAL ARCHITECTURE

UNDER THE COMMUNIST reign of Vladimir Ilyich Lenin, Joseph Stalin, and their successors, the geographical unity of what had been the Russian Empire survived more or less intact until the rapid decline and fall of the Soviet Union from 1989. The architecture that pervaded the pre-revolutionary Russian empire, from the Baltic to the Bering Straits via the Black Sea, and which had been handed down as from on high in Moscow and St. Petersburg, had all too often been heavy-handed Classicism, interspersed here and there with bursts of National Romanticism and even Art Nouveau. From the late 1920s, with Stalin installed in power as a new tsar in all but name, the newly christened Union of Soviet Socialist Republics, was a brutal, centralized tyranny with heavy-handed new architecture to match. While there were gems amongst the dross – the wedding-cake towers of Moscow University (1949–53) by Rudnev et al and the many unforgettable stations of the Moscow Metro – by the time of the Great Patriotic War (1941–45), Soviet architecture had declined into a generally sad state of affairs.

There was, however, a brief and exotic flowering of genuinely revolutionary architecture between 1919 and 1930 that has continued to inspire architects such as Zaha Hadid, Daniel Libeskind (see pp.220–23), and others at the beginning of the twenty-first century. The work of revolutionary Soviet Modernists was characterized by a collective love of breaking the grid of conventional buildings by the intrusion of sudden diagonal or spiraling elements, by a daring use of giant, sloganeering graphics, by dramatic intersections and even collisions of the various parts of willfully abstract buildings. This was architecture as Soviet propaganda, of liberation from bourgeois norms, a way of building as shocking as the new wave of Soviet cinema and graphic design.

NEW STRUCTURES

The most powerful and best remembered of the early Soviet designs was the vertiginous steel spiral Monument to the Third Communist International (1919) designed by the artist Vladimir Tatlin (1885–1953). But the first sight most outsiders saw of the new spirit in Soviet architecture was the Soviet pavilion at the 1925 Art Deco exhibition, Paris. Designed by Konstantin Melnikov (1890–1974), this was a cleverly "deconstructed" rectangular structure made of red, black, and gray timber and shot through with a diagonal stair. The entrance was, of course, topped by a dramatic hammer and sickle motif. Melnikov also built the one and only private house allowed in Moscow at the time. This was his own home and studio (1927–29), a bizarre circular tower pierced with elongated honeycomb pattern windows. The interior layout is equally odd. Luckily the house survived and is still

MELNIKOV'S STUDIO AND HOUSE, MOSCOW, 1927–29
Melnikov's house and studio consisted of two interlocking cylinders, one taller than the other. The building is made up of 200 hexagonal "modules"; 60 of them are windows and the other 140 are filled in with brick.

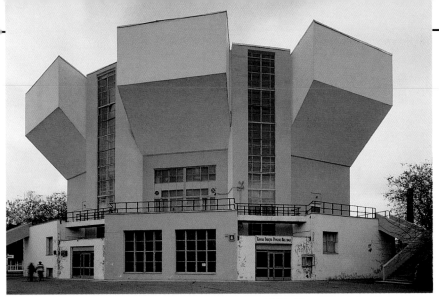

RUSAKOV CLUB, MOSCOW, 1927–28
The main auditorium of Melnikov's club for municipal employees can be extended into the three partitioned sections which are cantilevered off the back of the building.

lived in by the architect's son in the ultra-capitalist Moscow of the twenty-first century. The only other private houses were traditional "dachas" built as rural retreats for members of the Commuinist Party élite.

More importantly, Melnikov was also responsible for the development of a series of highly distinctive workers' clubs for political education and training in Moscow. He designed the rather aggressive Rusakov Club for employees of the Moscow City Soviet (1927–28). Echoes of this important building could be found in the design of conference centers and even motels throughout the Soviet Union built well into the 1970s. An alternative style was set by Ilia Golosov (1883–1945) with the Zuev Club for Moscow tram workers (1927–29), which boasts a superb glass stair tower at one end that appears to both anchor the long building and to turn it around the corner of the street. Who would commission and design such radical architecture for municipal workers in the Moscow, London, or New York of the 2000s?

NEW FORMS

Equally important, along with factory workers' kitchens and cafeterias, were new forms of collective housing. The most important of these was that built for employees of the Finance Commisariat (Narkomfin) Moscow (1928–30) by Moisei Ginzburg (1892–1946). This brick megastructure (it was rendered in white stucco) was a major influence on Le Corbusier's much later l'Unité d'Habitation, Marseilles (see p.183). Corbu not only visited Moscow at this time, but also entered the competition held between 1931 and 1933 to design a new Soviet parliamentary

building (Palace of Soviets), and he built the Tsentrosoyuz office building here (1928–36). The Ginzberg complex was designed around communal facilities (cooking, eating, washing) and was an experiment in collective living at a time when, to well-meaning outsiders at least, there was no obvious indication that the Soviet Union was about to be stripped of its revolutionary idealism as Stalin's grip on the former Russian empire tightened. Although radical new designs just about made it into the 1930s, the Stalin-backed school of Socialist Realism in art, music, and architecture stopped its development pretty much at once. In 1932, a decree was issued that abolished individual architectural practices; in future all architectural work would be organized through the Union of Soviet Architects. The revolutionary dream was officially over.

COLLECTIVE HOUSING FOR NARKOMFIN, MOSCOW, 1928–30
In contrast to Melnikov's flamboyant forms, the Union of Contemporary Architects (OSA) believed that the structure of their buildings should be determined by the residents' living patterns.

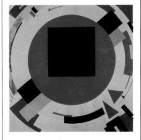

EL LISSITSKY
Born in Smolensk in 1890, Lissitsky first studied engineering in Germany and in 1919 returned to Russia, where Marc Chagall appointed him teacher at the revolutionary school of art in Vitebsk. There he was much influenced by the painter Malevich, founder of the Suprematist movement. He worked as a painter, typographer, and designer, becoming professor at the state art school in Moscow, working on a series of abstract paintings, *Proun* (see above). Later he moved to Germany, meeting Lásló Moholy-Nagy, who in his teaching at the Bauhaus took up many of Lissitsky's ideas on painting and mass communications. These were to have a major effect both in the US and Europe. Lissitsky died in Moscow in 1941.

"From each according to his abilities, to each according to his needs"
KARL MARX

THE BAUHAUS
RATIONAL DESIGN

THE BAUHAUS WAS TRULY a legend in its own brief and self-consciously designed life (1919–33). What was it? A combination at first of a German academy of fine arts dovetailed with a school of arts and crafts under the directorship of the architect Walter Gropius (1883–1969). There had been a widespread feeling in Germany before World War I that the world of the arts and crafts should be allied with that of industry to raise the quality of German industrial design.

One of the architects most involved in the discussion was Peter Behrens (1868–1940) who not only designed the AEG Turbine Factory, Berlin (1908–09), but also shaped many of its products, including electric fans and smoothing irons. One of his assistants (who for a brief period also included Le Corbusier and Ludwig Mies van der Rohe) was Gropius. Gropius' ultimate mission was to bring together artists, craftsworkers, and architects to recreate the world of medieval cathedral builders, but in a modern context.

The name Bauhaus (building house) was a sophisticated play on words. On the one hand it recalled the medieval *Bauhütte* (mason's lodge), and on the other it reflected the fact that Gropius and his colleagues wished to tackle the problem of rehousing in modern buildings the millions of people, most of them poor, made homeless by the destruction of World War I.

ART AND TECHNOLOGY UNITED

Gropius' fellow teachers were an extraordinary bunch. At first, the most influential was the increasingly mystical Swiss artist Johannes Itten (1888–1969). Itten, who looked like a monk and practiced yoga and vegetarianism, introduced such talents as the painters Oskar Schlemmer (1888–1943) and Paul Klee (1879–1940) to the Bauhaus in its first home at Weimar. He resigned, however, when the Dutch artist and Bauhaus teacher Theo van Doesburg (see pp.176–77) succeeded in making the school's courses immediately practical. This was a response to the Neue Sachlichkeit (New Objectivity) movement fashionable in Germany at the time. This was not the time to be mystical, but to join the engineer and the technician in shaping a truly Modern and functional world. From 1927 the Bauhaus began to teach architecture in earnest, and schemes

AEG TURBINE FACTORY, BERLIN, 1908–09
In his best-known work for the AEG (German Electricity Company), Behrens made a powerful statement about modern industry and production. The factory's classically inspired appearance lends it the character of a temple to industry.

FAGUS FACTORY, ALFELD-AN-DER-LEINE, GERMANY, 1911

In their design for the Fagus shoe-last factory, Walter Gropius and Adolf Meyer (1881–1929) introduced a style that was to set the architectural aesthetic for factories worldwide. The brick, glass, and steel building was not only elegant, but functional and Modern.

PAUL KLEE

Through both his art and his teaching, the Swiss-born painter Paul Klee (b.1879) was an important influence in 20th-century art. Trained at the Munich Academy, he later toured Italy and visited Paris. In 1911, he met Wassily Kandinsky (1866–1944), who persuaded him to take part in the second Blaue Reiter exhibition. Both artists were invited to teach at the Bauhaus (from 1921). It was here that Klee wrote his seminal work, Pedagogical Sketchbook (1925). Forced to leave Germany by the Nazis in 1933, he returned to Switzerland, where he died in 1940.

were produced for prefabricated mass housing and designs for ideal, low-cost homes were mocked up and exhibited.

This tendency toward functionalism was taken to an extreme after 1928 when Gropius resigned to concentrate on his architectural practice and the Swiss architect Hannes Meyer (1889–1954) took over as director. Meyer was very much a living caricature of the humorless functionalist; one can easily imagine him as the model for Professor Otto Silenus, the young architect in Evelyn Waugh's first novel *Decline and Fall* (1928) whose mission is to eradicate the human element from architecture. Meyer was persuaded to resign in 1930. Mies van der Rohe took over and the last two years of the Bauhaus were largely given over to the study of new architecture, although courses in graphic design, ceramics, painting, and metalwork continued.

THE BAUHAUS LEGACY

The Bauhaus had moved into Walter Gropius' fine new ultra-modern, purpose-built quarters at Dessau in 1926; now it was forced to move to Berlin. In 1933, Hitler came to power. The Bauhaus was seen as hotbed of decadent art and socialism and was closed, by order. This, however, was not the end of the story. Those who had taught or been taught at the Bauhaus became cultural refugees in the 1930s. Some, like Gropius, the artist László Moholy-Nagy (1895–1946), who

had replaced Itten, and the brilliant architect-designer Marcel Breuer (1902–81) went briefly to London before emigrating to the United States.

It was in the States that many Bauhaus talents were reunited, and after the arrival of Mies in 1937, the US enjoyed much of the cream of Modern Movement talent in painting, industrial design, and architecture. In fact, from the 1940s, this essentially practical country took the lead for the first time in both architectural theory and design. The Nazis managed to ditch or lose Germany's finest talent, as they had in science and engineering, as in music, art, and movies.

BAUHAUS BUILDINGS, DESSAU, GERMANY, 1925–26

The removal of the Bauhaus from Weimar to Dessau in 1926 provided Gropius with the perfect opportunity to give physical form to his philosophy – the synthesis of all the arts in a building.

MASS EUROPEAN HOUSING
REVOLUTIONARY EXPERIMENTS

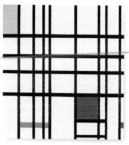

PIET MONDRIAN

Born in Holland in1872, Mondrian was one of the most important figures in 20th-century abstract art. He studied abstraction and developed his own theories about the horizontal-vertical axes. In 1917, along with Theo van Doesburg, he founded the De Stijl group. His geometrical, abstract paintings – such as *Composition with Red, Yellow, and Blue* (c.1937–42; see above) – employed the three primary colors and black, white, and gray. Mondrian's almost ascetic style of painting eschewed representation, three-dimensionality, and the curved line, and was to have a lasting influence on abstract art and graphic design. He died in 1944.

EARLY EXPERIMENTS in radical new housing tended to be for the most part in the realm of wealthy private patrons willing to experiment with untried and untested forms of architecture. Most mass housing before World War II tended to be fairly conservative in both form and function. The first truly revolutionary experiments, for better or worse, were made in the Soviet Union, but there were architecturally more important projects in Holland and Vienna after World War I. The adoption of Modern Movement architecture by city and other local authorities for the purpose of mass housing followed by and large after World War II. Massive military destruction on a continental scale led to a need for new homes that could be built quickly and efficiently.

It is significant, perhaps, that Gerrit Rietveld, the celebrated De Stijl architect, was one of a distinguished team (including Adolf Loos and Hugo Häring) who worked on the design of the Werkbund Estate (1930–32), Vienna. This was a development of Modern Movement housing based on Mies van der Rohe's Weissenhof Estate, Stuttgart. It was a communal effort aimed at raising the general standard of modern housing in the then-enlightened Austrian capital. Only a few years before, Rietveld's vision was (happily) confined to the solitary and rather whimsical aesthetic statement made by his admittedly exquisite Schröder House, Utrecht (1924), a colorful, two-story cube of immense sophistication. Equally significant is the fact that the Schröder House is tagged on to the end of a long row of uninspired apartment housing. The challenge for socialist local governments and radical architects in the aftermath of the Great War was to create mass housing that offered the sunshine, air, gardens, and healthy way of life hitherto accessible to the bourgeoisie in Continental Europe but not to the working classes. What was to be done?

RED VIENNA
Between 1919 and 1933 in socialist or "Red Vienna" (*Gemeinde Wien*) no fewer than 66,000 new dwellings were built under the direction of the City Architect, Karl Ehn. Some of these were small houses built in new garden suburbs adopted from England (notably Rannersdorf, 1921 under the direction of Hans Tessenow), but most were shoehorned into giant courtyard apartment blocks. The most impressive of these was the combined Karl-Marx-Hof and Svoboda-Hof (1926–30) by Karl Ehn; this was a 3,300-foot- (one-kilometre-) long wall of housing interspersed with well-tended gardens and laced through with communal amenities. The architecture was hardly radical, but the

SCHRÖDER HOUSE, UTRECHT, HOLLAND, 1924
Rietveld's white cube house was designed as a series of overlapping planes, a fact reflected in the interior, where spaces are defined by movable partitions. The architect uses the abstract principles of the De Stijl movement to create a uniquely suggestive sense of structure: "my main aim," Rietveld wrote, "[is] to give a yet unformed space a certain meaning."

spirit and program of this giant housing scheme was. Everybody, Ehn and the city of Vienna were saying, deserved a decent home, even if it was small. Unfortunately, this exemplary socialist housing program ended in 1933–34 when the Fascists came to power in Austria, paving the way for the *anschluss* ("unification") with Nazi Germany in 1938.

DUTCH PLANNING

Similar but less overtly political housing programs were initiated in Amsterdam and Rotterdam, although here the architecture itself was radical. A government law of 1901 insisted that all Dutch towns and cities plan and build for growth systematically decade by decade. This meant that planned or controlled housing was built into the way of life of communities that were in any case well ordered and had been so for at least the past 300 years. What was new in the 1920s was the marriage of this rational housing plan with Modern Movement design. It led to Europe's first multistory housing block, De Wolkenkrabbe at de Dageraad, Amsterdam (1927–30) by J. F. Staal. At much the same time, the young Rotterdam city architect, J. J. P. Oud, designed

SCHEEPVAARTSTRAAT, HOOK OF HOLLAND, 1924–27
City Planner for Rotterdam and a founding member of the De Stijl movement, J. J. P. Oud was responsible for several major housing programs. Here he managed to create mass housing but on a humane scale.

two ultra-modern low-rise housing blocks, Scheepvaartstraat, Hook of Holland (1924–27) and the Kiefhoek Estate, Rotterdam (1928–30). These estates were characterized by their squeaky-clean lines, free of all decoration, that suggested a healthy and efficient way of life. In formal terms, the design of these estates also marked a deliberate turning away from the rather flamboyant Dutch school of Art & Crafts social housing that to iconoclasts like Oud would have seemed fussy and even dishonest.

Appropriately, perhaps, Rotterdam was host to the first multistory, deck-access Modern housing, a form of design that made its mark in many cities across the world in the 1950s and 60s. It seemed radical then, so imagine how brave-new-worldly the Bergpolder flats (1932–34) directed by J. A. Brinckman (1902–49) and L. G. Van der Vlugt (1894–1936) must have seemed so many years earlier. Modern housing had come of age, yet its spread would only accelerate a generation and another world war later. And even then out of all proportion for the majority of people who found it as hard to look at as to live in.

KARL-MARX-HOF, VIENNA, 1926–30
In addition to offices and facilities such as laundries and a library, this vast estate contained 1,383 apartments. An attempt by Vienna's socialist council to provide affordable housing with fixed rents, such complexes became known as "workers' fortresses."

> *"Our own times demanded their own form... their own manifestation"*
> GERRIT RIETVELD

DE STIJL
This group of Dutch artists formed in Leiden in 1917 around the figures of Mondrian, van Doesburg, and Rietveld. It published a journal of the same name that continued until 1932. The group's principal tenets were laws of equilibrium and clarity in art and a belief that art and design should be incorporated in all areas of life. Its style was one of austere abstraction. The movement was largely influential in the areas of furniture design, graphics, and architecture – perhaps its greatest influence was on the designers of the Bauhaus (see pp.174–75).

LUDWIG MIES VAN DER ROHE
LESS IS MORE

LUDWIG MIES VAN DER ROHE (1886–1969) was a stonemason's son from Aachen in Germany. He had little formal education, yet the combination of practical building skills, a powerful will, and great intellect, drove him, along with Frank Lloyd Wright and Le Corbusier, into the position of one of the three most important and influential architects of the twentieth century.

To Mies, as he was universally known, we owe, for better or worse, the modern steel-and-glass office building, stripped of whimsical decoration. The Seagram Building, New York (with Philip Johnson, 1954–58), remains one of the finest of the type, a building of supreme integrity in which form, function, and the finest materials – bronze, brass, and marble, as well as steel and glass – are truly one and the same thing. Exquisitely proportioned, the Seagram Building, set back on its own plaza on Park Avenue, is a mid-twentieth century, commercially-driven successor to the Parthenon, a temple dedicated to Mammon. Although a finite structure, it is easy to imagine its lines – both vertical and horizontal – stretching into infinity. And, in this sense, Mies' architecture was a relentless and logical pursuit of perfection, of the infinite, and even of God.

A SPIRITUAL MAN
The first building the young Mies worshiped was Aachen Cathedral. His favourite authors were those great divines St. Augustine and St. Thomas Aquinas. Although in later life living in Chicago, dressed in immaculately tailored suits and never starting work until 2.00 pm after a

LUDWIG MIES VAN DER ROHE
One of the greatest architects of the 20th century, Mies was a pioneer of the skyscraper. He also designed the famous "Barcelona chair."

lunch preceded by two dry martinis, Mies was far from being the big businessman he resembled. Not only was he a fundamentally spiritual man, but his buildings can be experienced as much as works of contemplation as practical working tools. Although Mies believed in and practiced a more or less tireless logic in his work, his buildings can also be experienced as romantic ideals. They were designed to be models of perfection in what was a decidedly imperfect world.

EARLY PROJECTS
Mies designed his first building, a Neo-classical house in the style of Schinkel, for a Professor Riehl in Neubabelsberg. Mies was 21 years old. He went on to work with Peter Behrens, saw army service with the engineers during World War I, and then began to design a sequence of astonishing projects, built and unbuilt. The former included two unrealizable glass office towers in 1919 and 1921 (contemporary technology lagged behind Mies' purist dreams) and the striking brick-wall monument to Karl Liebknecht and Rosa Luxemburg (the martyred German communist leaders) of 1926. That same year, Mies was appointed first vice-president of the Deutsche Werkbund and given charge of creating the Weissenhof housing development, Stuttgart, as part of the Werkbund exhibition of 1927. Mies employed Walter Gropius (see p.174), J. J. P. Oud (see p.177), Le Corbusier (see pp.182–83), and Pierre Jeanneret, Bruno Taut, Peter Behrens, and others to create the first truly Modernist housing scheme, a remarkably desirable vista of white, flat-roofed Cubist villas. He also began to design his distinctive, purist furniture much of which remains in production at the beginning of the twenty-first century. Now in his stride, Mies was asked to

SEAGRAM BUILDING, NEW YORK, 1954–58
This elegant 38-story headquarters of the Canadian distillers stands on its own plaza set back from Park Avenue. The curtain walling uses gray tinted glass, bronze panels, and attached I-section bronze mullions.

design the German pavilion at the 1929 Barcelona exhibition. The result is one of the most exquisite of all Modern "temples," a single-story building contained under one sweeping horizontal roof, divided by glass and marble screens and set on a travertine plinth punctuated by a pool lined in black glass. A temporary building (reconstructed in 1986), it haunted the architectural imagination of the late-twentieth century.

MODERN STYLE

The Barcelona pavilion was translated into the exquisite Tugendhat House, Brno, Czechoslovakia (1928–30). A beautiful building making considerable use of glass and lavish materials, it is ranked with Le Corbusier's Villa Savoye and Frank Lloyd Wright's Robie House as one of the three most important twentieth-century houses. The theme was explored again when Mies was working in Chicago on the design of the exquisite Farnsworth House at Plano, Illinois (1945–51). As with the Tugendhat House, the quiet, near-neutral color scheme employed inside and out is offset by a glorious natural setting. "Less is more," Mies was famous for saying, along with "God is in the

detail": his buildings were pared down to be as refined as possible and crafted to the highest possible standard.

Finding it increasingly hard to work under Hitler's philistine regime, Mies left Germany in 1937, having closed down the Bauhaus (he was its third and last director) in the teeth of Nazi suppression. Encouraged (at first) by Frank Lloyd Wright and Philip Johnson, Mies went to teach a whole generation of architects at the Illinois Institute of Technology, Chicago, for which he designed the memorable Crown Hall (1952). At much the same time, he produced the twin apartment towers at 860 Lake Shore Drive, Chicago and would soon be at work on the Seagram Building. By now, Mies was often accused of being too rational, too objective, and thus, in the US where novelty was valued highly, old hat and even uninteresting. Mies retorted, "I don't want to be interesting. I want to be good."

His last designs included an unbuilt headquarters for the Bacardi company in Havana (the Cuban revolutionary war intervened) and the Neue Nationalgalerie, Berlin (1968). When the prefabricated steel roof of the latter, all 1,250 tons of it, was lifted into place, Mies was driven underneath it in an open-topped Mercedes to watch the daunting process. He was pleased to have come home to a democratic Germany. One of the greatest architects of all time – one who connected the spirit of ancient Greece with the Modern Movement – he died the following year. His influence was to be incalculable on architects and on the look of our homes and cities. Yet it was always going to be difficult to match his perfection.

"*God is in the detail*"

LUDWIG MIES VAN DER ROHE

GERMAN PAVILION, INTERNATIONAL EXHIBITION, BARCELONA, 1929
In this asymmetrical, single-story building divided by partition walls, Mies used the finest of materials — marble, onyx, and chromed steel.

FASCIST ARCHITECTURE
THE TRIUMPH OF THE WILL

ALBERT SPEER'S first commission for the Nazis was a villa in Grunewald, a wooded suburb of Berlin. The villa was refurbished for Karl Hanke, a minor official. Speer (1905–81) convinced his client to decorate some of the rooms with the latest wallpaper from the Bauhaus, a hotbed of Communists as far as Hitler's men were concerned. But this was 1932. It was to be another year before Hitler was elected to power. At this stage, Speer – the future Generalbauinspektor für die Reichshaupstadt (chief architect and planner of Berlin) and, from 1942, Hitler's armaments minister – was an unassuming young architect. In party terms he was no more than the head of the Wannsee sub-branch of the Nazi Corps of Motorists.

THE REMODELING OF BERLIN

By the beginning of 1937, the 32-year-old Speer was in charge of replanning Berlin, or – the same thing – creating Germania, the planned name for the capital after the projected German victory in Europe. The plans were grossly ambitious. At the heart of Germania, an avenue six times as long as the Champs Elysées would connect north and south railway termini, passing enormous Nazi palaces, giant hotels, vast department stores, titanic theaters, Brobdignagian government ministries, and Hitler's very own design for a triumphal arch that would dwarf Napoleon's Arc de Triomphe. There was also a meglomaniacal Great Hall that, topped with a dome reaching over 1,000 feet (300 meters) into the gray Berlin sky, would have a volume 16 times that of St. Peter's, Rome. So vast was the dome that US military engineers examining the design after the German defeat of 1945 reckoned that, when packed with crowds of the Nazi faithful, clouds would form inside and rain would fall in suitably Wagnerian fashion. At least this might have put a damper on tasteless events.

The crazy plan says much about the spirit of Nazi architecture. Designed for the most part on a gargantuan scale in a heavy-handed, stripped Neo-classical manner based loosely on that of the great Prussian architect Schinkel (see pp.130–31), it was meant not simply to impress but to crush the individual human spirit. This was the architecture of ogres, standing at attention along impossibly grand avenues.

In the event, the Nazis built relatively little. Most new housing was designed in a Hansel-and-Gretel style while factories adopted a proto-High-tech look. Civic buildings were designed to outdo the grandeur of imperial Rome. Werner March and Speer designed the colossal Olympic Stadium, Berlin (still very much in use): it was meant to outdo the Colosseum. Speer's best design was perhaps the airy studio for the sculptor Josef Thorak, Baldham (1938). His most impressive design – notably from the point of view of speediness of construction – was the new Reich Chancellery, Berlin (1938–39). This was a block-long

NEW REICH CHANCELLERY, BERLIN, 1938–39
Albert Speer's vast Chancellery building was built in less than 18 months. Though cleverly planned, its most notable architectural features were its use of lavish materials, such as marble, and the sheer scale of its intimidating rooms.

SANTA MARIA NOVELLA STATION, FLORENCE, 1932–33
Michelucci's Modernist station stands on the edge of Renaissance Florence. Its central, glazed section – shown here from the interior – was intended to stand out as a box of light.

Maria Novella railway station, Florence (1932–33) by Giovanni Michelucci (1891–1990) – the spirit of the Baths of Caracalla brought up to date – and the Casa del Fascio (now the Casa del Populo), Como (1933–36) by the supremely talented Giuseppe Terragni (1904–43).

The Casa del Fascio is an intriguing exploration of the cube, a building of astonishing complexity and delight that at first appears to be little more than a severe and humorless travertine-clad box facing Como's flamboyant cathedral. It can, perhaps, be seen as the architectural equivalent of Rubik's Cube.

Other buildings and developments of note in Fascist Italy were the Stadio Communale (1930–32) and two (destroyed) concrete aircraft hangars at Orvieto (1936) and Orbetello (1939–41) by the great engineer Pierluigi Nervi (1891–1979), the new towns – principally Sabaudia (1933 onward, by Luigi Piccinato, (1899–1983)) – built on decidedly rational principles on the formerly malaria-infested Pontine marshes to the south west of Rome – and the many seaside resorts – 3,800 buildings in all built in styles ranging from the pompous to the lighthearted for a generation of children who came to know a much more delightful Italy in the 1950s, even if the trains now failed to run on time.

civic palace that adopted its look from Schinkel's nearby Altes Museum. Using the latest construction techniques and laborers and craftsworkers from throughout the Third Reich, it was completed in record time. Most (childishly) impressive was the extremely long mirrored hall that (bigger than Louis XIV's at Versailles) led to Hitler's master-of-the-universe style study. Although Speer's became the house style of official Nazi architecture, the truly impressive autobahnen (highway) architecture and engineering of Fritz Todt was an equally important contribution.

FASCIST ARCHITECTURE IN ITALY

The architecture of Mussolini's Italy (1922–43) was always eclectic: "I am a revolutionary and a reactionary according to circumstance," said the jutting-jawed dictator. It was true. Despite a predilection for heavy-handed, stripped Neo-classical ministries of justice throughout the peninsula and the cold, bombastic Neo-classical architecture of the EUR district of Rome (built for the ill-starred Esposizione Universale di Roma of 1942), the regime oversaw the design and construction of many truly brilliant buildings. The very best are, without question, the Santa

CASA DEL FASCIO, COMO, ITALY, 1933–36
Despite its function as the headquarters of the local Fascist party, this stark, marble-clad building has become accepted by architects of all political persuasions as a masterpiece of Modernist design.

LE CORBUSIER
SWIMMING INTO THE SUN

A LONER, A RADICAL thinker, polemicist, painter, sculptor, provocateur, controversialist, urban planner, craftsman, and architect, Le Corbusier (the professional name of Charles-Éduoard Jeanneret, 1887–1965) was the most inventive and poetic architect who has ever lived. A cult figure among members of his profession even 50 years after his death – he drowned, deliberately, it is believed, swimming into the sun in the south of France – his ideas pervade the fabric of our lives in so many parts of the world, from his adopted France and the rest of Europe to Brazil, India, and Japan, and many points east, west, north, south, and in between.

LE CORBUSIER
The architect's work as an abstract painter – rejecting Cubism in favour of Purism – had a profound effect on the formation of his style.

Le Corbusier, who was born in the Swiss watchmaking village of La Chaux-de-Fonds, was known universally as "Corbu" (*corbeau* is French for "raven," which is what admirers and detractors thought he most resembled). His father engraved watch cases and this is what he did before winning a scholarship and setting off on travels not only through Greece, Italy, the Balkans, Asia Minor, and North Africa, but also through the studios and ateliers of some of the most radical European architects of the early years of the twentieth century, among them Peter Behrens in Berlin and Auguste Perret in Paris.

Although his first houses were designed in an Arts & Crafts style, he was to become an early master of the white, Modern Movement villa not long after he settled in Paris in 1917. Here, with the painter Amedée Ozenfant and the poet Paul Dermée, he published *L'Esprit Nouveau*, a magazine dedicated to "the modern aesthetic." In its vibrant pages, Corbu experimented with ideas that were to make his name. Many of these came together in his radical book *Vers une architecture* (1923) in which he made an intriguing link between Greek temples, Gothic cathedrals, aircraft, cars, and ocean liners with the new architecture that he famously described as "the masterly, correct, and magnificent play of masses brought together in light." He also described the house as "a machine for living in." This dictum was long misunderstood; Corbu was not arguing for machinelike homes, but for houses that were as beautiful and efficient as the best new machinery. Although it has often been ignored, in almost the same breath, he said "Architecture goes beyond utilitarian needs."

THE WORLD OF SUNLIGHT
As well as designing idealistic cities of the future and developing, over 20 years, his own proportional system – the Modulor – Corbu showed the world his first radical white villa in the guise of a hugely influential exhibition stand, the "Pavillon de L'Esprit Nouveau" at the famous Art Deco show, Paris, 1925. His first mature house was the Villa Savoye at Poissy, outside Paris (1929–30). Raised on columns called "piloti" by the architect, the house was intended to be an exercise in pure, white, abstract geometry: the mind of man set against the

VILLA SAVOYE, POISSY, 1929–30
Commissioned as a weekend country house, the Villa Savoye's raised piano nobile *allows light to pour into the main living quarters and the windows and roof terraces afford views out across the French countryside.*

UNITÉ D'HABITATION, MARSEILLE, FRANCE, 1946–52
Conceived as a self-sufficient neighborhood, the Unité was the only realized part of Le Corbusier's plans for Marseille. Three other unités were built at Nantes and Briey-en-Foret in France and one in Berlin.

natural world. An auto-age equivalent of a Palladian villa, the Villa Savoye is a magnificent example of how the world of sunlight and the elements can play throughout a highly sophisticated geometrical home to mutual advantage.

After World War II, during which time, much to his discredit, Corbu collaborated with the Vichy regime, his work changed course dramatically. Away went the lightness and whiteness of the 1920s and 30s; in came weighty, bush-hammered concrete, highly sculptural forms, and a rawness which, together, exposed Corbu's increasing withdrawal into his own spiritual world. The remarkable Unité d'Habitation housing block he designed at Marseille (1946–52) was a great concrete ocean liner berthed in the Mediterranean city. Held up by mighty piloti, this concrete megastructure housed around 340 apartments for about 1,600 people. With its double-height living rooms and internal shopping street (including a dog-grooming parlor), it was at once ultramodern and yet its dense, physical presence recalled, through the distorting lens of the twentieth century, the temples of ancient Egypt.

LATER WORK
Soon afterward, Corbu designed the deeply moving and highly sculptural pilgrimage church of Notre-Dame-du-Haut Ronchamp (1950–54) and then the magnificent Dominican monastery of Sainte Marie de la Tourette, Eveux (1957–60). La Tourette was built for a client with little money, yet its concrete starkness is also ineffably poetic. To stay here is to feel at peace with the world. The foolish thing is that, as with other buildings by Corbu, its design was mimicked worldwide by a younger generation of architects in settings and in situations where its asceticism was irrelevant and even demeaning.

His wife dead and finding himself very much alone, Corbu became increasingly religious in his vision (he was never interested in money and lived an almost monastic life set between a modest apartment in Paris and a seaside shack at Cap Martin on the Mediterranean). It seems strange that perhaps his most profound building – la Tourette – should have been built for the Dominicans. For St. Dominic had created the Inquisition and nearly wiped out the Cathars, the Albigensian heretics from whom Corbu was descended.

Before his death, Le Corbusier was also responsible for the design and principal buildings of Chandigarh, the new capital of the Punjab, India, as well as the author of numerous town-planning schemes (his various schemes for Algiers never took off), an unbuilt 1,200-bed hospital in Venice and, finally, the colorful steel "Maison de l'Homme" exhibition pavilion, Zurich (1965–67). "The drama of architecture," wrote Corbu, "is that of the man who lives by and through the universe." He swam out into the sun at Cap Martin at 11.00 am, August 27, 1965, to meet the greatest architect of all. He had never been a part of the architectural, political, or social establishment.

> **"*A curved road is a donkey track, a straight street, a road for men*"**
> LE CORBUSIER

MID-CENTURY MODERN
AN AMERICAN DREAM

CARNAGE ASIDE, World War II showed the United States at its best. When Uncle Sam went to war in 1941, the huge and astonishingly productive might of the US made victory in Europe almost inevitable. Despite its own productive efficiency, the German military machine was ground down by the Red Army on its eastern front and the Allies from the west. Uninvaded and untouched by bombs from Germany or Japan, the US enjoyed an economic boom during the 1940s. This was the great era of high-speed trains, Hollywood at its best, jazz, and the establishment of a new form of slick and assured International Style architecture that has become known as Mid-Century Modern.

THE AMERICANIZED SPIRIT
This is not really a style, but a way of designing and building that fused the indigenous energy and highly efficient prefabricated building skills of US industry, and architects, and the influence of European architects and designers, notably those from the Bauhaus (closed in 1933), and above all of Mies van der Rohe, who arrived in the States from Germany, via London, in 1937. Walter Gropius, founder of the Bauhaus, taught at Harvard; Mies at the Illinois Institute of Technology, Chicago. Both designed new campuses that represented the new Americanized spirit of Modern Movement architecture – US nuts-and-bolts technology married to the reductivist logic of the Bauhaus – and which drew many of the brightest young US architects to sit at the feet of the German masters.

Mies' Mid-Century Modern work (his highly assured Crown Hall, Chicago; Farnsworth House; Lake Shore Drive Apartments; and the Seagram Building, see pp.178–79) had a great influence on a number of US practices, notably Skidmore, Owings, and Merrill, whose Lever House, New York City (see pp.196–97), was the prototype for global corporate headquarters in the 1950s and 60s. Equally slick and equally convincing was the General Motors Technical Center, Warren, Michigan (1948–56), by Eero Saarinen, a skyscraper turned on its side that has a relentless quality. Working with the GM design team, whose studio was housed in a dome at the heart of the building, Saarinen made use of what later became known as "technology transfer," with components and materials used in automotive design – notably neoprene gaskets that were to become an important feature of High-tech architecture 20 years later – transferred to the building itself. It is easy to imagine this building stretching into the infinite. And this, in fact, is very much a part of the idea and the appeal of these supremely confident steel-framed American buildings: they are symbols of astonishing confidence, of the relentless American industrial machine. This is the architecture of a male culture that saw itself, not without justification at the time, as master of the universe.

PALM SPRINGS POETRY
This, however, was not the whole story. There was another, earlier European Modern tradition that had developed independently in California. Here, young architects in the 1920s and 30s were widely influenced by two Viennese emigrés, Richard Neutra (1892–1970) and Rudolph Schindler (1887–1953), who designed a number

LOEWY HOUSE, PALM SPRINGS, CALIFORNIA, 1946–47
A student of Corbusier, Swiss-born Albert Frey was drawn to the States by the new technology used in US architecture. His house for Raymond Loewy successfully integrates the house with the desert.

CASE STUDY HOUSE NO. 21, LOS ANGELES, 1958
Pierre Koenig was invited to build Case Study House 21 by John Entenza, owner of Art and Architecture *magazine, who began the Case Study Program to promote Modernism in Los Angeles.*

production techniques had a domestic beauty, if only the designer saw poetically. The Eames went on to design some of the finest industrial furniture yet seen; as the years advanced it simply got more and more fashionable.

LATER MODERN

The spiritual apotheosis of Mid-Century Modern is, however, best witnessed in the astonishing chapel designed for the US Air Force Academy at Colorado Springs, an origami-like folding of stylized aircraft wings raised and joined in prayer. Although if you believe that shopping is the new religion, it might equally be argued that the pure, hard, platonic forms of the Northland Shopping Center, Detroit (1954), by Victor Gruen, were equally important.

EXILES IN THE US
The US might have fought Germany for four years, but it welcomed some of that country's best inventors. Among them was the young rocket engineer Werner von Braun, who designed the V2 missile, and the Saturn rocket, which later took the first men to the moon. Architecturally, there were luminaries of the Bauhaus such as Mies and Gropius, and two Austrians, Rudolph Schindler and Richard Neutra, both of whom worked in Frank Lloyd Wright's office before developing their own styles in California.

of serene, single-story, open-plan houses in and around Los Angeles and Palm Springs. With their sliding glass walls and carefully considered relationship with nature, these houses connected the world of Japanese Zen Buddhism to the great American outdoors via the open-plan architecture of Frank Lloyd Wright and the functional sensibilities of the early Modern Movement. In short, they were a near-perfect marriage of form and function – architectural sonnets.

In the aftermath of the World War II, the Neutra-Schindler style was developed, again in Los Angeles and Palm Springs – a fashionable resort for Hollywood stars and moguls – by a younger generation of architects including Pierre Koenig (b.1925), a highly decorated young US Army engineer who fought across Europe and witnessed firsthand the hell of Nazi concentration camps. Inspired to create a clean new world free from the political and architectural horrors of the past, Koenig's Case Study Houses Nos. 21 (1958) and 22 (1959) were poetic steel structures that combined the strength and simplicity of the US construction industry and the sonnetlike qualities of the earlier desert houses by Schindler and Neutra.

Elsewhere in Los Angeles, at Pacific Palisades, the hugely successful and influential husband and wife team, Charles (1907–78) and Ray (1912–88) Eames, designed and built their own house (1949) of proprietary steel and other factory-made components. Their genius was to prove that mass-

NO.8 PACIFIC PALISADES, PALM SPRINGS, CALIFORNIA, 1949
Charles and Ray Eames' own home was a delightfully planned site. The house was built alongside a row of eucalyptus trees which filtered light through the floor-to-ceiling windows.

MODERNISM & FREEDOM
ARCHITECTURE OF LIBERATION

ALVAR AALTO

Born in Kuortane, Finland, in 1898, Aalto was the leading exponent of Scandinavian Modernism. His buildings unite the technological innovations of the Modern Movement with a typically Scandinavian appreciation for nature and natural materials, such as timber and stone. Indeed, in contrast to many Modernists he claimed that "Nature, not the machine, is the most important model for architecture." Aalto was also a talented designer of both glassware and furniture. He died in Helsinki in 1976.

MODERNISM implied two key freedoms: freedom from ill health, or ill-being, and political freedom. In its first incarnation, Modernism was a largely left-wing project, its open-plan architecture was free of historic detail and association with autocratic regimes. The latter had, for centuries, been propped up by heavyweight buildings encrusted with complex symbolism and lavish, sometimes histrionic, detail.

The first freedom – well-being – was intended to be built into, and expressed through, the outward form of buildings that aimed to be white, light, warm, and open to the natural world: a healthy body in a healthy house. The prewar apotheosis of this holistic Modern approach can be seen and experienced in the beautiful Paimio

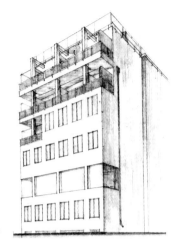

PAIMIO SANATORIUM, 1929–33
Aalto started work on his famous sanatorium when he was just 30. Its design and construction were paid for by 50 local Finnish communities.

Sanatorium, Finland (1929–33), by Alvar Aalto. Compared to the work of contemporary French, German, and British Modernists, Paimio was warm, humane, and subtle. This was the great contribution of Aalto and Scandinavia: to give Modernism a human face. During the 1930s, Aalto nurtured an ever-close relationship between Modern architecture and nature. His own house, the Villa Mairea (1938–41), broke down the hard-edged formality of so much new housing to date and made gently pointed use of natural materials indoors and out. Where much Modern architecture was antithetical to nature, Aalto's set his up in apposition to its natural surroundings. After the blood, mud, and carnage of World War I, Modernism offered sunlight, convenience, and liberation: it was, in the example of Paimio, literally a sanatorium, a place of healing in every sense.

NEW GERMAN ARCHITECTURE

After World War II, architects provided new forms of escape and liberation. In Germany, there was inevitably a strong reaction to the grandiose, militaristic architecture of the Third Reich. Architects, many of whom had served as officers in the armed forces, looked for a way of building that was free of political association. Two of the finest new buildings in this vein were the Philharmonie (1959–63) and State Library, Berlin (1967–78), by Hans Scharoun (1893–1972). Their swooping roofs and free-flowing interiors are a studied and successful fusion of rational and organic forms and planning. Sited close to No Man's Land and the Berlin Wall, they were intended from the outset to form a new cultural hub of a reunited Berlin that became a reality in 1989. Scharoun offered a powerful and highly individualistic architecture that was also an antidote to the vainglory and rigors of Nazi design. However, even as Scharoun was at work on the design of the Philharmonie, Mies van der Rohe was producing the New National Gallery

VILLA MAIREA, NOORMARKKU, FINLAND, 1938–41
The L-shaped form of Aalto's house curves around the swimming pool to the rear. The main structure of the building is of reinforced concrete, while both exterior and interior use timber and stone cladding to integrate the house with its surroundings.

STATE LIBRARY, BERLIN, 1967–78

Together with Scharoun's Philharmonie and Mies van der Rohe's New National Gallery, the State Library forms part of Berlin's Kulturforum. The interior of the building derives its shape from its function as a library, its open areas stitched together by stairways.

nearby, with its brilliant connection between the severe Neo-classicism of the great Prussian architect Schinkel, who built so many of Berlin's most distinguished monuments and the world of the Bauhaus: the former was admired by Speer and Hitler, the latter they despised.

Architecture, however, is in many ways prescriptive and deterministic – it tells us how to live – no matter how idealistic and ideologically free a particular architect might be. Only a very few architects have tried to create genuinely participatory buildings – ones in which clients and users take part and make a real contribution to the design and building process. An attempt was made by Lucien Kroll (b.1927) in the Students' Residence at the Catholic University of Louvain, Belgium (1969–75). This was an ad hoc design and represented the spirit of 60s "liberation" in timber and concrete, a cry for freedom that echoed around university campuses worldwide in a puff of reefer smoke, even though new college buildings themselves remained for the most part formal and the work of a much older generation of architects.

Rather sadly, revolutions and so-called liberations rarely produced radical new architecture in the postwar era, not even in countries such as Cuba which were otherwise willing to experiment with graphics, film, photography, philosophy, and literature. Only in the extraordinary dome-based architecture of the new ballet and art schools designed by Ricardo Porro in the Miramar district of Havana can the visitor see a new and liberating spirit at work. Underpinned for the most part by funds from Moscow or Beijing, revolutionary governments in Africa, Asia, and Latin America tended to build Soviet-style concrete housing blocks and other monstrosities utterly insensitive to locale and local culture. Such buildings were far from liberating, imposing, in fact, a new tyranny of their own.

UNIVERSITY OF LOUVAIN, LOUVAIN-LA-NEUVE, BELGIUM, 1969–75

Leuven University in the Netherlands was bilingual until the 1960s, when students took to the streets to claim it as Dutch-speaking. In 1968 the separate French-speaking university was built in Belgium.

NEW CITIES
THE NEW JERUSALEM

THE GARDEN CITY
The garden city was initially a reaction against the overcrowding and squalor of 19th-century industrial cities in France and Britain. The first projects for bringing green spaces to the urban center, such as Frederick Law Olmsted's Central Park, New York City (1850s) and Ebenezer Howard's ideal diagram for a garden city (1898), attempted to reestablish the link between humans and "nature." The concept found its greatest expression at the turn of the century in such schemes as Letchworth, England (see p.145), but also fed into the urban plans such as Garnier's Cité Industrielle (1917) and Berlage's plans for south Amsterdam (1902–20). In Le Corbusier's Contemporary City (1922) too, we see the fusion of elements of social planning with an idealistic concept of nature.

IN THE 1950s AND 1960s an attempt was made worldwide to create ideal new towns and cities. The ideal often proved elusive. The reason was pretty obvious; on the whole, most towns and cities have grown organically. They are accretions of many different ways and layers of planning and building nurtured, rejected, and superimposed over many centuries. To plan a large town from scratch is to expect the messy high and low drama of human life to conform to a neat pattern that, even if it made sense at the time it was drawn up, would, in all likelihood, be out of date within a few years or decades at the most.

New towns were nearly always outposts of older cities either splitting at the seams or with populations who wanted to escape a way of life that had become, for far too many of them, nasty, brutish, and short. New cities were something else again, set up for largely political reasons and usually to create a new national capital, as for example at Chandigarh, Brasilia, and Canberra.

The ways that people adopt a new city or adapt it are graphically presented in Chandigarh, the new capital of the Punjab. The traditional capital, Lahore had been ceded to the new Muslim republic of Pakistan in 1948, leaving thousands of Hindu refugees in need of a new center. Chandigarh was designed by Le Corbusier from 1951 (and by others, including the British architects Jane Drew and Maxwell Fry, who recommended Corbu for the job).

LE CORBUSIER AND CHANDIGARH
The plan itself was developed from Corbu's long study of the new city of sun, light, and greenery, although, unlike his famous plans for the rebuilding of Paris made in the 1920s, it eschewed glass towers in favor of low-rise, garden-city villas. The major buildings were a magnificent play of Corbu's postwar raw concrete manner and Mughal tradition, as witnessed in the provision of deep loggias, water gardens, deep-eaved roofs, as well as the architect's own highly characteristic concrete *brises soleils* (sunscreens), built into the window openings.

The result is a sequence of imposing, abstract monuments, buildings that echo drawings by Picasso and sculptures by Braque set against the mind-searing backdrop of the Himalayas. The major civic buildings are the Assembly (1955–60), the High Court (1952–56), and the Secretariat (1952–56). The designs were executed by Pierre Jeanneret, Corbu's cousin and long-time practice partner, who

THE ASSEMBLY, CHANDIGARH, INDIA, 1955–60
Le Corbusier's designs for Chandigarh are a mixture of his own themes with those of traditional Mughal forms. Here, the crescent-shaped roof is at once a practical sun-shield and a reference to earlier forms. The building manages to be both modern and monumental.

ANZAC PARADE AND PARLIAMENT HOUSE, CANBERRA, AUSTRALIA

In the foreground is the Australian War Memorial, with Anzac Parade leading down to the water. Across the artificial lake (part *of Griffin's original plan) is the white strip of the Old Parliament House and beyond, built into the hilltop, the new Parliament House.*

JANE DREW AND MAXWELL FRY

Pioneers of the International Modern Style in England, Jane Drew (1911–96) and Maxwell Fry (1899–1987) were married in 1942 and business partners from 1945. Fry established a name with designs for private homes in England, and Drew's work includes buildings in Nigeria, the Middle East, and a section of the Festival of Britain. The most famous example of their work is perhaps their housing projects at Chandigarh, where Fry was Senior Architect to the New Capital Project.

contributed his own subtle designs for the Peon village (1952–53) and the Gandhi Bhavan (1959–61). Much of the housing was designed by Drew and Fry. What is intriguing to experience, 50 years on from the founding of Chandigarh is just how these buildings have been occupied by local people. Behind rational two-story façades, visitors will find three and even four stories squeezed inside.

Partly because of this, the population density of Chandigarh is much higher than planned; and as a result it enjoys the theatrical bustle of other Indian cities even though planned partly on low-density, garden-city principles. Unlike Canberra, it enjoys, an architecture of great distinction, one that connects modern-day life to ancient traditions and has an energy lost in the ultra-low density of the Australian capital. Here, then, is a story of how a new city could work: its wealth is its life and its vibrancy, not its smooth organization and overt efficiency – not simply the stuff of grand plans and globalized architecture, lacking texture, depth, and meaning.

CANBERRA

The plan for the new Australian capital, Canberra, had in fact been established by Walter Burley Griffin in 1912, yet several of the major buildings that brought the city more or less to life were not completed until the late 1980s. These included

the High Court of Australia (1972–80), the National Gallery (1968–82) by Edwards Madigan Torzillo and Briggs, and the Parliament House of Australia (1979–88), by Mitchell Giurgola Thorp. What these hard-edged, willfully sculpted concrete buildings have in common is an anodyne quality that means they might be many other places in the world, but not necessarily Australia. Giurgola's Parliament House is the most interesting of these largely anonymous national monuments, although even here the design lacks feeling.

Ingeniously, the American architect of the Parliament House has neatly half concealed, half revealed the two political chambers within a hilltop and just as neatly connected the axes of the city plan to those of the internal logic of the building. Beyond this, there is a knowing, if not altogether clever fusion of a grand Neo-classical beaux-arts plan and the look of Le Corbusier's much-quoted competition entry for the Palace of the Soviets, Moscow. Equally, local people have said that the willfully curved walls resemble a pair of giant boomerangs placed back to back – although why anyone would need to do that is something of a mystery. What is certain is that such cleverness and these knowing references do little or nothing to make either the building or Canberra itself either more humane or likeable. Creating life in a new city is not ultimately an architectural task: it is up to the people themselves.

> *"The first expression of our native genius... flowering on our newly earned freedom"*
> NEHRU
> ON CHANDIGARH

OSCAR NIEMEYER
THE VIEW FROM COPACABANA

OSCAR NIEMEYER (b.1907) brought an unprecedented degree of sensuality to the Modern Movement. Inspired, he said, by the mountainous views surrounding Rio de Janeiro, those of the Atlantic Ocean, and the stupendous beaches his home and studio overlook, he has given Modern architecture a sculptural force that, on first encounter, can be almost overwhelming. Perhaps what so much Modern architecture needed all along was an injection of Latin passion to give the depth, shadow, and vibrancy it too often lacked. However, it is not Latin passion *per se* that made Niemeyer's often almost baroque buildings so special but the architect's own vision and the particular political circumstances that gave rise to modern Brazil.

The revolution of 1930 that brought Getúlio Vargas to power was remarkable in that the new ruling class was also the avant-garde. As a result, the design of the new Ministry of Health and Education (now the Palace of Culture), Rio

OSCAR NIEMEYER
The majority of Niemeyer's work was carried out in his native Brazil, though he spent the period 1964–69 in exile in France.

de Janeiro (1937–42), played an important role in the development of radical, state-sponsored architecture, planning, and design in twentieth-century Brazil. The competition for the design of the building was won by Lucio Costa (b.1902) who went on to plan the new capital, Brasilia, with Niemeyer, a Communist, as his principal architect. In 1936, Niemeyer was a part of Costa's team. The design was heavily influenced by Le Corbusier, who was invited to Rio to act as consultant architect.

EXPERIMENTAL FORMS
Niemeyer's own work, beginning with the Brazilian Pavilion at the New York World's Fair (1939), became increasingly florid and daring as he experimented with the new forms that modern concrete engineering made possible. His work for Juscelino Kubitschek, mayor of Belo Horizonte, included the light and elegant and Casino (1942) and Yacht Club (1943–44), Pampulha, and the astonishing wavelike chapel of St. Francis (1943–46), also at Pampulha.

The extraordinary nave of the chapel is one continuous and sinuous space contained beneath four parabolic, concrete arches that act as roof and wall without an obvious visual or structural break. The story of Saint Francis is told by Candido Portinari in traditional Portuguese painted and glazed ceramic tiles, which fill the spaces between the ground and the apexes of the arched vaults. The overall effect is one of great originality, yet rightness and serenity. Although Niemeyer took risks and played games with architecture, then, results were inevitably highly resolved and all of a piece.

In the late 1950s, Kubitschek was Brazil's president. His dream was to create a new, ultramodern capital in the heart of the rain forest. The plan, by Costa, was as simple as it was monumental; Niemeyer designed the principal public

NATIONAL CONGRESS BUILDING, BRASILIA, 1960
Niemeyer's towering Congress Building is the dominant structure of the Plaza of the Three Powers. Following Costa's original plan, the main north-south axis of the planned city of Brasilia runs between the two prisms of the building.

NIEMEYER'S KEY WORKS
Yacht Club, Pampulha, Brazil, *1943–44*
Chapel of St. Francis of Assisi, Pampulha, Brazil, *1943–46*
Government Buildings, Plaza of the Three Powers, Brasilia, Brazil, *1958–60*
Brasilia Cathedral, Brazil, *1959–70*
Museum of Contemporary Art, Niterói, Brazil, *1997*

BRASILIA CATHEDRAL, 1959–70
The cathedral consists of a group of concrete beams held together at the top by a girdle of concrete and steel. An illusion of space is created in the interior by the circular floor being set below ground level and therefore lower than the entrance.

buildings to match. These are set around the vast Square of the Three Powers and comprise the National Congress Building (completed in 1960), the Ministry of Justice and the Itamarati Palace (1958), and, slightly beyond, the spectacular concrete crown-of-thorns that forms the new cathedral (1959–70). These are buildings of immense power, especially when seen from a distance, each a work of monumental sculpture. They could, and were, criticized for being ultimately simplistic and overbearing; their role, however, was as much to serve specific functions as to imbue the new capital with an instant and recognisable identity. Ever since Brasilia, national and regional governments around the world, have sought to enhance their identity and tourist-pulling power with investment in theatrical and monumental architecture: Sydney Opera House (see pp.170–171) and the Guggenheim Museum, Bilbao (see pp.224–225) are two that spring instantly to mind. The architect's own house overlooking Copacabana Beach (1953) was entirely modest in comparison; it opens like a flower onto the surrounding land and seascape, and is designed in such a way that interior and exterior spaces flow seamlessly one into the other.

His later works include the powerful House of Culture, Le Havre, France (1972), with its space-station-like interior and the extraordinary seaside Museum of Contemporary Art at Niterói, near Rio (1997), a kind of flying saucer on a tall landing pod overlooking the sea. This is architecture that makes people stop and stare. It has immense power, yet, given its context by the sea, is not overpowering.

ESSENTIALLY BRAZILIAN
Niemeyer continued to work on major projects into the twenty-first century. His career was intriguing not only because it coincided with a rare moment in modern history when a national government was almost institutionally avant-garde in its taste and sensibility, but because, despite being connected to currents of thought internationally, Niemeyer was essentially a local architect, investing his undoubted skill in shaping an architecture for Brazil as readily identifiable as Gaudí's was in Catalonia, Schinkel's in Prussia, and Imre Makovecz's in Hungary. In fact, he rarely worked outside Brazil – he hated flying – and his international *oeuvre*, if distinctive, is slight for such a powerful giver of hugely distinctive forms.

> *"I must design what pleases me in a way that is naturally linked to my roots and the country of my origin"*
>
> OSCAR NIEMEYER

BRUTALISM
RAW CONCRETE DESIGN

DENYS LASDUN
Born in London in 1914, Denys Lasdun began his career with Wells Coates in 1935 before joining Tecton (1938–48), a group established by Berthold Lubetkin. Lasdun's style is characterized by his emphasis on horizontal lines. Notable buildings include the Royal College of Physicians, Regent's Park (1961–64), and the National Theatre (1967–76), both in London. He published Architecture in the Age of Scepticism *in 1984.*

THE NEW BRUTALISM was a name given approvingly by the British critic Peter Reyner Banham to a school of architecture that was as tough on the eye as it was to the touch. This was a peculiarly British moment in architecture and one that is still causing controversy half a century on from its inception. Brutalism was a willfully ugly moment in architectural history. Sadly, this rough, tough aesthetic, based in part on the later works of Le Corbusier (Unité d'Habitation in particular, see p.183) and unspokenly on the concrete architecture of Hitler's Atlantic Wall, was first expressed in social housing. After the destruction and deprivations of World War II, Britain needed new housing urgently. Postwar governments set targets of up to 300,000 new homes a year, a task that was met by using techniques of prefabrication learned during wartime arms manufacture or by working, as Corbu did, in rough-cast concrete poured into frames or "shutters" on building sites.

This hard new aesthetic went hand-in-hand with a theoretical underpinning created by, among others, Reyner Banham and the architects Peter (b.1923) and Alison Smithson (1928–92), who were also admirers of the Art Brut of the French artist Dubuffet. The Smithsons designed one of the hardest of all Brutalist monuments, the Robin Hood Gardens housing estate (1969–72) in East London. Tougher still, however were the earlier Park Hill (1955–60) and Hyde Park (1962–65) estates in Sheffield designed by the city architects Jack Lynn and Ivor Smith. Linked by "streets in the air" that, sadly, became quick getaway alleys for muggers, these muscular megastructures were largely unloved by those who lived in them, although much admired by conservationists who enjoyed the brutal honesty of their logical and exposed methods of construction.

URBAN LIVING

Significantly, two of the most subtle British concrete housing blocks of the postwar era that most observers would label "Brutalist" were to become highly fashionable addresses for the arty middle classes in the 1990s. Although their architects would have preferred to avoid the naming game altogether. These were Trellick Tower, London (1966–73), by Ernö Goldfinger (1902–87), and Keeling House, London (1960), by Denys Lasdun (b.1914). Lasdun eschewed all labels, yet his work, although more fundamentally rational than those of the younger Smithsons, is nevertheless uncompromisingly tough. While both of these housing blocks are austerely logical and realized in no-nonsense concrete, they have two saving graces. Both are highly sculptural and

TRELLICK TOWER, LONDON, 1972
Designed in the Brutalist style by Ernö Goldfinger as part of a local authority estate, the Trellick Tower comprises duplex flats with fantastic views. The building has a sculptural form with a distinctive detached elevator tower. In the 1990s it became a fashionable west London address.

thus fascinating to look at, and, more importantly to residents, both offer imaginative, light, and spacious accommodation.

BRUTALIST MONUMENTS

It is possible that some architects of this generation were influenced not only by Le Corbusier in his raw concrete period (1945–65), but also by the remarkable wartime German fortifications designed – all 15,000 of them – as front-line defenses against the threatened Allied invasion that finally took place on June 6 1944 (D-Day). Major Lasdun of the Royal Engineers was only one among many architects who took part in the D-Day landings and would have seen and visited these extraordinary Expressionist structures. Anyone looking at the major civic monuments of London's South Bank to the concrete architecture of the Atlantic Wall and back again would find it hard not to draw comparisons even if the influence was unselfconscious or subliminal.

Those major monuments include the Hayward Gallery (1964) and the Queen Elizabeth Hall (1964) designed by the young Turks of the London County Council's Architect's Department, and the National Theatre, a powerful and intelligent geological outcrop (that's what it feels like – an urban mountain – more than conventional architecture) in raw concrete by Denys Lasdun.

As simple and crude interpretations of the New Brutalist style were used in the design and construction of heavy-duty public works such as multistory parking lots and sewage treatment plants, it is hardly surprising that it was widely seen as a brutalizing experience for ordinary people. Architects, designers, critics, and historians, however, have always had more than a secret admiration for the bravura sculptural qualities of the most heroic of Brutalist monuments. A final irony, perhaps, is the fact that the grand civic buildings Hitler and his architects designed in a grand Neo-classical style to last a thousand years lasted, for the most part, between five and twelve years: the brutalist buildings of the Atlantic Wall that pockmark the Normandy and Brittany coasts are likely, unless powerful tides sweep them away prematurely, to make their millennium.

COASTAL DEFENSES, NEAR CALAIS, FRANCE, 1942

In preparation for the Allied invasion of Europe the German army asked the Todt Organization (headed by Albert Speer) to build a wall of gun emplacements from Calais to Bordeaux. The work seemed to prefigure the work of British Brutalist architects of the 1950s.

BRITISH BRUTALISM

Brutalism, as practiced in Britain, was a curiously perverse style. Le Corbusier admired the rugged, natural qualities of concrete (béton brut), he employed it because it was a cheap material and required little or no maintenance. His British admirers – although they would never have admitted it – saw it as a style, and used raw concrete even when they had decent budgets to work with. As was so often the case in the post-World War II era, materials were often used to express a style or point of view as much as for their inherent qualities.

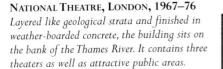

NATIONAL THEATRE, LONDON, 1967–76
Layered like geological strata and finished in weather-boarded concrete, the building sits on the bank of the Thames River. It contains three theaters as well as attractive public areas.

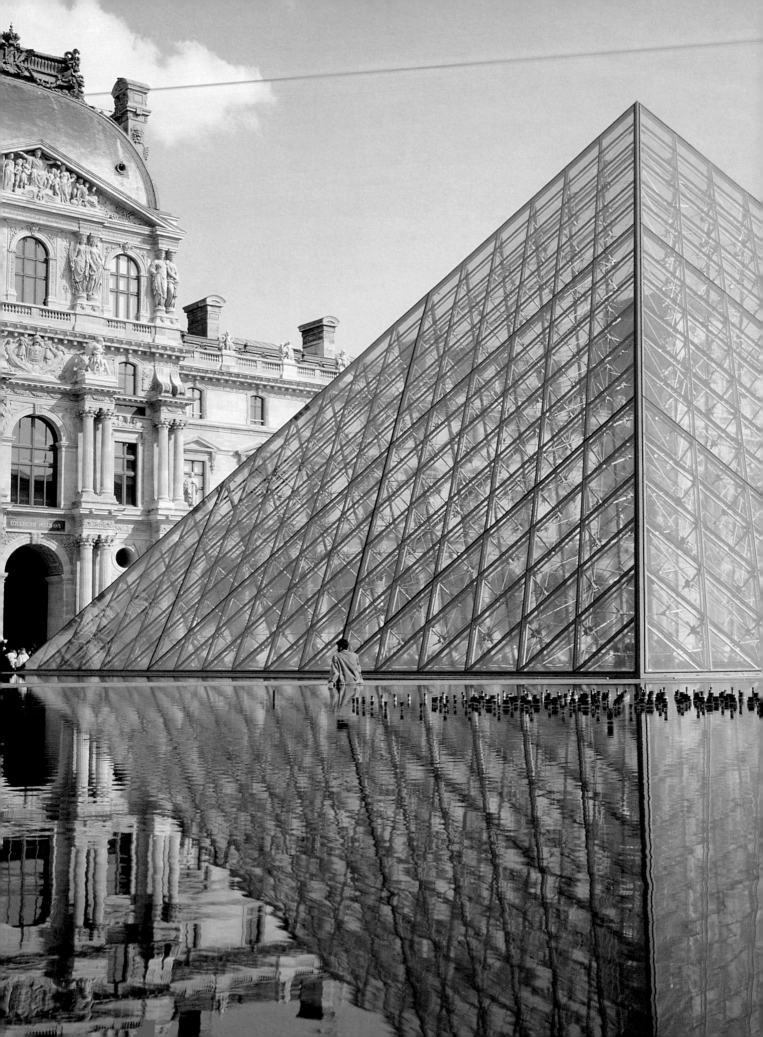

EVERY WHICH WAY

THERE WAS A POINT WHEN MODERN ARCHITECTURE HAD MATURED AND WAS REFINED TO A POINT WHERE MANY OBSERVERS BELIEVED IT HAD ESCAPED FROM THE AGE-OLD PURSUIT OF STYLE ALTOGETHER. MODERN ARCHITECTURE, IT WAS SAID IN THE 1950S, WAS A FUNCTIONAL, MORAL SOLUTION TO THE PROBLEM OF HOW TO BUILD. *THE* SOLUTION. THE TRUTH WAS SOMEWHAT DIFFERENT. ARCHITECTURE, LIKE THE PLANET IT STANDS ON, HAS ALWAYS BEEN CHANGING. JUST AS COMMENTATORS WERE SAYING THAT IT WAS A FIXED COMMODITY, ARCHITECTURE EXPLODED INTO A KALEIDOSCOPE OF NEW FORMS AND STYLES: POSTMODERN, HIGH-TECH, ORGANIC, CLASSICAL REVIVAL, DECONSTRUCTIVIST. AND IN BETWEEN THESE CONVENIENT CATCH-ALLS MANY OTHER APPROACHES. SOME OF THESE HAVE BEEN PASSING PHASES AND SOME LITTLE MORE THAN WHIMSY. OTHERS HAVE SHOWN HOW THE TECHNOLOGIES AND ECONOMIC, POLITICAL, AND ECONOMIC FREEDOMS AVAILABLE AT THE END OF THE TWENTIETH CENTURY AND THE BEGINNING OF THE TWENTY-FIRST CAN POINT ARCHITECTURE IN UNEXPECTED AND DESIRABLE NEW WAYS. THERE WILL BE MANY MORE IN THE FUTURE.

GLASS PYRAMID, LOUVRE, PARIS
I.M Pei's glass pyramid (1983–89) forms the entrance to the expanded galleries that lie beneath the Louvre's main courtyard. The structure provides a convincing argument for the integration of old and new styles.

CORPORATISM
THE BUSINESS OF ARCHITECTURE

"We deal with the oldest forms of man's concern: his shelter, and, even more, his need for beauty and personal expression"
NATHANIEL OWINGS

"MIES MEANS MONEY" was the word on the street amongst developers and senior corporate executives in the New York and Chicago of the 1950s. What they meant was that Mies van der Rohe (see pp.178–79), who was most certainly not a "commercial architect" in the sense of running a practice primarily as a means of making money or financing an expensive way of life, had struck on a form of architecture that proved to be ideally suited to the methods, organization, and ambition of big business.

Mies' steel-and-glass towers were always, in fact, an ideal, a dream of a pure, platonic architecture and he had been working at this dream from as early as 1919. His US disciples, however, quickly learned that Mies' philosophical and even spiritual idealism could be translated into a form of corporate office building that within the space of a single decade, the 1950s, would spread around the globe. The connection was first made, successfully, by the all-American team of Louis Skidmore (1897–1962), Nathaniel Owings (1903–84), and John O. Merrill (1896–1975), whose office, SOM, was to become the first multinational architectural business run on powerfully commercial lines.

THE PROTOTYPE
Founded in the late 1930s, SOM was the model and prototype for business-minded architectural practices. Its architects, dressed smartly for business, were encouraged to look like and even speak like corporate executives. SOM offices were neat and tidy; regimented rows of drawing boards and filing cabinets were the order of the day. This marked a fundamental change from the idea of the architect as bohemian intellectual or artist with a practical bent for building. The curious thing is that Mies, the master for the generation of SOM architects, who created the practice's most important building, Lever House, looked like a powerful tycoon, but was a man whose mind was on almost anything but making money and running a businesslike office. Mies happened to like finely tailored suits, Havana cigars, and dry Martinis, but he was more philosopher-king than business executive. Those he taught at the Illinois Institute of Technology learned, perhaps instinctively, to combine the

SOM OFFICE, CHICAGO, 1950s
Founded in 1936, SOM has completed over 10,000 architectural, design, and planning projects in over 50 countries. As well as five US practices, there are offices in London and Hong Kong.

LEVER HOUSE, NEW YORK, 1951–52
The smooth curtain of the glass wall effectively conceals the steel structure that lies beneath it. At ground level, the two-story base partially screens the building's inner courtyard.

KPF's London Office, 1990s
KPF's work includes the World Bank Headquarters in Washington DC, for which the company, with over 300 employees, was given an Honor Award by the American Institute of Architects.

formulaic qualities of Mies' architecture which superficially appeared to be a perfect partner for US industrial mass-production techniques with the might of US industry.

Over the previous four decades, the architect Albert Kahn (1869–1942) had built literally hundreds of steel-and-concrete-framed factories and assembly plants in the US and the Soviet Union. He saw his work as engineering and not as art, although European intellectuals, including Mies and Le Corbusier, interpreted them as models of the new architecture. It may well be that Mies himself was directly inspired by the example of Kahn: some of the lesser buildings on the IIT campus, including the chapel, have more than a look of Kahn about them.

SLICK EFFICIENCY

These two architectural traditions were brought together by SOM's Gordon Bunshaft in the design of Lever House, New York (1951–52). With its near ethereal curtain wall of blue-green glass criss-crossed with fine chromed-steel mullions and transoms, Lever House was a super-smooth container for corporate executives to make money in. It was as smooth, in fact, as the latest automobiles from Motown (Detroit).

What Lever House gave the business world was an image of modernity, of cleanliness and slick efficiency; here was a building that was lithe and fit, promising fast and easy bucks in an open and democratic world. The importance of Lever House cannot be overstressed. Its façades launched thousands of near-identical copies from New York to Nairobi on the way to San Francisco via Singapore. It was very different, however, from Mies' own Seagram Building (1954–58, see pp.178–79) which was built luxuriously, an exquisite one-off which bears comparison to Greek temples and Egyptian pyramids – it just happens to be a place of modern worship, dedicated to Mammon rather than to Athena or Ra. Lever House was a top-line Ford or Lincoln to Seagram's Rolls-Royce or Mercedes-Benz.

PROCESS AND PRODUCT

The business-minded spirit of SOM infused many new architectural practices worldwide. They aped its image and way of working and brought to the world of the property developer and business corporation a global house style that has endured, with slight changes of style – reserved largely for the "skin," or cladding, of office buildings – for half a century and more. SOM was also the model for what became known as "commercial architecture" designed by "commercial architects." Their progeny can be met worldwide, although in the US itself, the second generation SOM is KPF (Kohn Pedersen Fox), responsible for the creation of millions of cubic feet of slick office buildings and retail complexes. This is architecture as process and product, of brands and management speak: SOM and KPF are the Coca-Cola and McDonald's of architecture. Over time it has proved to be easy to build, adaptable to changes in style, durable and profitable. This corporate architecture is, however, a very long way indeed from Mies van der Rohe's glass tower dreams of 1919–21.

DG Bank Headquarters, Frankfurt, 1993
This mixed-use project by KPF attempts to link the residential community of Frankfurt's west end with the busy corridor of Mainzer Landstrasse, on which the building stands.

POSTMODERNISM
LESS IS A BORE

ROBERT VENTURI
Born in 1925 in
Philadelphia, Venturi
studied architecture at
Princeton University, and in
the 1950s worked in the
United States for one of the
pioneers of Modernism,
Louis Kahn (1901–74).
In the 1960s he reacted
against the International
Style and became a major
figure in Postmodernism
when he published
*Complexity and
Contradiction in
Architecture* (1966).
His designs include the
Vanna Venturi House,
Philadelphia, (1962) and
the Sainsbury Wing of the
National Gallery in London
(opened 1991).

BY THE MID-1960s an increasing number of
architects (and most of the public they designed
for) were questioning the blandness of the new
architecture that, in the wake of Mies van der Rohe
and the "commercial" style he spawned (without
being responsible for it) was beginning to smother
city centers. Characterless for the most part, the
new corporate style seen alongside mass-produced
housing projects and highways cut through the
heart of old communities was viewed as a travesty
of the brave new world promised by Le Corbusier
and the Bauhaus.

VENTURI'S MISSION
In 1966, Robert Venturi (b.1925) published
a manifesto, *Complexity and Contradiction in
Architecture*, in which he turned Mies' famous
dictum "less is more" upside down, announcing
"less is a bore." He was, he said, in favor of
messy vitality in architecture; he believed in
aesthetic ambiguity and visual tension; his
Postmodern vision was of an architecture of
"both-and" rather than "either-or." It was time to

bring richness and delight back into architecture
and to break away from what had, for the most
part, become an anodyne world of relentlessly
dull buildings owing nothing to a sense of place
and everything to their internal logic. Modern
architecture had become insensitive to the lives
and values of those it purported to serve.

Venturi's book was hugely influential.
It marked the beginning of a new epoch in
architecture – Postmodernism. This had been
brewing for some time and the term, drawn
from philosophy and literature, had been bandied
about for many years. In theory, it was a generous
notion. Architects appeared to have lost the
ability to play with what Edwin Lutyens called
"the high game," which was well understood by
architects of previous centuries and especially
during the Baroque era. At its best Postmodern

VANNA VENTURI HOUSE, PHILADELPHIA, 1962
*Venturi's first building – built for his mother – was influenced by
the work of Palladio and Le Corbusier, but also incorporated features
from the typical American house, such as the porch and gable.*

"*Architecture
is evolutionary
as well as
revolutionary*"
ROBERT VENTURI

design was a "high game" played at first by Venturi and a number of American architects – notably by Charles Moore, Michael Graves, Robert Stern, and the much older Philip Johnson – and then spreading worldwide just as low-rent copycat Miesian architecture had in the 1950s. At its worst it was a silly game for big kids who should have known better and led to a spate of candy-colored buildings in the 1970s and 1980s that were pastiche confections of historic and Hollywood styles pasted on to conventional steel- and concrete-framed buildings with the clumsy assurance of dangerous children.

Venturi's mission, however, was not to trash the best Modern Movement design. A pupil of the great formalist Louis Kahn – whose Kimbell Art Museum, Fort Worth, Texas (1969–72; see p.51) is one of the greatest buildings of all time – at the University of Pennsylvania School of Architecture, Philadelphia, he singled out Le Corbusier and Alvar Aalto for praise. What he was against was mindless tedium and unthinking repetition.

First Projects

His first building was a house for his mother at Chestnut Hill, Philadelphia (1962). This was a playful design with cartoonlike façades that drew on sources as diverse as Le Corbusier and Palladio and incorporated a folksy porch, gable, and other overscaled details drawn from the classic American house. The interior plan of the house was rich and complex, or ambiguous as the architect might prefer to say.

Venturi went on to establish a successful practice with Denise Scott-Brown. Together with Steven Izenour, a partner in the practice, they wrote a second much-read book, *Learning from Las Vegas* (1972), a celebration of populist and ad hoc architecture and details as witnessed in unselfconscious US streets. Their work included a wide range of playful houses as well as colorful art galleries and museums. It was fascinating to see how Venturi and Scott-Brown came to terms with London, when in 1991 they won a competition to design a new extension to the National Gallery, Trafalgar Square, to house a magnificent collection of early Renaissance Italian paintings. Here, they donned a rather tweedy suit and, although the galleries themselves are graceful, top-lit spaces, the façades to Trafalgar Square are, dare one say it, a walk on the tame side.

The danger with the Postmodern approach is that it could easily slip into the realm of bad visual puns and gimcrack design. And it did. In

PUBLIC SERVICES BUILDING, PORTLAND, OREGON, 1980–82
This 15-story municipal office building by Michael Graves has become a Postmodern landmark. Its windows are small and square, contrasting with the bold masses of color.

the Postmodern era anything went. But all that was involved was a change of dress, as it were, instead of the development of an appropriate and responsible architecture. Classic examples of skin-deep Postmodern design can be found throughout American and European cities and, sadly, in the fast-emerging cities of Southeast Asia too.

Michael Graves

The other "master" of the style, at its best, was Michael Graves (b.1934), whose Public Services Building, Portland, Oregon (1980–82) is a model of how to do Pomo. The building is a near-cube, 12 stories high, with playfully modulated and artfully applied motifs and features drawn from Ledoux (see p.126), among other historic architects. Quasi-trompe l'oeil effects and ambiguous finishes create an image of sophistication that is fundamentally skin-deep. This was architecture as stage set but without the depth or grandeur of Ledoux or Boullée or the great European Baroque architects.

POSTMODERN CERAMICS
The Los Angeles architect Peter Shire (1947–), who was a member of Ettore Sottsass' Memphis group, is noted for his highly individual ceramic designs. The California Peach Cup, made in 1980, is typical of his work and a good example of Postmodern design.

TV-AM Building, London, 1982
Terry Farrell's headquarters for the TV-AM breakfast-time station was the one of the first British Postmodern buildings. This view, alongside the canal at Camden Lock, shows the distinctive paintwork and the roof topped with glass-reinforced plastic eggcups.

Graves had started his career in the early 1970s as a member of the New York Five (alongside Richard Meier, Charles Gwathmey, Peter Eisenman, and John Hejduk). They had a fascination in common for the white, 1920s architecture of Le Corbusier and a desire to evoke its qualities in new buildings. If Graves' leap into Postmodernism seemed odd at the time, then Corbusier's fans were equally thrown off course when he adopted a raw concrete aesthetic from the late 1940s and abandoned the crisp, white style of his early success.

Graves had a number of imitators, not least Terry Farrell (b.1940), whose "Eggcup House,"

as it was popularly known, a headquarters for the short-lived TV-AM broadcasting station, Camden Town, London (1982), evoked a jokey journey across the world, a rising sun motif (TV-AM was a breakfast channel) together with workaday offices hidden behind an undulating crinkle-crankle façade. The building's canalside front, reworked from an old garage, was topped with GRP eggcups (GRP stands for glass-reinforced plastic, a material that characterized Pomo design in the 1980s). The building had a lightness of touch, a stage-set quality that Farrell was to lose as his later works, such as Embankment Place above Charing Cross Station, became grander in design. As the Eighties progressed, Postmodernism became a house style for brash new big business, notably in deregulated financial markets.

PHILIP JOHNSON

Philip Johnson was the man who brought Mies van der Rohe to the States in 1937 and who, together with the historian Henry-Russell Hitchcock, introduced New York to the Modern Movement (what they dubbed "International Style") in an exhibition of that name held at the Museum of Modern Art in 1932. He had been going Pomo for many years before designing the controversial AT&T Building, New York City (1984). Described as resembling a giant Chippendale cabinet, this mighty, stone-clad skyscraper raised a gigantic Italian Mannerist split pediment over the skyline of Manhattan. It was, detailing aside, the Seagram Building by other means, although far less sophisticated. Johnson had been Mies van der Rohe's

EMBANKMENT PLACE, LONDON, 1987–90
The profiled curved metal roof of Terry Farrell's office building above Charing Cross railway station make it one of the more imposing waterfront landmarks on the banks of the Thames.

partner on the Seagram project. It was always fascinating to watch how often he changed his style. Blink, it seemed, and the pioneer Modernist was a "historicist." Blink again and the wily maestro was a Postmodern. Soon enough he would abandon Postmodernism, dip into Deconstructivism and then, in his nineties, move on again.

EUROPEAN DEVELOPMENTS

In Europe, a Postmodern spirit affected some heavy-duty architecture in much subtler and occasionally deeply convincing ways. A good example is the civilized yet provocative Neue Staatsgalerie, Stuttgart (1977–84) by James Stirling (1926–92) and Michael Wilford (b.1934). Here, new technology, Neo-classicism, intelligent urban planning, and the colorful whimsy of Postmodernism come together in what was a wonderful climax to Stirling's prodigious career. He was a large, opinionated man who had served during the Allied invasion of occupied France in 1944, and made it vociferously clear that he detested labels. Again, here was proof that the best Postmodernists were architects who were passing through a particular phase. In effect they were abandoning what had become the arid certainties of an increasingly characterless Modernism and were searching for new meanings and attempting to connect, in fresh ways, with history.

AT&T BUILDING, NEW YORK CITY, 1984
Philip Johnson's Manhattan skyscraper was proclaimed a rejection of Modernism. The top has a broken pediment which journalists compared to Chippendale furniture.

JAMES STIRLING
After studying architecture at Liverpool University, James Stirling (1926–92) went into practice with James Gowan (1923–) in 1956. Early buildings, such as Leicester University Engineering Building (1959–63), established their reputation. From 1963 to 1971 Stirling practiced alone. Notable buildings from this period of his career include the Cambridge University History Building (1964–67). Michael Wilford became a partner in 1971.

NEUE STAATSGALERIE, STUTTGART, 1977–84
The Neue Staatsgalerie is an extension to the existing Neo-classical art gallery. The central courtyard forms a focal point for the gallery spaces and the public route through the site. The galleries are arranged in a U-shaped block, raised on a podium.

EXTREMES
THE CUTTING EDGE

JUST HOW FAR could the notion of Postmodernism be pushed in architecture? In the US, we have seen how in the end a style that began in a cartoonlike way ended up in the service of the Disney Corporation. This seemed right and fitting. What were missing in the US experience, perhaps, were irony on the one hand and on the other a sense of how to play with history seriously but in new ways. Architecture, as the Mannerists in Renaissance Italy knew, could be witty and playful without descending into pratfalls and heavy-handed jokes.

MUSSOLINI'S BATHROOM, CENTRO DOMUS, MILAN, 1980
Branzi worked for the Italian magazine Casabella *in the 1970s and was involved with the design groups Studio Alchemia and Memphis, all influences that are evident in the set shown above.*

Not surprisingly then, it was the Italians who, from the end of the 1970s gave Postmodern style-mongering a new and, initially, unexpected twist in two very different directions. Both emerged in Milan. One was a clever critique of both Modernism and the banality of the Postmodern condition as perceived by a loosely related group of sophisticated architects who were also distinguished product designers. The other was an earnest if sometimes chilling game that led to some of the most profound architecture of recent times. In between, there were experiments by other architects, notably in England, trying to connect currents in Postmodern music and fashion with those of a challenging, occasionally disturbing, but serious architecture.

MILANESE DESIGN

First, there was the work of two Milanese groups, Studio Alchemia and Memphis, gathered around Alessandro Mendini (b.1931), editor of *Domus*, a highly influential architecture and design magazine, and Ettorre Sottsass (b.1919). Both groups produced comical designs, from coffee-pots to interiors, making their public debut at the Milan Furniture Fair of 1980. The aim was, in part, to subvert the way in which people perceived the icons of everyday design they saw around them. In Sottsass' words, Memphis existed in a "gelatinous, rarefied area whose very nature precludes set models and definitions." They were involved in the process of "mutation

GRÖNINGEN MUSEUM, NETHERLANDS, 1984
Designed in collaboration with Philippe Starck, Alessandro Mendini's museum was put together on computer in California before these plans were sent to Dutch shipbuilders for the construction.

VILLA ZAPU, NAPA VALLEY, CALIFORNIA, 1984–88
Built of timber throughout, the house was designed for the Swedish wine-grower Thomas Lundstrom. A separate "guest tower" stands beyond the villa's long swimming pool.

of form and open to change". This was a deliberate challenge to the certainties of Modernism and rational design. The approach was often best expressed in exhibition displays rather than in real buildings. The Mussolini's Bathroom set by Andrea Branzi (b.1934) exhibited at the Centro Domus, Milan (1980) was a delightful parody of the absurdities of Fascist pomp and the Italian dictator's attempt to mix the imagery of Modernism with his repressive form of government. Stretched into full-scale buildings as in the Museum of Contemporary Art, Gröningen, Netherlands, by Mendini (1984), the limits of this "ironic" style were evident. A joke, no matter how sophisticated on paper or in the guise of a chair, translates awkwardly into a full-scale building.

Much more successful was the Villa Zapu, Napa Valley, California (1984–88) by the British architects Julian Powell-Tuck (b.1952), David Connor (b.1950), and Gunnar Orefelt (b.1953). They emerged during the Punk movement in London in the late 1970s, working with Malcolm McClaren and Vivienne Westwood, creators of this angular, streetwise style. An architectural

adventure, the house was theatrical, witty, and refined, a kind of Postmodern Palladian villa, at the heart of a Californian vineyard, seen through the distorting mirror of Punk experimentation and Deconstructivist gamesmanship. Built of local materials (redwood rendered in stucco) and beautifully set in its landscape, it was a good example of what a Postmodern attitude could achieve.

ALDO ROSSI

At the same time as Mendini and Sottsass were setting out to provoke in Milan, Aldo Rossi (1931–97) was working on such profound and extreme works as the Teatro del Mondo (1980) in Venice, a floating wooden theater composed of the key elements of his highly personal "Rational" architecture – based in part on the haunting, metaphysical townscape paintings of Giorgio de Chirico (1888–1978) – and the deeply moving if daunting San Cataldo cemetery, Modena (completed 1984). Rossi's powerful architecture was for the most part mournful, silent, funereal, and conveyed a sense of emptiness.

While this was in many ways perfect for the San Cataldo project it seemed out of place in the design of social housing. The Gallaratese 2 housing he designed at the end of a long tram ride out of Milan was spooky, a long and relentless arcaded row of white apartments without a single relieving feature. This appeared to be as much a city of the dead as the cemetery at Modena. The cemetery, however, is magnificent, a miniature city of memories and dreams, a superb sequence of hypnotic monuments etched with deep shadows and set along unyielding axes. This is an extreme form of architecture taken beyond life's extremity.

ALESSI
Founded by Giovanni Alessi in 1921, the first Alessi products were coffeepots and trays. After 1945 consultant designers were commissioned and the firm began to concentrate more on the appearance of its lines. However, it was in the 1970s that the firm really came to prominence, producing numbered, signed pieces by architects and designers, including Ettore Sottsass. In 1983 the company launched the Tea and Coffee Piazza project, commissioning 11 architects including Robert Venturi, Michael Graves (his kettle is above), Richard Meier, Aldo Rossi, and Alessandro Mendini to produce "architecture in miniature." This was a huge success and Alessi became known for playful, Postmodern design. Further projects have involved Philippe Starck and Frank Gehry.

MODEL OF SAN CATALDO CEMETERY, MODENA, COMPLETED 1984
Aldo Rossi's plans for this cemetery won a competition in 1971, and the site was built over the following years. The simplicity of Rossi's design owes much to 1930s Italian Rationalism.

HIGH-TECH

THE AGE OF THE NEW MACHINE

RICHARD ROGERS

Born in Florence in 1933, Rogers trained in London and at Yale. Apart from his pioneering buildings, such as the Lloyds Building, London, and the Pompidou Centre, Paris, Rogers has also created large-scale planning projects for London, Berlin, and Shanghai, and is the author of *Cities for a Small Planet* (1997), an attempt to outline a sustainable combination of architecture and inner-city planning. In 1998 Rogers was invited to chair the Urban Task Force, a government-appointed body concerned with urban regeneration in England.

ARCHIGRAM

Archigram was a group – almost a pop group – of inventive young architects who gathered around Peter Cook at the Architectural Association, London, in the early 1960s. Cook and his colleagues published their own magazine and held exhibitions of their drawings of buildings and cities in the style of superhero comic books. Some of these cities could be added to indefinitely, their facilities "plugged in;" another (by Ron Herron) walked and settled wherever its citizens wanted it to. Archigram's designs were playful and speculative. Few were realized, yet they had a profound influence on the young Richard Rogers and Norman Foster, an influence most clearly seen in Rogers' and Piano's Pompidou Centre.

IN THE US, HIGH-TECH was a fashionable interior style, something to do with a surfeit of matt black and chrome – tables, chairs, clothes, what have you – which dominated the 1980s. In Britain, Europe, and elsewhere it was a highly distinctive architectural movement championed by three major talents, those of Norman Foster (b.1935), Richard Rogers (b.1933), and Renzo Piano (b.1937). Piano and Rogers, with the Irish engineer Peter Rice, were the architects of the first High-tech monument, the Pompidou Centre, Paris (1971–77), a vibrant and colorful machine for exhibiting art with its insides displayed on the outside, a fact that prompted some waggish commentators to describe its style as "bowellist." The idea, however, was to liberate the maximum possible volume of space inside by positioning all its workings – stairs, elevators, escalators, structural supports, heating and ventilation ducts, and so on – outside the interior envelope of the building.

The net effect was extraordinary, a highly animated structure that owed precious little to convention, designed by a team of long-haired and bearded young hopefuls in the aftermath of the *événements* of 1968. For a moment it had seemed that left-wing students, militant workers, and other radicals might just topple the Fifth Republic. In the event they didn't, and three years later, the French president was the strictly conservative Georges Pompidou who, despite his initial shock, gave his assent to Piano and Rogers' radical design.

HIGH-TECH INFLUENCES

The Pompidou Centre was not entirely unprecedented. Its roots lay partly in Rogers' admiration of the Crystal Palace of 1851 (see pp.140–41), the world's first monumental prefabricated building. It also lay in Piano's fascination with modern engineering structure (and particularly in the work of the French engineer Jean Prouvé, whose iron, steel, and plywood buildings and furniture were designed up and out from highly resolved individual components), and in the work of Archigram.

POMPIDOU CENTRE, PARIS, 1971–77

Piano and Rogers competition-winning design is ideal for a modern art gallery. The external positioning of the building's color-coded service elements maximizes the uninterrupted floor space within.

SAINSBURY CENTRE FOR VISUAL ARTS, UNIVERSITY OF EAST ANGLIA, NORWICH, 1978

Commissioned to house a collection of tribal art, the center also functions as part of an academic institution, with offices and lecture rooms. An extension was built in the early 1990s, positioned below ground level at one end of the building.

NORMAN FOSTER

Born in Manchester, England, in 1935, Norman Foster is one of the world's preeminent architects. The headquarters of the Hongkong and Shanghai Banking Corporation, and the new German Parliament, Reichstag, Berlin (see p.11), are among his most important works. He received the Pritzker Architect Prize in 1999.

"I confess to being obsessed with invention"
NORMAN FOSTER

Together with Norman Foster, Rogers had received his postgraduate education at Yale. With friends they traveled across the States looking at new developments in architecture and technology. Foster, in particular, was fascinated by the work of the inventor Buckminster Fuller (see p.208) whose geodesic dome was one brilliant way of covering the maximum volume of space with the lightest possible strong materials.

He was also intrigued by the latest steel-based architecture in California where Ezra Ehrenkrantz, Craig Ellwood, and Pierre Koenig (see pp.184–85) had been developing a light, bright, clean technologically based architecture that was nevertheless poetic. Combined with his love of aircraft and flying, Foster was to develop an immediately recognizable style of his own that was smooth-skinned and taut, just as Rogers' work proved to be animated and held together by flamboyantly expressed structures.

Foster and Rogers worked together with Su Rogers and Wendy Cheeseman as Team 4 in London in the early and mid-1960s. Foster's first masterpiece was the Sainsbury Centre for Visual Arts, University of East Anglia, Norwich, England, (1978), a sleek aircraft hangar of a building infused with delicately filtered daylight. In a broadcast for BBC television a decade later Foster was asked to talk about his favorite building, characteristically he chose a Boeing 747 "Jumbo" jet.

What was curious, though, about High-tech architecture was the fact that it celebrated technologies that were passing rapidly into the history books. Not entirely, of course, but it is not hard to see in buildings by Rogers and Foster a nostalgia for Victorian machinery as well as a cool passion for the latest developments in materials and structural know-how. And notably in some of the earlier projects, High-tech buildings required a large input of skilled industrial craftsmanship.

A design like Foster's Hongkong and Shanghai Bank headquarters (1979–86) was exquisitely made, each component inside and out custom-made for the building. What Foster and other High-tech architects have tried to achieve is an impeccable standard of fit and finish comparable to the best new cars, and even aircraft. This was a lofty goal and only achievable when the architects were able to have complete control over the building process, an increasingly difficult role to obtain and maintain as the 1990s gave way to the 2000s and the architect's position in the building team was being marginalized.

HONGKONG AND SHANGHAI BANK HEADQUARTERS, HONG KONG, 1979–86
The main piers of the building stand at its corners, surrounding a vertical atrium at the center. Floors are suspended from trusses positioned in stages up the building.

CHEP LAP KOK AIRPORT, HONG KONG, 1998

Three 300-ft (100-m) hills off the south China coast were flattened to create the largest construction project of its time. Foster's

terminal building is shaped like a giant aircraft and consists of a lightweight steel roof laid over a base structure of exposed concrete.

Appropriately, given their fascination with the design and technology of travel, in the 1990s Foster, Rogers, and Piano were all involved in the design of major airports: Rogers with the long-delayed Terminal Five, Heathrow, London; Foster with Chep Lap Kok, the new Hong Kong airport; and Piano with Kansai airport (1991–94, see p.224), built on an artificial island on Osaka Bay.

VISIONS OF AEROSPACE

By the turn of the twenty-first century, Foster was, by common agreement and most measures the world's most successful architect, designing major galleries and museums, as well as corporate headquarters, schools, bridges, furniture, electricity pylons (for the Italian national grid), vehicles, and even speculative offices. It was partly Foster's dynamism that made this so, and partly the highly able team he surrounded himself with. More than this, however, was the fact that his architecture clicked into place with his generation of business, political, and cultural leaders as surely as Mies van der Rohe's had with the movers, shakers, and moneymakers of 1950s Chicago and New York. Foster offered a vision of aerospace grace, and efficiency. His practice was also businesslike and efficient. In effect he bridged the gap that had existed in 1950s New York and Chicago between the artistry of Mies and the machinelike competence of SOM (see pp.196–97).

Renzo Piano, meanwhile, moved High-tech away from the machinelike intensity of Foster and the almost baroque aesthetic of Rogers, to a softer and more organic approach. He investigated the

world of the "soft machine" and was as likely to investigate the properties and possibilities of timber, brick, and plywood as he was to push the frontiers of new materials technology. On the one hand he has designed perhaps the most sophisticated of all airports — Kansai — and on the other produced two very different but equally beautiful and important museums. The first of these was the Menil Collection, Houston, Texas, a home in the relentless suburban grid of this sun-baked city for a particularly fine collection of tribal art. Working with Peter Rice, Piano devised a simple structural device — a concrete leaf extruded in rows across the tops of the museum walls — that throughout the day filtered light into a gentle procession of galleries and internal courtyards without glare. The result was a simple building, clad externally in clapboard,

RENZO PIANO

The son of builders, Piano was born in Genoa, Italy, in 1937 and studied and then taught at the Milan Politecnico before forming a partnership with Richard Rogers in 1970. His first important commission was the Italian Industry Pavilion at Expo '70 in Osaka. His work has concentrated on the use of new technology and materials. These include the mile-long Kansai Airport (see p.224), the football stadium at Bari, and the reconstruction of the Potsdamer Platz in Berlin. Piano has practices in Genoa, Paris, and Berlin, and in 1998 was awarded the Pritzker Architecture Prize.

MENIL COLLECTION, HOUSTON, TEXAS, 1986

The frame of this "soft machine" is of steel and the wall of weather-board. The protective leaves of the roof are made of thin sections of reinforced concrete integrated with the steel lattice girder.

and filled with gentle and changing light that as far as possible allowed the exhibits to be seen as they were intended to be. Here the technological input was in the thinking and the process that led to the shaping of the concrete roof assembly which, in turn, allows nature to do what far too many architects rely on fluorescent lights to do.

GREENING TECHNOLOGY

In marked contrast, the Jean-Marie Tjibaou Cultural Centre (1991–98), set on a bay beyond Nouméa, capital of the French colony of Nouvelle Caledonie (New Caledonia), is a highly expressive timber and steel structure that feels at once futuristic and like an extension of nature. Piano's center was the last of the *grands travaux* commissioned by the French president François Mitterand, partly as a sop to local sensitivities – many were upset that the French have no plans to give up this South Pacific island (rich in nickel deposits and a key part of France's independent and global nuclear weapons program).

The center celebrates the culture of the indigenous Kanak people. Collections, a library, a multimedia centre, café, bookshop, and conference and performance spaces are housed in ten tall podlike structures clad in long strips of sustainable hardwood that sing gently as the wind rushes through them and appear to mingle with the surrounding trees. The center is not air-conditioned, but subtly arranged so that fresh air breezes through most of the tropical day.

JEAN-MARIE TJIBAOU CULTURAL CENTRE, NOUMÉA, NEW CALEDONIA, 1991–98
The curved structures of the center are made of glass, stainless steel, and laminated timber. Piano described them as "archaic containers of an archaic appearance, whose interiors are equipped with all the possibilities offered by modern technology".

Despite its very different aesthetic, the Jean-Marie Tjibaou Centre is like the Menil Collection in that the great input of computer and other high technology has gone into making buildings that are fundamentally simple and very much in tune with their natural setting. It is significant that the architects most concerned with sophisticated technology at the end of the twentieth century were also those generally most interested in the conservation of energy. Perhaps their goal can be summed up as an energetic attempt to bring architecture in line with the very latest technological developments while seeking to minimize the expenditure of energy and paying homage to the human machine maker.

There was a great satisfaction to be had from landing in the latest aircraft at an airport such as Kansai or Chep Lap Kok, where the technology of machine and architecture overlapped, or arriving at Nicholas Grimshaw's Waterloo International Station (1993) in a 185-mph (300-kph) Eurostar train where the prognathous trains fitted like steel fingers in a well-tailored metal glove.

NICHOLAS GRIMSHAW
Born in 1939, Grimshaw has completed a number of ambitious projects in his native England. These include the Financial Times Printworks, London (1988), Sainsbury's Supermarket at Camden in London (1988), and the RAC Centre in Bristol (1995). His work has many of the qualities of other Hi-tech masters, and like them he has used technology to create a more responsible architecture. His British Pavilion at the '92 Expo in Seville had glass walls cooled by a continuous cascade of water, the pumping fueled by solar electric panels. His Eden Project (2000) in Cornwall, England, is a biosphere that attempts to recreate key global microclimates.

ARCHITECTS' ENGINEERING
THE WELL-TEMPERED MACHINE

BUCKMINSTER FULLER
Engineer, philosopher, and architect, Richard Buckminster Fuller was born in Massachusetts in 1895. One of his first ventures was a company that created housing from fiber blocks. He developed various theories about the uses of technology, which he believed would solve problems of human shelter, nutrition, and transportation through "anticipatory design." His greatest contribution to architecture, however, was the geodesic dome, a self-supporting structure that increased in strength as it increased in size. Fuller died in 1983.

HIGH-TECH WAS a distinctive approach to architecture in which architects working closely with engineers made a style out of engineering developments and skill. In lesser hands than those of Renzo Piano, Richard Rogers, or Norman Foster, High-tech became a fussy and over-the-top aesthetic in which the structures of buildings could become over elaborate simply to satisfy some whim of the designer's.

During the twentieth century many architects came close to designing almost pure engineering structures, as for example did the prolific Albert Kahn (1869–1942) with huge, efficient, and well-planned structures such as the Chrysler Half-Ton Truck Assembly Plant, Detroit (1937–38) which covered an area of no less than 11.5 acres (4.6 hectares). Equally there were engineers and inventors like Buckminster Fuller, who designed impressive structures such as the Freight Wagon Repair Shop, Baton Rouge, Louisiana (1958), which relied for their strength and appearance wholly on the sum of machined components with no architectural pretensions whatsoever. Wall and roof were one.

Somewhere in the middle of these two extremes sprouted an architecture that owed its logic and aesthetic to engineering design, but not the self-conscious stylistic and idealistic way of Rogers, Foster, and Piano. Two of the most impressive loom over the center of Chicago. These are the John Hancock Center (1965–70) and the Sears Tower (completed 1974), two skyscrapers, both at the time of completion claiming the record for the world's tallest building, and both designed by SOM (see pp.196–97). The former tapers up into the clouds, its stacked floors of offices and apartments held together by giant external steel X-braces. In other words, the structure of the building is on the outside and this gives the tower its striking appearance. The sense of a pure engineering structure is heightened by the tall red-and-white communications masts on the roof that reminded most commentators of ICBM missiles.

The Sears Tower is similarly equipped, but its structure is a simple expression of the US steel-framed building taken to new heights. The building steps back as it climbs over 1,500 feet (457 meters) above the Chicago sidewalks, losing bulk as it approaches the realm of aircraft rather than architecture. Both buildings represent the increasingly important role of the structural engineer in the architectural process. Both have something of the feel of ancient temples and monoliths. Both, like the pyramids of ancient Mexico and Egypt, stare blankly out over their surroundings as if utterly indifferent to them.

ARCHITECTS IN AEROSPACE
Another deeply impressive SOM project was the Hajj Terminal, Jeddah (1982). The aim was to provide a vast concourse for the huge numbers of Muslim pilgrims: as many as two million

HAJJ TERMINAL, JEDDAH, SAUDI ARABIA, 1982
This ground-breaking structure was one of the first to combine earlier architectural forms with the latest High-Tech materials — here, the tensile fabric used to roof the airport building.

OLYMPIC PARK, MUNICH, 1967–72

The arena, main stadium, and the swimming pool of the Munich Olympic complex were all linked by Frei Otto's tentlike roof.

It was made of PVC-coated polyester fabric, which was held in tension by large cables slung from supporting masts.

INTELLIGENT BUILDINGS

Advances in technology have enabled architects and engineers to build intelligence into buildings, to create structures that can respond to changes in environment, and thus adapt to human needs. The Institut du Monde Arabe (1983–89) was built as a symbol of the partnership between France and 21 Arab countries. The southern façade is composed of 240 "diaphragms"(one is shown above) arranged in a geometric pattern. These are regulated by light-sensitive cells and open and close with the sun, allowing filtered natural light to enter the building without harming the artworks within.

people can be here at one and the same time on their way to and from Mecca, as every Muslim is expected to visit the holy site at least once in their lifetime. The solution, which was principally the work of the structural engineer Fazlur Rahman Khan, was to erect a sequence of huge modern tents using the latest tensile roof technology, yet reminiscent the tents in which nomadic tribespeople once sheltered across the deserts of Arabia and of early air terminals, which were usually little more than a few canvas tents pitched on the edge of grass runways.

What was special about the Hajj Terminal, its scale aside, was the fact that it was a modern airport without walls, glazing, or air-conditioning. The tents were, in effect, giant parasols, their sides open to catch desert breezes. To have built on this scale for so many passengers using accepted building technology would have been exorbitantly costly in terms of energy consumption. Designed after the "Energy Crisis" of 1973–74, when Arabian countries withheld supplies of crude oil to the West and thus raised fuel prices to unprecedented limits, the Hajj Terminal was a model of how to design a low-energy building that was also a handsome match for its purpose and surroundings.

Equally impressive were the swooping tensile steel roofs of the sports buildings at the Olympic Park, Munich (1967–72), designed by Gunter Behnisch (b.1922), a U-boat commander during World War II, and the brilliant engineer Frei Otto (b.1925). Behnisch's later Hysolar Research Institute, Stuttgart (1987) was an exciting building

to look at, but here the accent was on a willfully playful engineering style closer to High-tech than an artistically modified engineering structure.

PURE ENGINEERING

An example of an architect moving into pure engineering is Norman Foster's multispan Millau Viaduct over the Tarn Valley, in the Massif Central in the south of France. By way of contrast, a particularly fine example of an architect adapting new engineering know-how for a purely visual effect, yet integral to the spirit and structure of the building is the Institut du Monde Arabe, Paris (1983–89) by Jean Nouvel (b.1946). A whole wall of this much-liked complex is composed of a screen of what the architect has called "modern mashrabeya work," or the sunscreens of traditional Arabic buildings. They are very beautiful, evoking a past tradition, yet utterly modern.

MILLAU VIADUCT, MASSIF CENTRAL, SOUTHERN FRANCE, 2000
This slender, cable-stayed bridge, which carries the motorway that links Paris and Barcelona, impacts minimally on the majestic landscape. Yet at its highest point it is taller than the Eiffel Tower.

JAPANESE METABOLISTS
THE RISING POP ART SUN

JAPAN'S STRUGGLE to find a new architectural identity after the nuclear blows of Nagasaki and Hiroshima was, until the beginning of the 1960s, a painful one for those involved. As Japan entered the modern world with a new determination and energy, how could it find an architectural language of its own? How could its architects avoid being caught up in wholesale Westernization?

To begin with, the major influence on a new generation of post-war Japanese architects was Le Corbusier, who designed the National Museum of Western Art, Tokyo (1955–59), built by the Japanese architects Kunio Maekawa and Junio Sakakura. Corbu was to inspire the work of two of Japan's most distinguished Modern architects, Kenzo Tange (b.1913) and Tadao Ando (b.1941). Although the Swiss master's influence was paramount in the 1950s, by 1960 a group of young architects and critics had emerged with a philosophy (of sorts) that fused ideas drawn from traditional Japanese design, Pop architecture (notably the work of the British design group Archigram; see p.204) and Le Corbusier. This they labelled Metabolism, introducing the new creed to a group of distinguished overseas visitors at the World Design Conference, Tokyo in 1960.

AN ISM OF ONE'S OWN

The group was led by the twenty-six-year-old Kisho Kurokawa, along with Fumihiko Maki, Kiyonori Kikutake, Masato Otaka, and the critic Noboru Kawazoe. They were determined to have a fashionable and influential "ism" of their own and one to compete with those that young Western architects appeared to invent at the drop of a T-square. The name was meant to suggest a biological or biomorphic approach to design, buildings, and cities that grew to meet new demands in a way parallel to nature yet making full, and even exaggerated use of the latest building technologies and emerging forms of communication.

Metabolism first showed its colors in a series of collaborative fantasy projects along the lines of Archigram's Plug-In and Walking Cities. These included Ocean City, Helix City, and Space City. In reality these led to a small number of striking buildings including the much-published Nagakin

Capsule Tower, Tokyo (1972) by Kisho Kurokawa. Here, two concrete shafts incorporating elevators, emergency stairs, and services supported 140 individual "pods." These were highly serviced studio rooms equipped with the latest technological and electronic gizmos of the time, all very James Bond (*You Only Live Twice*, a Bond

NAGAKIN CAPSULE TOWER, TOKYO, 1972
Kurokawa's bizarre capsule structure was an attempt to use modern technology to resolve the problems of Japan's overcrowded urban centers. The building's playful functionalism makes a virtue out of its visual incongruity.

film set in Tokyo, had been released in 1967); they were, in fact, highly modified sea-containers, each with a porthole for a window. The idea of the building was to suggest either the possibility of continual change or of permanent incompleteness. It was also great fun.

Several buildings were realized in a similar vein, including Youji Watanabe's Sky Building No. 3, Tokyo (1971), which looked like a stack of Airstream trailers piled high into the sky, and Tatsuhiko Nakajima's Kibogaoko Youth Castle, a rather crazy looking hostel in Shiga Prefecture (1973) complete with a tower of pods and a reproduction of Michelangelo's statue of David inside its lobby.

EXTENDABLE ARCHITECTURE

Perhaps the best of the Metabolist buildings was by the older architect, Kenzo Tange, a designer who proved able to move through a number of styles and approaches over a long career that began with the Corbusian Hiroshima Peace Center (1949–55) and entered a dramatic Postmodern phase in the 1980s.

The Yamanashi Communications Center, Kofu (1964–67) built against the backdrop of Mount Fuji was a muscular and theatrical building, a twentieth-century Samurai castle, its floors of offices, studios, and printing presses held up by mighty service towers. These gave the appearance of being infinitely extendable, although, in practice as with most "extendable" architecture, its form stayed pretty much finite. One of the great strengths of Tange's design was the fact that it suggested a not quite still point in a fast-changing world, where its post-and-beam construction were reminders of the roots of architecture (Oriental and Western). This was offset by the building's implicit celebration of the new communications technology that was truly revolutionizing life in the last third of the twentieth century – with much of the technology being developed and made in Japan, and revolutionizing the Japanese economy and society in the process.

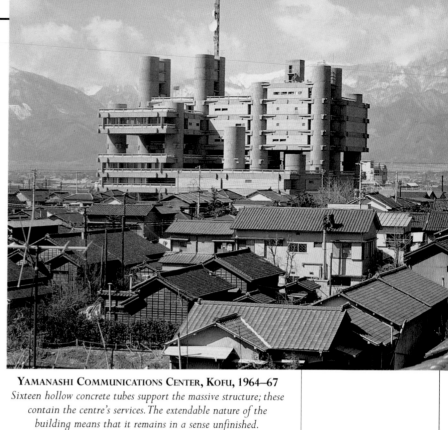

YAMANASHI COMMUNICATIONS CENTER, KOFU, 1964–67
Sixteen hollow concrete tubes support the massive structure; these contain the centre's services. The extendable nature of the building means that it remains in a sense unfinished.

SONY TOWER, OSAKA, 1976
A forerunner to both the Pompidou Centre and Rogers' Lloyds Building, Kurokawa's Sony Tower has its service elements – the lift and the steel-clad toilet capsules – hung off the main frame.

For the rest, the Metabolists proved to be masters of exhibition design and created such entertaining pavilions as Kisho Kurokawa's Takara Beautilion at the Pop-age Expo 70, Osaka (1970). This plug-together structure, squeezed full of entertaining "happenings" was also suggestive of the imagery that was to be used in sci-fi films some years later, notably Ridley Scott's *Alien* (1979), in which space-age structures appeared to be more organic than metallic. Very much like Metabolism itself.

Kurokawa's Sony Tower (1976) in Osaka was a showroom for the company's new products and as such required maximum display space inside and free access from without. The solution is to attach services to the exterior of the building. The structure is known as an "information tree," each function of the building being segmented, and to some extent autonomous, but serving the whole as leaves and branches sustain the whole tree. A typically biological metaphor for this most biomorphic of architecture.

KISHO KUROKAWA
Born in Nagoya, Japan in 1934, Kurokawa studied at Kyoto and Tokyo Universities. A founder member of the Japanese Metabolists, he worked with Kenzo Tange before setting up his own office in Tokyo in 1961. His major projects have included the National Ethnological Museum, Osaka, the Hiroshima City Museum of Contemporary Art, the Pacific Tower in Paris, and Kuala Lumpur International Airport. He was recently awarded first prize in the competition for the master plan and design for Astana, the new capital of Kazakhstan.

THE CLASSICAL REVIVAL
NEW WORLD ORDERS

THE REACTION AGAINST the certainties of global Modernism led to Postmodernism and a branch of this led into the cul-de-sac of the sometimes soggy and at other times megalomaniac revival of Classicism. While in Britain especially, and to an extent in the US, there were architects working in a modest way on the design of Classical villas and the very occasional public building, Classicism had all but disappeared by the mid-1950s when even Soviet architects abandoned the style in favor of concrete and prefabrication. Its revival on a large scale began with the references to Classicism made by a number of Postmodern architects in the late 1970s (notably by Charles Moore and Philip Johnson in the US, see p.200), and by the more substantial dialogue between Modern and Classical architecture made by James Stirling in the design of the Neue Staatsgalerie, Stuttgart (see p.201).

Another young architect working in Stirling's office was Quinlan Terry (b.1937), who believed that the canons and orders of Classicism had been ordained by God. This divine missionary set up practice in rural England (in Dedham, Suffolk, known to the world through John Constable's famous paintings *Dedham Vale* and *The Haywain*) and built a number of precious new Georgian-style town and country houses for those made newly rich in Margaret Thatcher's newly money-crazed Britain (1979–90), and for the Crown Estate. Terry also rebuilt a major part of Richmond-upon-Thames, Surrey (1988) in the guise of a massive riverside development in which modern, fluorescent-lit shops and offices hid with their low-ceilings and air-conditioning behind lovingly detailed 18th-century brickwork, sash windows, and tall chimneys.

TALLER DI ARQUITECTURA

In Malibu, California, the Getty Foundation commissioned a brand new museum by Landon, Wilson et al which proved to be more or less an ancient Roman villa brought accurately to life. Very much the opposite approach was adopted by the Taller di Arquitectura, a maverick architectural practice based in both Barcelona and Paris. The Barcelona studio was housed in an imaginatively converted cement works at San Just Desvern. Here, in the early days of Ricardo Bofill's idiosyncratic yet highly effective practice, poets and parrots, painters and philosophers mixed with musicians and the architects themselves. Originally the Taller worked in a powerful Pop idiom, but from the mid-1970s, its chief designer, Peter Hodgkinson, an English

RICHMOND RIVERSIDE, SURREY, 1988
This riverside development alongside the Thames was designed by the Classical revivalist architect Quinlan Terry. Georgian-style exteriors conceal modern air-conditioned shops and offices.

architect from Bath, took the studio down the Neo-classical route with outrageous designs for mass-housing, built in pre-colored prefabricated concrete. Despite their modern materials, from a distance, these buildings appeared to be as imposing as the grand palace of Versailles itself.

The first of these housing projects were intended as a kind of Versailles for the people, but, although impressive in a stage-set manner from a distance and in the architects' drawings, the reality was rookeries of small, low-ceilinged apartments. In later projects, the Taller was able to raise ceiling heights and incorporate a degree of Classical detailing into concrete molds and so bring a touch of Rome and "the high game" of Classicism into the living rooms of French citizens at the bottom of the social pile.

NEW ESTATES

The first Taller estates were at St. Quentin-en-Yvelines (1978–82) and Marne-la-Vallée (1978–83), new suburbs of Paris. Within a few years they were home to a downtrodden immigrant community. Perhaps the people lived here in a little more comfort and style than the courtiers who thronged the attics and roof timbers of Versailles during the reign of Louis XIV. Perhaps.

These were huge projects inspired as much by Piranesi and Boullée as by Versailles. The main block at Marne-la-Vallée was 18 very substantial stories high. At St. Quentin-en-Yvelines, a giant terrace of Neo-classical apartments strode across a lake in the manner of the famous French renaissance château at Chenonceaux. In 1982, Peter Hodgkinson described these controversial designs as "the Classicism of yesterday's great masters reduced to the essences of today," adding that "concrete is the new stone." Not everyone agreed, but many further schemes emerged elsewhere in France.

LE PALAIS D'ABRAXAS HOUSING, MARNE-LA-VALLÉE, FRANCE, 1978–83
In this development of monumental prefabricated concrete apartments in suburban Paris, Bofill created a powerful sense of place. Giant columns in precast concrete and glass are attached to the façade.

Perhaps the most impressive of all Classical revival exercises was the National Museum of Roman Art, Mérida (1980–85) by the Spanish architect Rafael Moneo (b.1937). This beautifully built museum with its breathtaking collection is based around a central atrium, an interpretation of the vaulted naves and aisles of the major Roman basilicas. Built in shallow Roman bricks leading up to lofty arches, the effect was monumental yet washed with daylight. Moneo's genius was to match this evocation of ancient Rome with overtly Modern elements. Beyond this, the museum was raised over a cavernous undercroft of excavated Roman remains.

In Moneo's hands, Classicism had a real purpose and even a future. In Britain, it was tied up with the nostalgic vision of the Prince of Wales and in the US with Las Vegas, Hollywood stars, and rich institutions – not much different from ancient Rome itself.

NATIONAL MUSEUM OF ROMAN ART, MÉRIDA, SPAIN, 1980–85
The arches of the brick central atrium act as natural divisions between displays. Natural light enters through skylights marking the rhythm of the walls.

FUTURES

Ᏼʏ ᴛʜᴇ ᴇɴᴅ ᴏꜰ ᴛʜᴇ ᴛᴡᴇɴᴛɪᴇᴛʜ ᴄᴇɴᴛᴜʀʏ, ᴀʀᴄʜɪᴛᴇᴄᴛᴜʀᴇ ᴄᴏᴜʟᴅ ɢᴏ ᴀɴʏ ᴏɴᴇ ᴏꜰ ᴍᴀɴʏ ᴅɪꜰꜰᴇʀᴇɴᴛ ᴡᴀʏꜱ. Nᴇᴡ ᴍᴀᴛᴇʀɪᴀʟꜱ, ᴄᴏᴍᴘᴜᴛᴇʀꜱ, ᴀɴᴅ ᴀ ꜱᴇɴꜱᴇ ᴏꜰ ꜰʀᴇᴇᴅᴏᴍ ꜰʀᴏᴍ ᴏᴠᴇʀᴀʀᴄʜɪɴɢ ᴘʜɪʟᴏꜱᴏᴘʜɪᴇꜱ ᴀɴᴅ ᴅᴏᴍɪɴᴀɴᴛ ᴍᴏᴠᴇᴍᴇɴᴛꜱ ɢᴀᴠᴇ ᴀʀᴄʜɪᴛᴇᴄᴛꜱ ᴀ ɢʀᴇᴀᴛᴇʀ ʀᴀɴɢᴇ ᴛʜᴀɴ ᴛʜᴇʏ ʜᴀᴅ ᴇᴠᴇʀ ʜᴀᴅ ʙᴇꜰᴏʀᴇ. Tʜᴇʀᴇ ᴡᴇʀᴇ ɴᴇᴡ ʀᴇꜱᴘᴏɴꜱɪʙɪʟɪᴛɪᴇꜱ ᴛᴏ ꜰᴀᴄᴇ ᴜᴘ ᴛᴏ – ᴄᴏɴᴄᴇʀɴꜱ ᴀʙᴏᴜᴛ ᴇᴄᴏʟᴏɢʏ, ᴛʜᴇ ᴜꜱᴇ ᴀɴᴅ ᴀʙᴜꜱᴇ ᴏꜰ ꜰᴏꜱꜱɪʟ ꜰᴜᴇʟꜱ, ᴀɴᴅ ᴛʜᴇ ɪɴᴠᴏʟᴠᴇᴍᴇɴᴛ ɪɴ ᴛʜᴇ ᴅᴇꜱɪɢɴ ᴏꜰ ᴛʜᴏꜱᴇ ᴡʜᴏ ᴜꜱᴇᴅ ᴛʜᴇ ʙᴜɪʟᴅɪɴɢꜱ. Aɴ ᴇxᴘʟᴏᴅɪɴɢ ᴜʀʙᴀɴ ᴘᴏᴘᴜʟᴀᴛɪᴏɴ ᴡᴀꜱ ᴘᴀʀᴛɪᴀʟʟʏ ᴀᴄᴄᴏᴍᴍᴏᴅᴀᴛᴇᴅ ʙʏ ᴛʜᴇ ᴀᴅᴅɪᴛɪᴏɴ ᴏꜰ ɴᴇᴡ ʙᴜɪʟᴅɪɴɢꜱ ᴛᴏ ᴛʜᴇ ꜰᴀʙʀɪᴄ ᴏꜰ ᴏʟᴅ ᴄɪᴛɪᴇꜱ. Tʜᴇ ᴄᴏᴍᴘᴜᴛᴇʀ ᴘʀᴏᴠᴇᴅ ᴛᴏ ʙᴇ ᴀ ʀᴇᴀʟ ᴀʟʟʏ, ᴀʟʟᴏᴡɪɴɢ ᴀʀᴄʜɪᴛᴇᴄᴛꜱ ᴛᴏ ᴛᴀᴋᴇ ᴇxᴛʀᴀᴏʀᴅɪɴᴀʀʏ ʟᴇᴀᴘꜱ ᴏꜰ ᴛʜᴇ ᴠɪꜱᴜᴀʟ ɪᴍᴀɢɪɴᴀᴛɪᴏɴ. Aꜱ ᴛʜᴇꜱᴇ ɴᴇᴡ ꜰʀᴇᴇᴅᴏᴍꜱ ᴏᴘᴇɴᴇᴅ ᴜᴘ, ᴛʜᴇ ɪʀᴏɴʏ ᴡᴀꜱ ᴛʜᴀᴛ ᴛʜᴇ ᴀʀᴄʜɪᴛᴇᴄᴛ ᴡᴀꜱ ɪɴᴄʀᴇᴀꜱɪɴɢʟʏ ᴍᴀʀɢɪɴᴀʟɪᴢᴇᴅ ɪɴ ᴛʜᴇ ʙᴜɪʟᴅɪɴɢ ᴘʀᴏᴄᴇꜱꜱ, ᴡʜɪᴄʜ ʙᴇᴄᴀᴍᴇ ɪɴᴄʀᴇᴀꜱɪɴɢʟʏ ɪɴᴅᴜꜱᴛʀɪᴀʟɪᴢᴇᴅ. Mᴏʀᴇ ᴛʜᴀɴ ᴇᴠᴇʀ ᴀᴛ ᴛʜᴇ ʙᴇɢɪɴɴɪɴɢ ᴏꜰ ᴛʜᴇ ᴛᴡᴇɴᴛʏ-ꜰɪʀꜱᴛ ᴄᴇɴᴛᴜʀʏ, ᴀʀᴄʜɪᴛᴇᴄᴛꜱ ɴᴇᴇᴅᴇᴅ ᴛᴏ ꜱᴛʀᴇᴛᴄʜ ᴛʜᴇɪʀ ɪᴍᴀɢɪɴᴀᴛɪᴏɴꜱ ᴀɴᴅ ᴀɪᴍ ꜰᴏʀ ᴛʜᴇ ꜱᴛᴀʀꜱ.

Eᴅᴇɴ Pʀᴏᴊᴇᴄᴛ, Cᴏʀɴᴡᴀʟʟ, Eɴɢʟᴀɴᴅ
Grimshaw's geodesic domes for the Eden Project (2000) display all the effortless advantages of the new technology. They are triple-glazed with a strong, lightweight, highly transparent material that offers better insulation than glass.

ORGANIC ARCHITECTURE
BACK TO NATURE

HUNGARIAN ARCHITECTURE

After the Soviet repression of the 1956 uprising, Hungarian architecture came under state control. The most significant projects were the renewal of historic buildings in Budapest – an attempt to attract foreign investment and tourism. In the early 1970s the Pécs group emerged, attempting a reinvention of a native "organic" architecture. The most notable product of this group was the work of Imre Makovecz (above).

BRUNO ZEVI

The architect and architectural historian Bruno Zevi (1918–2000) was an innovator in modernist architecture. In his book *Towards an Organic Architecture* (1947), Zevi argued that organic form, not classical symmetry, was the key to modern design. He taught at the universities of Rome and Venice and wrote a number of works that popularized the work of Frank Lloyd Wright and the theory behind organic architecture.

THE SPIRIT of the disparate Green movement in architecture might best be summed up in the remarkable career of Imre Makovecz. A carpenter's son, Makovecz was born in Budapest in 1935. As a small boy he helped to blow up Nazi tanks. During the 1956 Hungarian uprising against the invading troops (and tanks) of the Soviet Union, he was arrested and initially sentenced to death. At architecture school he was rebellious both politically and academically. He railed against the impact of Soviet-style prefabricated design that was destroying major Hungarian towns and cities. A naturally religious man, Makovecz proposed instead an architecture that would connect heaven and earth.

DEVELOPMENT OF A STYLE

Initially this was difficult because Makovecz was effectively banned from working in state studios and from teaching. He did, however, find a job working for the state forestry commission where he built up a team of carpenters and young architects whom he taught on train journeys through rural Hungary. In the forests above the Danube he built timber shelters, ski huts, and other small buildings in an organic style that was a complex interpretation and reworking of the ideas of Frank Lloyd Wright, of Hungarian poets, of Rudolph Steiner, Antoni Gaudí, Odon Lechner, and of traditional Hungarian-Celtic motifs, from ancient crowns to totemic burial markers.

Throughout the 1970s and 80s, Makovecz worked with this group in the forest and lakeside communities and built new village halls in the form of giant birds of prey and other creatures. These were cheap to build (using trees as columns), easy to maintain, and acted as an uplifting focal

CHURCH OF THE HOLY SPIRIT, PAKS, HUNGARY, 1992
The interior of Makovecz's three-spired church is realized throughout in timber. The space is lit from the top by a stained-glass window shaped like an ancient Celtic symbol.

point for villagers who feared the threatened industrialization of rural Hungary. In the event this never happened because of the fall of Communism.

Makovecz described his designs as "building beings." None is wholly symmetrical because neither are humans, nor flora nor fauna. His first work to be critically acclaimed (by the *Architectural Review* in 1981) was his mortuary chapel at Farkasret (1977), a suburb of Budapest. This was a model in timber of the human rib cage. Between 1986 and 1989 he designed and built the highly expressive Roman Catholic church at Paks.

A further powerful Lutheran church at Siofok (1986–89) in the form of spreading wings was built at the same time.

After the fall of the Communist party, Makovecz became a local hero and was chosen to design the Hungarian Pavilion – a churchlike structure topped with many belfries – at the 1992 Seville Expo. Makovecz was not entirely alone. Aside from his own team, a number of Hungarian architects, notably Gyorgy Csete (b. 1937) based in Pecs, instilled a similar organic and anti-establishment spirit in a group of like-minded architects and craftsmen.

PERSONAL VISIONS

Carlo Scarpa (1906–78), a Venetian architect steeped in the rich tradition of his native city crafted an architecture that was close in spirit but never slavish to the older buildings and landscapes it both joined and enhanced in an organic fashion. His most mysterious work is the Brion Tomb (1970) at the cemetery of San Vito di Altivole, Asolo, at once formal yet highly personal and embedded into its surroundings. In Vienna, the artist Friedensreich Hundertwasser (1928–2000) developed a form of colorful, crazy-paving-like apartment blocks drawn as if from the illustrations of a children's book.

Elsewhere in the west, the desire to shape an architecture close to nature was realized using new technology and materials by a small number of architects who believed that the new technology could be enjoyed and ecologically correct at one and the same time. One of the most convincing practices in this field was Future Systems (Jan Kaplicky, b. 1937, and Amanda Levette, b. 1955) which was fascinated with the potential lightness of modern materials and technology. Following partly in the footsteps of Bukminster Fuller (see p.208), Future Systems investigated beautiful forms that were light, elegant, and which touched the ground as gently as possible. Kaplicky illustrated the concepts in the delightful picture books he published of insects standing on water, of NASA lunar modules on the moon's surfaces, of jellyfish, ultralights, bamboo shelters and other animals, organisms, and forms of structure in which lightness was all. The aim was to reduce the materials and energy to a minimum.

Cleverly, Future Systems designs, while being Space Age-modern, fitted in well to natural landscapes. This was because their forms were – like Makovecz's but in a modern, technological idiom – ultimately drawn from nature. The Ark, an elegant visitors center and museum planned for The Earth Centre, an educational ecology park at Doncaster, England (originally scheduled to open in 2001) was shaped in the guise of a giant, translucent-winged butterfly. And like even the most brilliantly colored insect, it promised to be a natural foil to the undulating reclaimed industrial landscape it was to be set in.

An even gentler design was a weekend house, dug into the hills of Pembrokeshire in rural Wales. Malator (1998), known as the "Teletubby House" after a children's television program in which strange humanoids live in underground homes. It was a delightful interweaving of landscape and an architecture of lightweight materials.

LOWENGASSE AND KEGELGASSE APARTMENTS, VIENNA, 1985
In this municipal apartment block the artist and architect Friedensreich Hundertwasser broke away from conventional restraints by deploying irregular bands of color and onion-dome cupolas.

FRIEDENSREICH HUNDERTWASSER
The decorative style of the Austrian painter and architect Friedensreich Hundertwasser (1928–2000) follows in the tradition of Gustav Klimt and Egon Schiele. His work shows a preoccupation with spiral forms and his coloring demonstrates an Asian and Persian influence, with a concentration on gold and silver and phosphorescent reds and greens. In 1971, he began work on town planning projects for Vienna and New Zealand. His design for the Lowengasse and Kegelgasse apartments involved a dialog with future residents in an effort to anticipate their needs.

REUSE OF BUILDINGS
MAKING DO AND MENDING

THE WAVE OF DEMOLITION of historic buildings that smashed through cities worldwide in the 1950s and 60s, and which continued to surge through the developing world (notably China) into the twenty-first century, led to the consolidation of conservation movements committed to saving our architectural heritage. It was not realistic, however, to expect every building of historic or architectural interest to be preserved as a folly. If new uses could be found for old buildings however, then they would have a viable future. The tendency in the twentieth century was to demolish redundant buildings and start afresh. Historically, however, buildings had often been reused.

Beginning in the 1960s, sympathetic architects learned how they could adapt old buildings while imbuing them with a new and often unexpected character. In fact, the new use could often enhance the character of an old building, the original purpose of which — as in the case of power stations or factories built in city centers — had become unacceptable to later generations. One of the most influential conversions of an old building in the 1960s was that of the medieval Castelvecchio, Verona into an art museum (1956–64) by the Venetian architect Carlo Scarpa

CASTELVECCHIO MUSEUM, VERONA, 1956–64
Scarpa intermingled past and present with interlocking floor slabs set up against roughly plastered walls. His attention to materials enabled him to blend the two without jarring.

(1906–78; see p.217). Scarpa had a great love of rich materials and of complex architectural forms and surfaces. He understood how to use these in fresh ways, so that his restoration work offered new ways of experiencing old buildings, steering well away from kitsch on the one hand or slavish imitation of old forms on the other.

In the Castelvecchio Museum the fabric of the old castle is respected for what it is while "interventions" by the architect were clearly expressed. In other words there was a pronounced interplay of old and new and the result was a museum of great distinction, which serves the art on display as well as the old building and its visitors. The building was successful and won critical acclaim. For many architects worldwide, it pointed the way to what could be done in the name of intelligent conservation.

THE MUSÉE D'ORSAY

In a similar, if more dramatic vein, the conversion of the florid Beaux-Arts style Gare d'Orsay, Paris into the Musée d'Orsay (1984–86) by the Milanese architect Gaia Aulenti (b.1931) was another of the renovation success stories of the 1980s. The strength of the design is Aulenti's obvious enjoyment of the great sweeping, processional space of a major railway station with its extensively

MUSÉE D'ORSAY, PARIS, 1984–86
Built for the 1900 World's Fair, the original station was designed to complement the nearby Louvre. A hotel was planned to replace it, a scheme scuppered by renewed interest in 19th-century architecture.

TATE MODERN, LONDON, 1999
The height of Scott's original chimney was limited to 325 feet (99 meters) so as not to compete with St. Paul's Cathedral. The new two-story glass structure, or lightbeam, spans the length of the roof and admits daylight to the galleries on the top floors.

glazed concourse. While new side galleries have been introduced from one end of the museum to the other, these do not interrupt the principal flow and the central space.

The art on display at the Musée d'Orsay covers the period 1848–1914 and this sits perfectly in the lofty spaces of the deliciously decadent interiors of the former station. The original building had been designed by Victor Laloux (1850–1937) and it was opened to coincide with the 1900 World's Fair, a more significant moment in the history of art than railways: it was here that Braque and Picasso began to immerse themselves in African and other "primitive" art and so begin the experiments that led them to Cubism. From Cubism it was a short step to the architecture of Le Corbusier, the Modern Movement, and the process by which ornate old buildings were torn down to make way for the insistently functional architecture of the 1950s and 60s.

Some of the grandest of all city buildings in the twentieth century were power stations. These were dressed up in a variety of heroic styles by architects working as consultants to the engineers who built them. The idea was to civilize these generators of energy and transform them into temples of power. Two of the finest were built on the banks of the Thames River in London. These were at Battersea (1955) and Bankside (1963), the latter facing directly across the Thames from St. Paul's Cathedral. Both Battersea and Bankside were given impressive profiles and heroic façades by Sir Giles Gilbert Scott (1880–1960), architect of Liverpool Cathedral (see p.149) and Waterloo Bridge. Both were made redundant in the 1970s.

Battersea passed through several owners, each promising to turn it into an entertainment venue, but nothing had happened by the beginning of the twenty-first century. Bankside was more fortunate. It was transformed into Tate Modern (Tate Gallery of Modern Art, 1999) by the Swiss architects Jacques Herzog (b.1950) and Pierre de Meuron (b.1950). This involved the installation of five floors of galleries on the river side of the building and the conversion of the former turbine hall into a massive lobby and gallery for giant sculpture and other events. The gallery was connected to St. Paul's Cathedral by a footbridge designed by Norman Foster with the sculptor Anthony Caro and Chris Wise, an engineer with Ove Arup and Partners.

THE REICHSTAG

Foster produced one of the last great "remolds" of the twentieth century: this was the Reichstag, Berlin (see p.11; originally, 1884–94 by Paul Wallot, 1841–1912), ponderous Baroque home of the parliament of the Second Reich. Gutted by fire in 1933, knocked about in the Battle of Berlin, 1945, it was restored without its dome as government offices in the 1960s. Foster stripped the building to its bare walls, and added a great horseshoe-shaped chamber topped with a glass dome open to the public. This was a case of a building finding a modified version of its original role having witnessed the rise and fall of the Second and Third Reichs, the Weimar Republic, and the German Democratic Republic (DDR, or East Germany).

THE TURBINE HALL, TATE MODERN, LONDON, 1999
After original machinery had been removed, a brick-clad steel frame remained. A vast concrete foundation raft was built, then the steel framework that supports the seven floors.

FRANK GEHRY

Gehry was born in Toronto in 1929. His family later moved to Los Angeles, where he established his own practice in 1979. Gehry's early work was notable for its unusual materials – his design for the Temporary Contemporary Museum in Los Angeles used chain-link and corrugated metal. More recent work such as the Schnabel Residence (1986), the Vitra Design Museum (1987–89), and the Guggenheim, has an almost sculptural quality, made possible by computer design.

DECONSTRUCTIVISM
BREAKING THE BOX

DECONSTRUCTIVISM is a mouthful of an architectural movement inspired by the French philosopher Jacques Derrida's (b.1930) notion of Deconstruction. By this he understood that the meaning of a given text (essay, novel, newspaper article) is a result of the difference between the words used rather than their reference to the things they stand for. In other words, the different meanings of a text can be uncovered by taking apart the structure of the language in which it is written.

In the US in the 1980s this philosophical system was translated into the design of buildings under the label Deconstructivism. A number of architects began to take apart and reassemble conventional buildings to imbue them with new meaning or simply to follow an exciting new fashion. Of course they did not take existing structures to pieces, but designed deconstructed buildings on the drawing board or computer, these would sometimes look incomplete and sometimes highly distorted. At their best, in the hands of master architects, such buildings were highly sophisticated games, brave experiments and even thrilling experiences; at their worst they were gimcrack designs, slaves to fashion, and rather annoying.

EARLY DESIGNS

The movement was kick-started by Peter Eisenman (b.1932) who, as part of the New York Five, had made a conscious return to the pure, white Modern architecture of Le Corbusier in the 1920s. Bit by bit, Eisenman began to break the new American houses apart on the drawing board, to slide walls away from one another, to create elisions and illusions of space; in other words, to break and even splinter the rational geometry of classic Modern Movement orthodoxy.

VITRA MUSEUM, WEIL-AM-RHEIN, GERMANY, 1987–89
The deconstructed form and provocative façades of Gehry's building create a unique series of display spaces, which are lit by light towers and swooping glazed roofs.

By 1988, there were sufficient examples of Deconstructivist designs, most of them in model form and on paper, for an exhibition to be held (under the aegis of the 82-year old Philip Johnson; see pp.200–01) at the Museum of Modern Art, New York, where in 1932 the International Style had been curated by the 26-year old Johnson, with Henry-Russell Hitchcock. As it emerged and took root in major built projects in the 1990s, the new stars of the movement were Daniel Libeskind (b.1946; see p.222), Zaha Hadid (b.1950; see p.223) and, although he hated to be labeled in any way, Frank Gehry (b.1929; see opposite).

DESIGNS FOR VITRA

Gehry's own house in Santa Monica, California (1978–79) was a fascinating breakdown and reassembly of a family home that made wilful use of such basic home-improvement store materials as chickenwire, corrugated steel, and chain-link fencing. Walls and ramps slid here and there at unexpected angles. Ten years later, Gehry built the Vitra Museum, Weil-am-Rhein, Germany. It was built for the Swiss-German furniture company dedicated to making some of the best office furniture, including designs by Charles and Ray Eames and Gehry himself. The museum was a playful and utterly convincing flow and intersection of curved and diagonal planes, its interiors inventively yet quite practically arranged. The image of the museum was extremely strong and did much to put Vitra on the map of modern design and manufacturing. By the end of the century, Gehry's most powerful work was represented by the Disney Concert

VITRA MUSEUM, WEIL-AM-RHEIN, 1987–89
Ralph Fehlbaum, director of Vitra, commissioned Frank Gehry to build a museum to house the Fehlbaum family's collection of chairs. Gehry's own Beaver Chair (1987), made of laminated cardboard, stands in the foreground on the right.

Hall, Los Angeles (1995–) and the Guggenheim Museum, Bilbao (1993–97; see p.225), two spectacular, major buildings that drew applause from a cross-section of society. This was modern architecture at its most daring, and perhaps part of its popularity was that it offended the sensibilities of those who preferred architecture as plain as a plate of meat and potatoes.

DANIEL LIBESKIND

Born in Poland in 1946, Libeskind studied music in America and Israel before turning to architecture. His work draws on mathematics, music, and painting, creating, theoretical forms which are then developed architecturally. He was a teacher and theorist of architecture at Harvard, UCLA, and the University of London before establishing his own practice in Berlin in 1989. Apart from the V&A extension (see below) his current work also includes a design for a new theater in Bremen and the Imperial War Museum of the North in Manchester, England.

Perhaps more striking still were three projects by Daniel Libeskind, a Polish-born musician-turned-architect who was well known as a teacher in England and the US before winning the competition to design the Jewish Museum, Berlin in 1989. This astonishing lightning-bolt of a building took ten years to complete after much negotiation and political delays. Shooting in zig-zag fashion across its site alongside the existing Baroque Berlin Museum, the Jewish Museum was meant to be an extension to the earlier building but ended up as the tail that wagged the dog. Even without exhibits, hundreds of thousands of people came to see and to experience this extraordinarily powerful building the year after construction was completed. It was a highly emotional work that, through the experience of the architecture alone, told the story of the disappearance of Berlin's Jews. In this sense it could be said to have a Baroque quality, a sense of theatre as well as a powerful impact and meaning.

The building was characterized by its zinc skin, the slashes of the windows, and inside by the concrete void that ran through the galleries and reminded visitors of the cultural and human void left at the heart of Berlin with the absence of a Jewish population that had thought of itself as patriotically German. The atonal quality of the architecture was in part inspired by the resonant

JEWISH MUSEUM, BERLIN, 1989–99
Given the experience of his family in the Holocaust, the museum has a personal significance for Libeskind. He has described the building as "deliberately ambiguous… as wrenching as the history of the city. As difficult as the implications of its history."

echoes of Arnold Schoenberg's (1874–1951) unfinished opera *Aron und Moses*, a haunting work that Libeskind turned to again and again during the design process.

The museum has no obvious entrance and is reached through the old building down a long, tapering stair that leads into the undercrofts and ramped walkways. These allow visitors to take one of three routes up, through, and out of the building. One leads into the Holocaust void, a terrifying, unheated raw concrete tower filled with a heartbreaking absence and lit only by a tiny slit of daylight. This was inspired by the story of those who recalled such slits of light as their only sight of the outside world and their only symbol of hope in the obscene cattle-car journeys many of Berlin's 250,000 Jews were forced to take on the trains that led to the concentration camps.

SPIRALS AND OUTCROPS

The Jewish Museum established Libeskind as one of the most radical form-givers of his age. It was followed by the Felix Nussbaum Museum, Osnabruk (1998), devoted to the work of the Jewish painter who died in a Nazi concentration camp, and by the Spiral (planned completion, 2005), a radical extension of the Victoria & Albert Museum, London, designed with the engineer Cecil Balmond. This takes the form of a complex, crystalline spiral rising up out of an existing museum courtyard, its form based on fractal geometry that involved successive subdivisions of multi-surfaced, three-dimensional space.

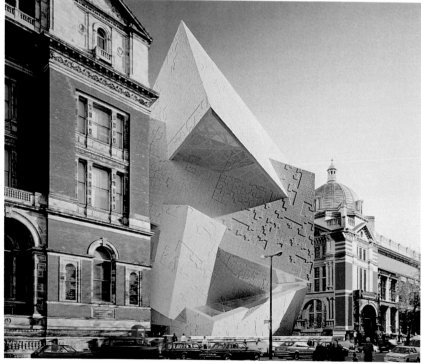

DESIGN FOR BOILERHOUSE WING, VICTORIA & ALBERT MUSEUM, LONDON, 2005
Libeskind's extension to London's museum of decorative arts is located in a restricted courtyard and manages to create varied gallery space by breaking the confines of the original site.

The Spiral was intended to be a highly innovative and dynamic design for a museum in which interactive technology would be a part of the very fabric of the structure.

Libeskind's first house, and studio, for sculptor Barbara Weil, Majorca (planned completion 2002), is sited on a cliff face and designed to be as much a geological outcrop as an architecture of serpentine and even sensual geometry.

DYNAMIC SPACES

Zaha Hadid, an Iraqi-born architect, studied and taught at London's Architectural Association before coming to prominence for her stirring drawings and paintings of schemes for competitions – notably for the Hong Kong Peak. These fused the dynamic geometry of Russian Constructivists with the new intellectual and aesthetic sensibilities of Deconstructivists. Hadid's first building was a fire station for the Vitra furniture factory at Weil-am-Rhein (1991), a thing of dramatically elongated horizontals and angular projections. In 1999 she completed an exhibition building close by for the Weil-am-Rhein landscape and gardening show which incorporates an environmental research center dug into the ground.

In London, Hadid designed a dramatic enclosed bridge for the University of North London, Holloway (2001) to connect the various parts of the campus which were separated from one another by the busy Holloway Road. The steel structure meets the various buildings it connects in "sky lobbies," spaces that could be used

as cafés, libraries, and seminar rooms. The walkways themselves are woven through with interactive computer technology so that internally they read as a digital newspaper for students dawdling, or scurrying, between the different parts of the campus. Externally from the road, they are an "urban newspaper carrying moving images and projections to make a dynamic cinematic space across Holloway Road." This was a good example of dramatic new architecture being used to serve a particularly useful service, yet also giving life and character to a pedestrian muddle of buildings and to a road that otherwise seemed no more than a gully full of cars.

Hadid's first major building was the Center for the Contemporary Arts, Rome, won in an international competition in 1999. For those without a secure grasp of architectural design the geometry of the competition drawings are difficult to comprehend, but the experience of the building when completed (c.2005) promises to be as delightful as it will be intriguing.

The proposal was for a gallery that acted as a kind of second skin over an old city site flanked by military barracks. It would flow in a complex sequence of spaces from indoors to outdoors. Artworks are encountered in unexpected settings to help break the often stifling uniformity of art gallery interiors. The sinuous, daylit galleries are intended as a gentle challenge to curators, calling on them to interact with the architecture. This was very much in the spirit of Deconstructivism in that it takes apart formal and spatial certainties and encourages those charged with running the museum to think afresh, in this case about the relationship between art and architecture.

ZAHA HADID

Born in Baghdad in 1950, Hadid studied at London's Architectural Association from 1972. She later taught there with Rem Koolhaas, leading her own studio from 1987. She set up her own practice in 1979, and is renowned for her stunning architectural drawings and plans, winning first prize for designs in competitions for the Kufurstendamm, Berlin (1986), for an Art and Media Center in Dusseldorf (1989), and for the Cardiff Opera House (1994). Her work also includes two projects in Tokyo (1988) and a folly in Osaka (1990). Hadid has had several exhibitions of her paintings and drawings, and has also taught at Harvard and Columbia.

EXHIBITION SPACE FOR GARDENING SHOW, WEIL-AM-RHEIN, GERMANY, 1999
Hadid's design aims to dissolve the boundaries between architecture and landscape through a network of paths running around and though the building, and by suggesting rather than enclosing the exhibition and café spaces.

THE COMPUTER
DIGITAL DREAMS

REM KOOLHAAS

Born in 1944, Dutch architect Rem Koolhaas worked as a journalist before leaving for London to study at the Architectural Association. His paper *The Berlin Wall as Architecture* (1970) created a sensation and he obtained a scholarship to study in the US, where he became fascinated by New York City, and published *Delirious New York, a Retroactive Manifesto for Manhattan* (1978). In 1975 he established the Office of Metropolitan Architecture (OMA). He has worked on the Netherlands Dance Theater (1987) and the restructuring of Lille, France. In 1996 he published *OMA: S, M, L, XL*. Frank Gehry has called him "the most comprehensive thinker in the profession today."

MOVIEMAKERS of the early 1960s loved them. Computers, that is. Great banks of the things were housed in tall, gray cases and were the stuff of tape turning on plastic wheels, with professorial men in white coats tending them studiously. Computers occupied buildings, usually Miesian designs, but while they appeared to manage many of the more sinister aspects of late twentieth-century life – mainly nuclear warfare – and were widely considered to be sinister (for example, the Alpha 60 computer in Jean-Luc Godard's *Alphaville*, or the HAL 9000 computer that has a breakdown in Stanley Kubrick's *2001: A Space Odyssey*), they seemed to have curiously little effect on the design of buildings themselves.

Early applications of what was called CAD (computer-aided design) appeared to have little or no effect on the aesthetics or nature of buildings. They helped architects, mostly those engaged in the rapid design of rentable office space and industrial parks, to produce working drawings at great speed. If the computer was a tool in the 1980s, it was a crude one – a pickax or shovel – in the hands of the majority of architects.

Two of the first major buildings to show how the computer could not only help with the design of complex projects but actually suggest how they might look and how they should be built were Kansai International Airport, Osaka Bay, Japan, (1988–94) by Renzo Piano's Building Workshop, and the Guggenheim Museum, Bilbao (1993–97), by Frank Gehry.

Kansai Airport is remarkable for its mile- (1.6-km) long terminal building that appears to rest as gently as a stork on an artificial island in the Bay of Osaka. Honshu, the main island of Japan, is mountainous, with precious little land on which to build. To construct a major new airport in the sea was sensible for two key reasons: it saved valuable land elsewhere, and it kept aircraft noise away from existing settlements. The complex profile and engineering of the winglike terminal building, designed to cope with typhoons, was generated as much by the suggestion of computer programs as by function and aesthetics. The result is a highly technical building with elegant, almost organic, free-flowing lines. It is easy to imagine it going through its paces on computer screens.

COMPUTERIZED AIRPORT DESIGN

Kansai International also marked the mature development of a new wave of airport terminals in which the nature of flight and the aesthetic of aircraft were celebrated, and through which passengers could, from the moment they entered the building, see their aircraft. All too often in the 1980s and 1990s the international air terminal had been viewed by its owners as a form of shopping mall with aircraft attached somewhere down the line and out of sight. The two best new 1990s airport buildings other than Piano's were the second terminal at Stansted, London, and Hong Kong, both designed by Foster and Partners. The same principles applied at Hong Kong and Stansted: clear routes through the building, maximum deployment of daylight, and a look that matched the ambition of the Wright brothers and their successors.

THE GUGGENHEIM

Frank Gehry's much praised Guggenheim Museum, Bilbao, has almost completely redrawn the world's image of the Basque capital. Until its opening, Bilbao was best known as the stomping ground of

KANSAI INTERNATIONAL AIRPORT, OSAKA BAY, JAPAN, 1988–94
The low, gentle curve of the building's aerodynamic roof is covered with 90,000 identical stainless-steel panels, enabling it to withstand hurricanes. Inside, the form of the roof allows air to circulate freely around the terminal building.

COMPUTER-GENERATED DESIGN FOR THE EDEN PROJECT
The structure of Nicholas Grimshaw's series of giant conservatories in southwest England was based on a 3-D computer model, itself linked to a machine shop, where sections of the domes were made.

the explosive ETA (Euzkadi ta Askatsuna, or The Basque People and Liberty), a nationalist group determined to rid the Basquelands of Spanish rule. To a great extent Euzkadi (the Basque country) is free from direct rule from Madrid. Its independence of spirit and the originality of its people (the first-known settlers in Europe speaking a unique language) is celebrated by Gehry in his wilful, idiosyncratic, and eye-catching building, which occupies a site in the city-center docklands. The complex curves, and the cut of the many different-shaped titanium tiles that cover them, were worked out with much help from computer-aided design. Yet what one sees here is very clearly the hand and eye of

a great modern Baroque architect working intelligently in partnership with the almost infinite possibilities suggested to him by the process of computer modeling.

CYBER DREAMS

At the beginning of the twenty-first century the use of computers in architecture had become commonplace. Young Chinese architects, straight from college, could be found sitting with colleagues in cramped kitchens in Shenzen and Guangzhou designing the facades of instant-build office towers on laptops. They would cull images of office towers from around the world seen in glossy magazines, scan them into their computers and stretch the images vertically or horizontally to fit the concrete frame of the latest Chinese office block. The results were built soon afterward.

A more subtle use of computers has been made by many young architects worldwide attempting to create new forms of free-flowing structures and interior space. New materials technology — lightweight metals and polycarbonates — allows architects to get closer to the dream of infinitely malleable structure and space. Although the realization of such cyber-dreams is still some way off in the 2000s, it is exciting to see architects trying to shrug off the limitations imposed by forms of structure and space that had changed in fundamental terms remarkably little over the previous 2,500 years.

CATIA
The computer application used in the design for the Guggenheim was developed in the late-1980s by the French aeronautical industry. The program works on surfaces rather than polygons. The distances between surfaces of stone, metal, glass, and plaster and their connections are determined before the underlying structure, as they would be in a conventional design. Once the surface design has been completed, the computer can begin to calculate the volume and nature of the structure – in this case a steel frame – that will be needed to support these surfaces.

GUGGENHEIM MUSEUM, BILBAO, 1993–97
The billowing forms of the Guggenheim are unified by its great central atrium. The titanium-sheathed museum is built to resemble a vast ship, reflecting Bilbao's role as a major port.

ENJOYABLE CITIES
THE CITY RESPLENDENT

> " *The essence of the metropolitan culture is change — a state of perpetual animation* "
> REM KOOLHAAS

IN THE FIRST CHAPTER of our story we learned how architecture emerged with the rise of the first cities. The two were pretty much synonymous. Architecture adorned the streets and squares of cities from ancient times and the two emerged as an organic whole. Over the centuries, however, it is possible to trace a subplot in which individual architects and clients began, pediment by colonnade, arch by vault, to build to their own greater glory. As they did so, the nature of the city began to fragment. It could no longer be an organic whole when individual buildings came to express the ambition of powerful clients.

Even so, a common aesthetic, the use of local building materials, and the fact that everyone knew everyone else meant that until remarkably late — beginning with the spread of the Industrial Revolution from Britain in the mid-eighteenth

century — cities worldwide were often no more flamboyant than they had been hundreds or thousands of years before — with the possible exceptions of Rome or Istanbul.

It was only with the coming of the Industrial Revolution that they were taken apart, reworked, and often brutally treated. Wide new roads and railway lines were driven through them. These not only ripped apart old communities but also allowed the easy movement of building materials from different parts of a country and eventually from around the world. Cities were no longer to

CANNON'S WALK, SOUTH STREET, SEAPORT, NEW YORK CITY
In the nineteenth century industry was traditionally situated at the heart of the city. But as services moved elsewhere, certain areas fell into disuse. This left the old city ripe for redevelopment, like this pedestrianized street in New York City.

THE URBAN MIX

Although the growth of industry led to the efficient segregation of different parts of the city for different purposes, more recently architects and city planners have recognized the benefits of a more integrated approach. These include conservative proposals such as Rob Krier s plans for the center of Amiens in France, where older building types are preserved and even imitated in order to create an environment which can provide diverse uses, and Pier Luigi Cervelatti s restoration work in Bologna. In Berlin the International Building Exhibition (IBA) has encouraged a group of young architects to build within the confines of existing structures, but using more modern architectural styles.

LAS RAMBLAS, BARCELONA, SPAIN

This historic avenue at the heart of the old city serves as both a circulation route for traffic and a place where pedestrians can stroll. Its tree-lined central walkway is a mix of newsstands, flower stalls, and entertainers — an example of a liveable urban environment.

CONCERT HALL OF THE NATIONAL ORCHESTRA OF LYON

Originally opened in 1975, this famous concert hall with its distinctive scallop-shell profile was renovated 20 years later as part of Lyon's redevelopment scheme. New lighting and facilities integrate the concert hall more fully with its surroundings.

AERIAL VIEW OF DETROIT, MICHIGAN

When the demands of industry, such as major arterial routes and services, are emphasized at the cost of human living conditions, urban sprawl can result. Such environments make community problematic, and are prone to crime and pollution.

have a homogenous look either in terms of the stones from which they were built or in terms of building types. New types of what we now call global buildings grew rapidly with industrialism – train stations, freight yards, central markets, factories, warehouses, hospitals, asylums, libraries, professional institutions, office buildings, department stores, and places of mass entertainment from music halls to sports stadia.

DECLINE AND REBIRTH IN THE CITY

In the rush to build this brave and volcanic new world, the etiquette of urban planning, customs and rules that had built up since the rise of Jericho (c.7000 BC) was abandoned. All too often new buildings and vast new industrial developments were plonked down wherever land could be grabbed. By the second half of the twentieth century, the unholy alliance of insensitive Modern architecture, fast urban motorways, many of them elevated on concrete stilts, a rush to live in the suburbs, and the subsequent decline of everyday life in urban centers, saw cities worldwide on the decline as places to live and to enjoy. The city was being split apart.

In the last two decades of the century, however, a passionate commitment was made by architects, the best planners and politicians, critics, and the people who wanted to live in them, to tackle the problem of urban degeneration. The efforts made were prodigious. Conservation groups, notably in Europe and the US, began to save and restore historic downtown housing and to find loving owners. New buildings were increasingly required to take into account their neighbors and surroundings. While initially this led to much pastiche design, by the beginning of the twenty-first century, many architects had learned how to build in innovative styles that nevertheless enhanced rather than detracted from their locale.

Conferences were held with astonishing frequency at which architects, their critics, and supporters debated the issue of how to create "green" cities, ecologically sound and a pleasure to live and work in. This became a cause for concern because even as architects found this new voice in many parts of the world, in others, rapid industrialization or the brutal clearance of rain forests, saw urban and suburban sprawl spreading like wildfire. Increasingly, people from poor rural districts whether in China, or in Africa or Asia, were flooding into cities spiraling out of control, not because they wanted to live there through choice or to enhance its culture, but to earn a crust of bread or a bowl of rice and to be able to send a few dollars earned in the city home to families left in remote rural areas. Shantytowns grew virulently around the city centers of the developing world.

Herculean efforts were made, late in the day, to restore the inner life of old cities: effective public transportation; the car kept at bay; affordable new homes; new cultural venues; old quarters cleaned up; new city parks; the planting of thousands of trees; the encouragement of wildlife – and finally, a demand for high standards of architecture.

THE ENJOYABLE CITY

Such improvements, driven by political will, have transformed cities like Barcelona, Antwerp, Lyon, Berlin, and at least some of New York City and London over the last 20 years. There is a long way to go, although it is true that throughout history, no matter how glorious their appearance, the greatest cities have also been the most vibrant. It is the balance between order and chaos, the sensual and the rational, the drama of human life and the implied order of a dignified city plan that makes a great city what it is. At the beginning of the twenty-first century there was clearly much urgent work to do to make cities better and more environmentally sound places to live and work, but as the old saying goes, Rome wasn't built in a day. And that, at its peak in c. AD 200, was possibly the most ordered and disordered capital city of all time.

> " *The city is built To music, therefore never built at all And therefore built forever* "
> ALFRED, LORD TENNYSON

REDEVELOPED CITY SQUARE, LYON, FRANCE
Since 1989 more than 150 public spaces in Lyon and the surrounding area have been remodeled by famous French architects, urban designers, and landscape artists. Here, the Hotel de Ville towers over one of the redeveloped squares.

GLOSSARY

A

Abacus The flat slab between the top of a capital and the architrave.

Abutment Solid masonry that resists the lateral pressure of an arch.

Acropolis A Greek citadel containing temples, usually situated on the highest point overlooking a city.

Adobe Unbaked brick dried in the sun, commonly used in the American Southwest, Spain, and Latin America.

Aedicule A wall recess framed by columns supporting an entablature and pediment, and intended as a shrine or as a shelter for a statue.

Agora Ancient Greek market place.

Aisle Lateral divisions parallel with the nave in a basilica or church.

Ambulatory A continuous aisle around a circular building; the aisle around the east end of a church.

Apse A large semicircular or polygonal recess terminating the chancel at the eastern end of a church.

Arcade A series of arches supported by columns or piers. An arcade attached to a wall is called a blind arcade.

Arch A curved structure of masonry spanning an opening.

Architrave The lowest division of the Classical entablature; also the molded frame around a door or window.

Ashlar Masonry of smooth-squared stones laid in horizontal courses.

Atrium Courtyard at the center of a building that rises through consecutive floors.

B

Balcony A platform projecting from a wall, enclosed by a railing or balustrade, supported on brackets or cantilevered out.

Baldacchino An ornamental canopy supported by columns generally placed over an altar or tomb.

Baluster A pillar or column supporting a handrail or coping.

Balustrade A railing supported by a series of small posts or balusters.

Baptistery A building, within a church or separate from it, containing the font for baptism.

Basilica A public hall, with nave and aisles used for the administration of justice.

Bay A compartment of a building, as defined by columns, pillars, windows, or other prominent vertical features.

Beam One of the principal load-bearing horizontal members of a building.

Boss An ornamental projection at the intersection of the ribs or beams of a vault or ceiling.

Bracket A small supporting member projecting from a vertical surface to form a horizontal support.

Buttress A projection of masonry or brickwork from a wall to give additional strength, particularly where the wall supports a vault.

C

Campanile The Italian name for a belltower, usually freestanding.

Canopy A projection or hood over a door, window, niche, etc.

Cantilever A structural member projecting outward beyond its point of support and counterbalanced by the fixing of the inner part of the member.

Capital The crowning feature placed on to the shaft of a column.

Caryatid A column carved as a female figure.

Centering A temporary framework, usually made of timber, used for support during the construction of arches, vaults, and domes.

Chancel The section of a church reserved for the clergy and containing the principal altar.

Choir The part of a church where the services are sung.

Cladding Material used to cover the main structural material of a building, for protection or decoration.

Clapboard Overlapping horizontal boards that cover the timber-framed wall of a house.

Classical The architecture originating in ancient Greece and Rome, the rules and forms of which were largely revived during the Renaissance.

Clerestory The upper story of a building with windows above adjacent roofs.

Cloister A covered passage connecting the monastic church to the domestic parts of the monastery.

Coffering Decoration of a ceiling with recessed panels, generally square or polygonal in shape.

Colonnade A range of columns supporting an entablature or arches.

Column A vertical supporting member normally circular in plan and including base, shaft, and capital.

Corbel A bracket projecting from a wall used to support a roof beam, vault, or other feature.

Cornice In Classical architecture the projecting upper section of an entablature; also the projecting horizontal molding along the top of a building or wall.

Crocket Motif or leaf design carved into the projecting ribs that decorate the parapets and towers of Gothic buildings and their derivatives.

Crossing The space at the intersection of the nave, chancel, and transepts in a cruciform church.

Cruck Pair of large timbers used as a frame to support a cottage.

Cupola A dome or domed roof; also the inside ceiling of a dome.

Curtain wall A lightweight outside wall held off the main structural frame and serving no load-bearing purpose.

D

Dado The portion of a pedestal between its base and cornice; also the lower part of the walls of a room when decorated separately.

Dome A convex roof or ceiling of even curvature erected on a circular or polygonal base.

Drum A circular or polygonal vertical wall that supports a dome.

E

Eave The underpart of a sloping roof projecting beyond a wall.

Elevation The vertical face of a building, whether external or internal, or a drawing of this.

Entablature The upper part of a Classical order of architecture, between columns and pediment, consisting of architrave, frieze, and cornice.

Entasis A light swelling or curving outward along the outline of a column shaft, designed to counteract the optical illusion that it is thinner in the middle.

F

Façade The face or elevation of a building.

Facing A covering applied to the outer surface of a building.

Fanlight A window, often semicircular, with radiating bars suggesting an open fan.

Fan vault Vaulting peculiar to the Perpendicular period, in which all ribs have the same curve, and radiate from the wallshafts in a fanlike pattern.

Finial Crowning ornament placed at the top of a spire or roof pinnacle.

Ferro-concrete Concrete with steel reinforcement.

Fluting Shallow, vertical grooves running on the shaft of a column, pilaster, or other surface.

Flying buttress A buttress that stands away from the wall it reinforces, providing support via an arch at the main point of stress.

Formwork Temporary casing of woodwork, within which concrete is molded.

Frame The structural skeleton of a building made up of members of timber, iron, steel, reinforced concrete, etc.

Fresco A painting made on a wall with water-based colors while the plaster is still wet.

Frieze The middle division of a Classical entablature; also any broad horizontal band decorated with sculpture.

G

Gable The upper, triangular part of an exterior wall between the top of the side walls and the slopes of the roof.

Gallery A long room, often on an upper floor, for recreation, entertainment, or display of artwork. In a church, a gallery runs above an aisle and opens on to the nave.

Gargoyle A projecting waterspout, usually carved in the form of a grotesque human or animal figure.

Gazebo A small lookout tower or elevated summerhouse with a view, usually in a garden or park.

Greek cross A cross with four equal arms.

H

Hammerbeam The short horizontal beam that projects at the top of an interior wall and supports roof braces.

Hexastyle A portico with six supporting columns.

Hipped roof A roof with sloped instead of vertical ends.

Hypocaust An ancient Roman central heating system using hot air ducts in the floors of the building.

Hypostyle A pillared hall in which the roof is supported by many columns.

I

Insula An ancient Roman apartment block.

K

Keep The inner stronghold of a castle, equipped to serve as the main living quarters in times of siege.

Keystone The central, wedge-shaped stone of a semicircular arch.

L

Lantern A small, windowed tower on top of a roof or dome admitting light to the space below.

Lintel Horizontal supporting beam that spans an opening in a wall or between columns.

Loggia A gallery with an open arcade or colonnade on one or more sides.

Lunette A semicircular window or wall panel framed by an arch or vault.

M

Machicolation A projecting defensive wall or parapet with floor openings through which molten lead, pitch, or stones could be dropped on attackers.

Mansard roof A roof with four sides, having the lower part steeper than the upper.

Mastaba An ancient Egyptian tomb, with sloping sides and a flat roof, covering a burial chamber below ground.

Metope The space between Doric triglyphs, often decorated with sculpture.

Mezzanine A low, intermediate story between two higher ones.

Mihrab A niche oriented toward Mecca in an Islamic religious building.

Minaret The slender tower of a mosque from which the faithful are called to prayer.

Module A unit of measurement to which parts of a building are related by simple ratios. In Classical architecture it is usually the diameter of a column immediately above its base, which is divided into sixty parts or minutes.

Molding An ornamental edging or band, often enriched with decorative carving, projecting from a wall or other surface.

Mullion Slender post or upright member dividing windows or other openings set in a series.

N

Naos The principal chamber in a Greek temple containing the statue of the deity.

Nave The main body of a church to the west of the central crossing. Often flanked by aisles.

Niche A recess in a wall.

O

Oculus A round window.

Ogee An S-shaped double curve consisting of one concave and one convex part.

Oratory A small private chapel in a church or house.

Order A Classical column and entablature proportioned and decorated according to accepted modes. The Greeks recognized three orders: Doric, Ionic, and Corinthian. The Romans added the Tuscan and the Composite.

P

Pagoda A multistoried Chinese or Japanese tower with projecting roofs at each story.

Palladianism A style of architecture derived from the the buildings and publications of Andrea Palladio (1508–80). The Palladian revival began in Italy and England in the early 18th century and spread to America in the mid-18th century.

Panopticon A building with corridors radiating from a central observation point.

Parapet A low screening wall alongside a roof, bridge, or quay.

Pavilion An ornamental building placed in a landscaped setting; also a projecting section of a larger building.

Pedestal The support for a column, statue, or vase.

Pediment In Classical architecture, the triangular section of wall above the entablature; later, any similar crowning feature over a window or door.

Pendentive The curved triangular surface formed between the base of the dome and the corners of the supporting structure.

Peristyle A range of columns surrounding a building or courtyard.

Piano nobile The main floor of a building, raised one floor above the ground floor and containing the principal living rooms.

Picturesque The term used to describe the 18th-century taste for architecture and landscape gardening characterized by irregularity, wild ruggedness, and a variety of form and texture.

Pier A heavy masonry support, as distinct from a column, often rectangular or square in plan.

Pilaster A flattened, rectangular column or pier attached to a wall of the same design as the order with which it is used.

Piloti The French term for pillars or stilts that raise and support a building, leaving the ground floor open.

Polychromy Architectural decoration using a variety of colors or varicolored materials.

Porch The roofed entrance to a house.

Portal A monumental entranceway to a building.

Portico A covered entranceway or porch with columns on one or more sides.

Post and beam A construction system using vertical supports (posts) spanned by horizontal beams (also called lintels).

Precast concrete Components are cast and molded at a factory and then placed in position.

Pylon The gateway structure to an ancient Egyptian temple.

R

Relief Carved or embossed decoration raised above a background plane.

Reinforced concrete Steel rods are inserted in beams to help them withstand longitudinal stress without collapsing. This development has allowed the construction of very large structures using concrete beams.

Rib Projecting band on a ceiling or vault, often forming the primary structural frame.

Rose window A round window with tracery and stained glass radiating out like the spokes of a wheel.

Rotunda A round hall or building, usually topped with a dome.

Rustication The separation of regular masonry blocks by deeply cut, often wedge-shaped grooves.

S

Shaft The main part of a column, between the base and the capital.

Span The distance between the supports of an arch, roof, or beam.

Spandrel The triangular area between the sides of two adjacent arches and the line across their tops.

Stoa Detached colonnade found in Classical Greek architecture.

String course A continuous horizontal band set in the surface of an exterior wall or projecting from it and usually molded.

Stupa A Buddhist memorial mound that enshrines relics or marks a sacred site.

T

Tatami A straw floor mat used in Japanese architecture.

Tie-beam The main horizontal beam connecting the lower ends of rafters to prevent them from moving apart.

Tongue and groove A system of joining boards by fitting a projection along the side of one into a groove in the next.

Trabeated Built of horizontal beams and vertical posts.

Tracery The ornamental patternwork in stone filling the upper part of a Gothic window.

Transept The projecting transverse arms of a cross-shaped church, crossing the main axis at right angles.

Transverse rib A rib that extends at right angles to the wall across a bay or other vaulted space.

Travertine A type of limestone.

Triglyph A vertically grooved block separating the metopes in a Doric frieze.

Triumphal arch A freestanding monumental gateway developed in Roman architecture.

Truss A rigid framework of timber or metal members designed to span an opening.

Tufa A rough, porous building stone formed from Volcanic dust.

Tympanum The area between the lintel or beam over a doorway and the arch above it; also the triangular space enclosed by the moldings of a pediment.

V

Vault An arched ceiling or roof.

Vestibule An anteroom to a larger apartment.

Volute A spiral or scroll occurring in Ionic, Corinthian, and Composite capitals.

Voussoirs The wedge-shaped blocks that are used in an arch or vault.

Z

Ziggurat A Mesopotamian temple-tower in the form of a stepped pyramid.

INDEX

ACKNOWLEDGMENTS

The publisher would like to thank the following for their kind permission to reproduce the photographs. t = top, b = bottom, a = above, c = center, l = left, r = right.

p.1 © Michael Holford c. **p.2** AKG London Erich Lessing. **p.3** © Guggenheim Museum Bilbao Erika Barahona Ede c. **p.4** Arcaid Joe Cornish br. **pp.4–5** Corbis UK Ltd Bob Krist (background image). **p.5** View Pictures Peter Cook/© FLC/ADAGP, Paris and DACS, London 2002 br.
p.7 Art Directors & TRIP A. Ghazzal b. **p.8** Sonia Halliday Photographs. **p.9** Robert Harding Picture Library r. **p.10** Corbis UK Ltd Jonathan Blair l. **p.11** Foster & Partners Nigel Young b. **pp.12–13** Bridgeman Art Library, London/New York Stapleton Collection. **p.14** Ffotograff Charles Aithie b; Robert Harding Picture Library Richard Ashworth tr. **p.15** AKG London tr; Bridgeman Art Library, London/New York Musée du Louvre, Paris cr. **p.16** AKG London tr; Robert Harding Picture Library Guy Thouvenin bl. **p.17** Corbis UK Ltd: Gianni Dagli Orti br; Robert Harding Picture Library tr. **p.18** Robert Harding Picture Library bl. **p.19** AKG London Erich Lessing tr; Corbis UK Ltd: Martin Jones tl; DK Picture Library Geoff Brightling b. **p.20** Werner Forman Archive tl; Art Directors & TRIP P. Bucknall bc. **p.21** Scala, Musée du Louvre, Paris tr; Tony Stone Images Gavin Hellier b. **p.22** Art Directors & TRIP tl. **pp.22–23** Axiom James Morris b. **p.23** Robert Harding Picture Library tr. **pp.24–25** Robert Harding Picture Library Roy Rainford. **p.26** © Michael Holford: bl; Scala, Museo Pio-Clementino tl. **p.27** AKG London tl; Trireme Trust Paul Lipke br; © Dorling Kindersley Simon Murrell tr. **pp.28–29** AKG London t; © Dorling Kindersley Andrew Evans bl. **p.29** British Museum, London tr; Scala br. **p.30** Art Directors & TRIP Robin Smith bl; © Dorling Kindersley Simon Murrell tl. **p.31** National Gallery of Art, Washington Samuel H. Kress Collection/Photograph by Richard Carafelli. **p.32** AKG London tl; Corbis UK Ltd Mimmo Jodice bl; Ffotograff Charles Aithie tc. **p.33** Architectural Association Anthony Hamber b; © J. Paul Getty Trust John Stephens tr. **p.34** Archivo Iconografico, S.A. tr. Archivision, Toronto l; Robert Harding Picture Library br. **p.35** Corbis UK Ltd Wolfgang Kaehler br. **pp.36–37** Sonia Halliday Photographs. **p.38** Scala, San Vitale, Ravenna cl. **pp.38–39** Powerstock Photolibrary/Zefa b. **p.39** Bridgeman Art Library, London/New York Fogg Art Museum, Harvard University Art Museums, US tr. **p.40** A. F. Kersting bl; Scala tr. **p.41** Petrushka © V. Gritsuk bc; Scala, State Museum of Russia, Leningrad tr; © Dorling Kindersley Simon Murrell br. **p.42** AKG London Trinity Collage, Dublin tl; Eye Ubiquitous Hugh Rooney tr; Angelo Hornak Library bl. **p.43**

Archivo Iconografico, S.A. b. **p.44** Angelo Hornak Library bl; Courtesy of The Dean and Chapter, Durham Cathedral tr. **p.45** Joe Cornish tc; Domkapitel Speyer, Dombauamt br; © Dorling Kindersley Simon Murrell tr. **p.46** British Museum, London tl. Corbis UK Ltd Paul Almasy b. **p.47** A. F. Kersting t; Pictorial Press Ltd br; © Dorling Kindersley Simon Murrell tr. **p.48** © Dorling Kindersley Simon Murrell cl; Robert Harding Picture Library Michael Jenner bl; Art Directors & TRIP H. Rogers cr; M. Good br, crr. **p.49** Werner Forman Archive cr; Robert Harding Picture Library Schuster b. **p.50** Art Directors & TRIP H. Rogers b. **p.51** Ffotograff Patricia Aithie tl; Christoph Kicherer br; Kimbell Art Museum, Fort Worth, Texas cr. **pp.52–53** Angelo Hornak Library. **p.54** Corbis UK Ltd Angelo Hornak bcl; Scala, Galleria degli Uffizi, Florence tl. **p.55** Art Directors & TRIP G. Taylor t. **p.56** Bibliothèque Nationale De France, Paris c; Angelo Hornak Library br; © Crown Copyright. NMR Royal Commission on the Historical Monuments of England © The Dean and Chapter Library, York Minster bl. **p.57** Ulm/Neu-Ulm Touristik G. Merkle tc. **p.58** © Michael Holford tl. **p.59** Tony Stone Images br. **p.60** The Art Archive tl; Robert Harding Picture Library bl; Hulton Getty tr. **p.61** Archivo Iconografico, S.A. tr; Bildarchiv Preußischer Kulturbesitz Staatliche Museum, Berlin/Photograph Jörg P. Anders bl; The J. Allan Cash Photolibrary bc. **p.62** Robert Harding Picture Library Michael Jenner bl; © Dorling Kindersley Simon Murrell tl. **p.63** Archivo Iconografico, S.A. b; Corbis UK Ltd Jonathan Blair t. **p.64** A. F. Kersting bl. **p.65** Angelo Hornak Library Courtesy of the Dean and Chapter, Westminster Abbey bl; Pictures Colour Library tr. **pp.66–67** Corbis UK Ltd Massimo Listri. **p.68** Ikona tr. **pp.68–69** AKG London Galleria Nazionale delle Marche, Urbino/Photograph Erich Lessing b. **p.69** Scala tr. **p.70** AKG London AKG Berlin/S Domingie bl; Ikona tr. **p.71** Robert Harding Picture Library Christopher Rennie tl; Ikona Osvaldo Böhm, Italy br. **p.72** Corbis UK Ltd Michael Nicholson tl; Angelo Hornak Library br. **p.73** Spectrum Colour Library t. **p.74** Arcaid Joe Cornish cr; Corbis UK Ltd Catherine Karnow bl; Jonathan Blair cl; DK Picture Library James Strachan br. **p.75** AKG London Erich Lessing br; Edifice Darley tl; Esto Photographics Norman McGrath tr. **p.76** Arcaid Joe Cornish b; Bridgeman Art Library, London/New York Private Collection tc. **p.77** Corbis UK Ltd tc; John Heseltine bc. **p.78** Ikona Archivo Vasari bc; Scala, St. Carlo alle Quattro Fontane, Rome tl; © Dorling Kindersley Simon Murrell bl. **p.79** Bridgeman Art Library, London/New York Santa Maria della Vittoria, Rome, Italy t. **p.80** Archivi Alinari tr; Bridgeman Art Library, London/New York National Gallery of Victoria, Melbourne, Australia/Everard Studley Miller Bequest

tl; Rafael Valls Gallery, London bl. **p.81** Archivi Alinari Archivo Seat c. **p.82** Angelo Hornak Library l. **p.83** Corbis UK Ltd Stephanie Colasanti, Karlskirche, Vienna b; Robert Harding Picture Library tl; A. F. Kersting tr. **p.84** A. F. Kersting tc; © Dorling Kindersley Simon Murrell tl. **p.85** Bridgeman Art Library, London/New York, City of Westminster Archive Centre, London crb; Edifice Darley tl; Fotomas Index tc; Angelo Hornak Library b. **p.86** Archivo Iconografico, S.A. b; Scala: Galleria Palatina, Florence tl. **p.87** Photographie Giraudon tr. **p.88** Angelo Hornak Library bl. **p.89** Corbis UK Ltd Tony Arruza bcr; A. F. Kersting tl; Rodney Wilson tr. **p.90** Bridgeman Art Library, London/New York Hove Museum and Art Gallery tl; Scala, Mauritshuis Museum, The Hague b. **p.91** Axiom Chris Coe t; Link Picture Library Orde Eliason br. **pp.92–93** Mireille Vautier. **pp.94–95** Archivo Iconografico, S.A. tl; Robert Harding Picture Library Adina Tovy b. **p.95** Art Directors & TRIP H. Rogers tr. **p.96** South American Pictures Robert Francis bl; Art Directors & TRIP Ken McLaren t. **p.97** Ancient Art & Architecture Collection Ronald Sheridan b; Art Directors & TRIP S. Grant tl. **p.98** Corbis UK Ltd Jeremy Horner b. **p.99** Corbis UK Ltd Peter Wilson t. **pp.100–101** Arcaid Bill Tingey. **p.102** Axiom Gordon D. R. Clements tl; **pp.102–103** Robert Harding Picture Library Schuster b. **p.103** British Library, London 15258.cc.3. tr; Tony Stone Images Jean-Marc Truchet tc. **p.104** AKG London clb; Tony Stone Images D. E. Cox tl. **p.105** Ffotograff Roy Lawrence b. **p.106** Archivo Iconografico, S.A. b; Axiom Jim Holmes tl. **p.107** Moh Nishikawa tr; Nigel Paterson br. **p.108** Edifice Darley clb; Nigel Paterson br, t. **p.109** Axiom Jim Holmes tr; Nigel Paterson crb. **pp.110–111** A. F. Kersting. **p.112** © Michael Holford Victoria & Albert Museum tl; A. F. Kersting: b. **p.113** Corbis UK Ltd Sheldan Collins tr; Scala br. **p.114** A. F. Kersting b; V&A Picture Library tl. **p.115** British Library, London Add Or 948 tr; V&A Picture Library crb. **p.116** Axiom P. Rayne b. **p.117** Robert Harding Picture Library tl; Art Directors & TRIP T. Bognar br. **pp.118–119** A. F. Kersting. **p.120** Photographie Bulloz tl; **pp.120–121** Angelo Hornak Library b. **p.121** Edifice Jackson tr; Fotomas Index tl; National Trust Photographic Library Nadia MacKenzie br. **p.122** National Trust Photographic Library Andrew Butler b. **p.123** AKG London Galleria Palatina, Palazzo Pitti, Florence/Photograph S. Domingie tr; Bridgeman Art Library, London/New York Guildhall Library, Corporation of London b; Corbis UK Ltd Historical Picture Archive tl. **p.124** Special Collections and Archives, James Branch Cabell Library, Virginia Commonwealth University, Richmond, Virginia www.library.vcu.edu/jbc/speccoll/ post/ postmain.html bl; DK Picture Library cl. **p.125** Corbis UK Ltd Bettmann tr; Angelo Hornak Library tc, br.

AUTHOR'S ACKNOWLEDGMENTS

I would like to thank those, alive and dead, who have helped to open my eyes to architecture of all types, schools, fads, fashions, nations, and locales: John Betjeman, Ian Nairn, Hubert de Cronin Hastings, John Summerson, Colin Boyne, Dan Cruickshank, Gavin Stamp, Peter Buchanan, Augustus Welby Northmore Pugin, Berthold Lubetkin, John Ruskin, Bill Slack, Martin Pawley, Penelope Chetwode, Renzo Piano, Imre Makovecz, Ricky Burdett, Tudy Sammartini, Lance Knobel, Ilse Crawford, Nigel Coates, Daniel Libeskind, and the very many architects, engineers, critics, historians, clients, and owners of buildings who have generously given me their time over the past twenty years.

Thanks too to the long-suffering team at Dorling Kindersley – Anna Kruger who commissioned this book; Stephen Knowlden who oversaw the design; Rowena Alsey, Simon Murrell, and Carla De Abreu who designed it; Peter Jones, Neil Lockley, and Jo Marceau who edited it; and Sam Ruston who researched the pictures – and to everyone else who believed in the project.

DORLING KINDERSLEY WOULD LIKE TO THANK Mihály Katona, Judith More, Tim Scott, Louise Thomas, and Hilary Bird for the index.